Fly Fishing the Hex Hatch

by
Leighton Wass

Fly Fishing the Hex Hatch

Copyright © 2022 by Leighton Wass

All rights reserved. No part of this book may be reproduced or transmitted in any form or by any means without written permission of the author.

ISBN 978-1-943424-74-0

LCCN 2022938282

All photographs are by, or attributed to, the author unless stated otherwise.

All drawings and illustrations are by Terry Van Veghten unless stated otherwise.

North Country Press
Unity, Maine

For my parents, Henry and Thirza Wass

Without their influence and guidance during my younger years, it's doubtful that I would have become a teacher, and even more doubtful that this book would have been written. My father introduced me to the world outdoors and my mother kept my nose to the grindstone. I'm indebted to both.

AND

For my two beloved Labradors

Gilley and Scoter passed away during the last few months of writing this book. They brought more joy and happiness than mere words can explain.

Acknowledgments

When I looked at all the names that I have amassed of people who helped me with this book, it was abundantly clear that this book would not have happened without them. These kind folks include authors, regional magazine writers, fishery biologists, friends, guides, sporting camp owners, fly shop owners, publishers, fly tiers, editors, former students, college professors, and new friends found from working on the book. That's one heckuva group.

I hope in the following lists that I have included everyone! But, if perchance I missed you, please forgive me, and may I have a bucket of mayfly shucks dumped on my head. Your efforts, of course, were valuable, too.

I finally see a use for all the English exercises that I had for homework in school. I plan for all the following lists to be in alphabetical order, or may the ghosts of English teachers past rise up and castigate me.

Because of their initial involvement, my opening accolades go to the authors who willingly met with me before any writing took place. They helped me understand the basics needed to write a book, and the meetings were often accompanied by an ambiance of doughnuts and coffee. Those authors would be David Adams, Bernie Marvin, Gary Moore, and Peter Shea. Thanks, fellers!

I'm also grateful to contributors who reviewed/edited portions of my manuscript. Their reviews indeed nabbed a few errors and helped keep me on the correct track. They are David Adams, Greg Burr, Scott Davis, Sean Fowler, Ken Grimes, Jud Kratzer, Bob Mallard, Bernie Marvin, Gary Moore, Tim Obrey, Jim Pellerin, Drew Price, V. Paul Reynolds, Andy Schafermeyer, Jason Seiders, Peter Shea, Elizabeth Thorndike, Mary Van Veghten, Terry Van Veghten, and Jane B. Wass. Thank you, all.

Very special recognition is in order for my wife, Jane, Terry Van Veghten, and state fisheries biologists. My wife not only had complete confidence that I was capable of writing a book, but also answered questions regarding computerese, and reviewed/edited the majority of chapters in the book. I must admit, though, it was with a tad of reluctance at times, thus earning the title of "reluctant reviewer". Thank you, deah.

Terry Van Veghten is the book's freehand artist. He offered to do drawings for the book when I was first wondering who I could ask for that task. This was a total surprise to me since after 20 plus years of knowing him, I had no idea that he could even draw a straight line. He didn't even ask for remuneration for the drawings, but he will indeed be paid – if only in peanuts. I might add that the genes he acquired from his mother show up in many of his humorous drawings. Terry also supplied me with many quality photographs, reviewed parts of the manuscript, constantly kept in touch, and supplied me with valuable doughnut reports. His knowledge of parts of Maine and New Hampshire, areas that I was unfamiliar with, became a huge asset. Kudos, Guru.

Three dips of the net go to all the fishery biologists I contacted from all three states. They were an immense help to me by supplying factual information dealing with specific ponds and lakes, many of which I had never even seen, let alone fish. Some of these biologists reviewed sections of the manuscript appropriate to their assigned state areas and some just helped with their innate knowledge and expertise. Without exception, every state fishery biologist I contacted replied to my questions. I will highlight a biologist from each state for putting up with my incessant emails: Jud Kratzer (VT), Andy Schafermeyer (NH), and Tim Obrey (ME). Thanks to all for your participation.

The following people were more than willing to preview my book before it was published. I am indebted to these learned folks. They are David Van Wie, Will Lund, and V. Paul Reynolds. I should mention that when I was trying to decide on a topic, V. Paul was the person who really stoked the fire for this book's topic, the Hex Hatch. After sending him a list of ideas, he told me,

"...the Hex Hatch has potential." Then later, after I had written seven or eight chapters and needed a little assurance that what I had written was at least close to the mark, I sent him the chapters to review. V. Paul, never to be on the wordy side in an email, replied to me, "You've got a book there!" But that was all I needed. Thanks, V. Paul!

Originally, George Smith was also planning to review my book. I had emailed with George off and on through 2020 and early 2021, and he always answered my emails, and in a very timely manner, even though he was struggling with ALS. When I didn't get a reply to my Feb 11, 2021 email, I suspected the worse. This icon of the Maine sporting world passed away on Feb 12, 2021.

Then there is this cast of characters who sent or gave me photographs and/or articles. Each of these items was used in some manner and thus added to the book's overall integrity. They are Josh Adams, Jen Brophy, Greg Burr, Mark Dunton, Sean Fowler, Frank Frost, Ken Grimes, Jud Kratzer, Will Lund, Doug Lyons, Aaron Moore, Tim Obrey, Dave Oles, Joe Overlock, Drew Price, Jeff Reardon, Andy Schafermeyer, Peter Shea, Igor Sikorsky, Mary Van Veghten, Terry Van Veghten, and Matt Whitegiver. Plaudits to all!

I'm also appreciative of those who made multiple contacts with me, either via email or by phone. Their interest in helping me did not go unnoticed. They are Brett Damm, Dee Dauphinee, Mark Dunton, Frank Frost, Shawn Good, John Holyoke, David Howatt, Jud Kratzer, Will Lund, Bob Mallard, Tim Obrey, Jim Pellerin, Drew Price, Jeff Reardon, V. Paul Reynolds, Tom Roth, Andy Schafermeyer, Peter Shea, Igor Sikorsky, George Smith, Elizabeth Thorndike, Kevin Tracewski, and David Van Wie. In some cases, it was just one or two emails or a phone call that became part of the book-writing process, as with Steve Angers, Scott Biron, Michael Blanchette, Francis Brautigam, Steve Carpenteri, Andy Cobb, Ken Cox, Jim Deshler, Kevin Dunham, Rick Forge, Bill Graves, Don Hibbs, Matt LaRoche, George Liset, Mike Maynard, Declan McCabe, Kevin McKay, Ben Nugent, Lawrence

Pyne, Tom Seymore, David Smith, Tim Traver, Lou Zambello, and Daniel Mencucchi. Much obliged to everyone!

Some people offered detailed information on how I should go about writing a book and/or who I might look at for a publisher. These folks are David Adams, Bernie Marvin, Gary Moore, Bob Romano, Peter Shea, George Smith, Kevin Tracewiski, David Van Wie, Lars Walker, James Walker, Dee Dauphinee, Sarah Fowler, and Al Raychard. Thanks to this group as well.

My publisher, Pat Newell of North Country Press is one busy lady. On top of being a publisher, she handles over 280 tax returns for clients, so when I kept sending emails to her asking about this and that, I was probably putting her way over the top. So, I offer my gratitude for her perseverance with all my email falderal, as well as dealing with the 260 plus images I sent her with the manuscript. Thanks, Pat.

When writing a book for the first time, it's nice to hear from others who are interested in how things are going. It gives the wanna-be author a chance to explain some of the idiosyncrasies of writing and serves somewhat as an endorsement of what the writer is doing, as well as a way of offering support. A personal thanks go to two friends who often asked me, "How's the book coming?" They are Diane Nicholls and Anne LaBossiere. Bless you.

I have shared many Hex waters over the years with an assortment of regular companions who contributed to the enthusiasm, excitement, and overall hullabaloo of the Hexagenia mayfly hatch. They include Tom Beauregard, Jay Boomer, Joe Bottiggi, Mike Brown, Chris Crumbley, Steve Foster, Neil Hilt, Pat McCormack, Dave Oles, Lawrence Pyne, Terry Van Veghten, Jane B. Wass, and especially the three I partnered with the most, my brother Stan Wass and my devoted Yellow Labradors, Toller and Widgeon.

Most of the following people are already mentioned in this book because they will not be here to sit in their recliners and peruse the book's chapters. They were friends who have passed away and I believe deserve special recognition. These gentlemen were all great fishermen and I bet are still leading the "Anglers

Parade" for St. Peter. I know that each of them would have fully enjoyed this book. They are Angelo Ambrosini, Erland Coombs, Jay Boomer, Basil Day, Carl Decoster, Steve Foster, Harold Gassett, and Shawn Dutil. A special tip of my hat goes to fellow educator and Norwich alumnus, Jim Call, and teaching colleague, Phillip Nelson. See you in the future, guys, with fly rod in hand.

Foreword

As a teenager in Southwest Harbor, Maine, I had a bit of a flair for writing. Geez, I even got good marks on several English essays in high school. But no nerd here I must say. I would rather have been catching trout in Marshall's Brook, shooting hoops at White's outdoor basketball court, or shooting pool at Jim's underground pool hall (as long as my mother didn't know) than doing homework.

I started writing fishing and hunting journals in 1955 when I was an eighth-grader. By my rough math, that was about 66 years ago. I was emulating my father, Henry "Shorty" Wass, who also kept records of fishing trips, although a bit sketchier than mine.

Then in 1972, as a transplanted Downeaster teaching high school science in Vermont, I wrote my very first article to be published. It was titled, "Limit Out on Lakers" and dealt with ice fishing. It appeared in the now-defunct *Vermont*

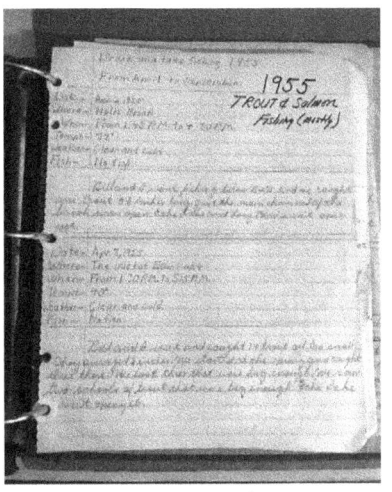

The author's first fishing journal page at age 13.

Sportsman with John Randolph as editor, and he paid me $30 for that article.

Since then, I have had a little over 80 articles published in a variety of magazines including *The Maine Sportsman, Vermont Outdoors, New England Game & Fish, Vermont Life, Northern Woodlands,* and, yes, even *Varmint Hunter Magazine*. I think you get it. I like to write. Also, like many other first-time authors, I have been prodded often by the question, "Why don't you write a book?" from many friends and relatives.

So now at a chronological age of 78, I have begun to look at what I want to accomplish in my remaining years. One idea popped up as if it came out of a Jack-In-The-Box. Write a book. Maybe it was the teacher in me erupting once again. Writing *is* a form of teaching and I did spend 33 enjoyable years teaching, sharing knowledge with thousands of high school students. Dammit Wass, grab the buck by the antlers and do it. And I did.

The author working on his book, 2020. (JANE B. WASS PHOTO)

First, I did some research online about "How to Write a Book." I needed at least a scintilla of an idea of what the heck I was getting into. Then I emailed a few scribes who have authored outdoorsy New England books to get their suggestions and recommendations for my project and met face to face with a few of them. I also got in touch with a few of my former students who have had books published. Everyone I contacted was more than eager to help. A former student even offered to review my manuscript – for free. Wait just a minute though. Is this a set-up? Could it be this is the chance to get back at Wass by red-marking **his** papers? "Hey, Mr. Wass, remember that biology paper of mine that you used two red pens to correct? Well, guess what…"

Who are these kind-hearted folks?

Robert J. Romano, Jr., author of *Shadow in The Stream* (2005) and others

David A. Van Wie, author of *Storied Waters* (2019) and co-author of *The Confluence* (2016)

Gary W. Moore, author of *Four Seasons in Vermont* (2018)

Peter Shea, author of *Vermont Trout Ponds* (2014), *Long Trail Trout* (2015), and many others

Bernie Marvin, author of *The Best of Bernie's Beat* (2019), *The Best of Bernie's Beat Volume II* (2021)

And I'm proud to list my former students who also contributed to my plea for help:

David Adams, author of *Why Do They Kill?* (2007)

Lawrence R. "Lars" Walker, coauthor of *Landslide Ecology* (2012) and others

Doug Walker, author of *Gaia Twist* (2018)

I kept the book idea close to my vest for a while. I was a bit afraid of failure and embarrassment. But on the way home from my coffee interview with Gary Moore, former VT Fish & Game Commissioner, I found myself saying, "This is going to work! It really is." And after repeating those same words to my three labs and one wife at home, they all exultantly smiled and wagged their tails. What support I thought! Here I do need to mention that my wife, Jane, has been a stalwart believer from the day I first uttered the words, "I think I'll write a book".

Next question. Why this topic, the *Hexagenia* mayfly, when I had three or four other subjects that I was pondering? All but one of my ideas had to do with fishing. Hell, I've cast a fly, tossed a

The author's father had his son fishing at an early age. This nice salmon was caught trolling with a Grey Ghost streamer on Long Pond in Southwest Harbor, Maine.

worm, hand-lined the ocean, trolled a streamer, tied some flies, jigged a jig, and bobbed a shiner for almost 70 years. Common sense said there's got to be something worthwhile to write about from all those years of fishing.

I was leaning towards an anecdotal memoir of my life of fishing, tilting a tad towards the humorous side. But then my fuzzy mind cleared, and I realized - there are a million of those books out there. I need to hone it down to more of a laser point. The Hex Hatch was one of my original ideas for a book since I had fished this hatch for three decades. In addition, I had written three articles about the hatch for outdoor magazines in the past. For sure it would be a focused topic aimed at a very specific contingent of readers – fly anglers. But I reasoned, could any red-blooded fly fisher pass by a book stand after seeing the words "HEX HATCH" in bold print, and not pick that book up? Good God no. Just whisper the word "Hex" in a fly shop around the end of June and the silence becomes deafening. All ears move like radars to focus on the next words uttered, and then these questions follow: "Where did he say?", "When was it?", "What was the name of the fly he intentionally mumbled?"

I searched the internet to see how many books had already been written about the Hex Hatch. To my surprise, and absolute

HEXAGENIA LIMBATA

delight, I could not find a single one. This looked indeed promising.

I tossed out a few of my book ideas to publisher V. Paul Reynolds of Maine Outdoor Publications (also editor of *Northwoods Journal*) and mentioned that I couldn't find a single book written entirely about the New England Hex Hatch. V. Paul emailed back and nut-shelled this answer for me. "For your book topics, the Hex Hatch has potential." Right then and there, a book was born.

So, why this book? Why not? Enjoy.

Table of Contents

1. Great Expectations 1
2. Dopplers, Snowplows and Hexagenia 6
3. Intro — Hexology 101 10
4. Heavy Panting — Hexology 102 14
5. Domiciles for Naiads — Hexology 103 18
6. Scuba Gear and Ice Fishing 22
7. Onset Temperatures & Journals 26
8. Five Steps to Heaven 30
9. Who Shops at the Hexagenia Supermarket? 35
10. Ducks, Duns and a Grumpy Fisherman 46
11. What's in a Name 51
12. Doughnuts Make it Special 61
13. Secret Ponds 67
14. Skinny on Vermont 72
15. Granite-Lined Waters of New Hampshire 83
16. Pine Tree State Has It All 97
17. A Triple Play, A Dunk and Strawberry Shortcake 174
18. Getting There Early and Puttin' on the Ritz 187
19. It's All About Timing & Temperature 202
20. Rising Like Bread Dough 215
21. What to Take to the Mayfly Dance 226

22. Trophy Trout and the Four Qs	242
23. The Value of a Chesster Ice Cream Sandwich	256
24. John-Boy's Journal	288
25. Endgame	295
About The Author	303
Resources	304
Index of Lakes, Ponds & Rivers	305

1. Great Expectations

Slurp. Slurp. "Lead him by at least six feet. He's moving fast and left!", my fishing partner shouted. My cast was on the money. Slurp. Slurp-splash. "I got 'im!!" Zzzzzzz complained my fly reel on the rainbow's first run and jump. Then silence. "Dammit, I lost him. Broke the f'er off." I *knew* it was my fault. I had never bothered to get rid of that wind knot.

The action just described might be familiar to some of you if you have ever cast to a cruising fish during a mayfly hatch. It may not have been a wind knot, but instead a frayed leader, or a walloping set of the hook on a light leader.

For a little over three decades, the author has chased trout and salmon during the Hexagenia mayfly hatch in Northern New England. He has condensed his experiences, buttressed with the skills and knowledge of others, to produce this book that you are about to read. Enjoy.

1. Great Expectations

For three decades, I have garnered enough information during my fishing adventures with Hex hatches to share with others by writing a book. Not only is the presentation of material in this book a condensation from my many years of fishing over *Hexagenia* mayflies, but it also includes a distillation of facts from many other sources, including fishing enthusiasts, professional ichthyologists, fellow anglers, and a variety of other contacts. Although my experiences are limited to Northern New England, I believe the information that you are about to read can be applied almost anywhere there is a Hex Hatch. Even anglers who are veterans of Hex mayfly fishing will find some snippets of enlightenment to enhance their fishing. To the novice Hex angler, I'm as sure that I haven't yet seen my last fly-fishing cast, that you will learn enough from old-timer Wass to raise one helluva ruckus at the scene of your next Hex Hatch. You are going to go into it "guns-a-blazing".

In this book, I will offer tips, tricks, and ruses to hoodwink

Every fly angler should have the chance to fish the noble Hexagenia mayfly hatch more than once in their lifetime.

trout and salmon, both prior to and during the *Hexagenia* mayfly hatch. I will draw from many years of experience at being seduced by this elegant, aquatic insect. By listing over 160 Hex ponds and lakes, coupled with a barrelful of how-to advice, I hope to make readers of this book competent Hex anglers. Make no mistake, casting to a Hex Hatch is dry fly fishing at its best. It's the essence of winter dreams. It's real maple syrup on pancakes. Some folks even base their social calendars on it. It's what I believe is one of nature's most remarkable events.

My introduction to this Paul Bunyan of the mayfly clan came on a trip to Maine's **Nesowadnehunk Lake** with my brother, Stan Wass, in the late 1980s. We had stopped at a well-known fly-fishing shop, the Maine Guide, in Greenville to buy a few last-minute items. (Don't we always need those no matter how much we plan?) After explaining where we were headed, the owner, Dan Legere, showed us an assortment of dries and nymphs that would be just the ticket because, as he said, "huge Green Drake mayflies"

Brothers Stan and Leighton Wass have chased trout and salmon all over Maine during the Hex Hatch.

1. Great Expectations

were beginning to hatch on this legendary lake. To my recollection, which I admit is as faulty as a Ford Edsel at times, that was the first time I heard someone mention Green Drakes. Most Mainers have called this mayfly a Green Drake for years and still do. Entomologically speaking it is the Hex mayfly, *Hexagenia limbata*. Dan hit the nail right on the head, as he almost always does. The largest mayflies that I had ever seen were indeed hatching at the lake, and the flies he recommended worked like charms.

I do need to address one last topic after reading David Van Wie's wonderfully written book, *Storied Waters*. Van Wie quite humorously fesses up his opinion of pond fishing, aka flat-water fly fishing, as something like Cow Flop Bingo. You know, that game played at fairgrounds that has you betting your life savings where a cow will crap. As he "flippantly" says, "You flip your fly out there and hope you put it in the correct (Bingo) square, where a trout is waiting." But he reasons that still-water trout don't just stay in one place, so you end up chasing rings and rises (*very* guilty as charged), "while fish cruise in random directions sipping mayflies".

Chasing rises.

Van Wie chooses moving water as his fishing cathedral. But, oh, David, hold your "hosses". This is war. It's Hendricksons versus Hexes. It's flowing water versus placid water. It's Dartmouth (David, 1979) versus Norwich (Leighton, 1964). Agreed, fly anglers generally belong to one clan or the other. It's either the Catch-Me-If-You-Can-I'm-Right-Here stream fishing gang or the rise-chasing Trout Pond Bingo fraternity. I proudly admit that I am of the latter. And I am not exactly sure why. I do know that water courses through my soul. Any water. Yet it's flat water, Walden Pond water that is my calling. I have come to believe part of that reason deals with those huge, abominable-looking *Hexagenia* nymphs that inhabit silty bottoms and metamorphose into graceful, elegant duns that we reverently call – The Hex Hatch.

The hat says it all.

So, what's the big deal? Why the Hex Hatch? Simply put, it's because *big* fish come to the surface for *big* mayflies, allowing you to land a fish of your dreams on a *dry fly*. That's why. And not only that, fishing a Hex Hatch will blow away your cobwebs. It will become a highlight of your fishing season. The very first trout that I learned was caught during this hatch turned out to be a 3 3/4-pound wild brook trout netted out of Pierce Pond, Maine. I've been infected ever since. I call it **Hexitis**.

2. Dopplers, Snowplows and Hexagenia

You may recall the stunning news about the "invasion" of mayflies in the mid-west during the summer of 2019. Bleary-eyed weather forecasters were watching their Doppler radars one even-

Doppler radar showing a huge mass of mayflies over Lake Erie around the first of July.

ing, only to discover a "sudden, rapidly expanding blob" near the shores of Lake Erie. The Dopplers weren't picking up a dastardly weather bomb but instead *billions* (that's with a **B**) of mayflies in their nuptial flights, and primarily our friend, *Hexagenia limbata*.

2. Dopplers, Snowplows and Hexagenia

A car in a Midwest parking lot during the annual Hexagenia Hatch on Lake Erie. Parking lot lights attracted the insects by the tens of thousands. Imagine getting ready for work on those mornings. SUE BIXLER PHOTO

Adult Hex mayflies are attracted to light, like moths, and will feebly fly a few miles towards those lights as long as the wind is light. After arriving at the source of light, they can completely coat parked vehicles under street lights, and turn roads and bridges into such a mess that snowplows may be called. Bridges are especially affected since they span water where the mayflies are hatching and are bedecked with numerous mayfly-attracting lights. Windshield wipers are necessary to keep a driver's vision of the road at least partly clear. Even electrical transformers have been known to shut down because of the enormous numbers of insects interfering with transmissions. These mayflies can show up on Doppler radar covering an area as much as 15 miles long and several miles wide. Talk about blanket hatches.

Can you imagine, though, driving over a bridge, after dark, and squashing so many-egg laden mayflies that the road becomes a veritable skating rink, causing accidents like driving in snow? It happens. Mind you, this is June and July, so it makes you wonder how prepared those snowplow drivers really are. Bridges may even be closed because of dangerous driving conditions.

I recall something a bit similar to this (in reality a comparative pittance) in the area of **East Grand Lake,** Maine in the 1950s. While riding with my father one evening, there were so many mayflies splatting the windshield that he couldn't see and had to use the wipers, as well as slow to a crawl. I'm not sure if those mayflies were *Hexagenia,* but as a teenager, I was most assuredly impressed.

2. Dopplers, Snowplows and Hexagenia

Nope. We don't need to worry about all that in Northern New England, but the inconveniences these mayflies cause are a small price to pay for their potential benefits, primarily to fisheries. Food. Lots of food. Biologists have found a multitude of fish species that make use of this insect as a source of food, either as a "nymphic soup" or a "mayfly BLT". A study done in a Canadian, walleye-infested lake found that young walleye, as well as adults, use the different Hex life-stages as a major source of food. What an opportunity to net a walleye on a fly rod.

A Hexagenia mayfly resting on the author's knee while fishing the Hex Hatch.

Also, many scientists consider *Hexagenia* mayflies a type of bellwether, an indicator of how biologically healthy a water body can be, or as the old tried but true saying, the "canary in a coal mine". These mayflies are very intolerant of pollution. In the 1950s, Hex mayflies disappeared from Lake Erie for 30 years. The cause? Pollutants. In fact, the demise of these insects was one of the primary factors that forced government agencies to get on the stick and improve water quality. Excessive phosphorous was a

2. Dopplers, Snowplows and Hexagenia

major culprit, but, once the phosphorus and other pollutants were curbed over the years, mayflies began to reappear in the 1980s, and have now become prevalent once more. Time and again, the importance of this mayfly (as well as several others) as an indicator of ecosystem health has been demonstrated.

Can you fish a Hex Hatch in Texas or Loozeeana? You can, but don't expect to land many trout. *Hexagenia limbata* has been found in every US state but Alaska and Arizona and is widespread in the Canadian provinces. There are large numbers of this mayfly in states you wouldn't expect, but a problem for pursuers of trout is that water temperatures in most of these states are too warm to support trout populations. But the Hex mayfly earned its ribbons in the Midwest - primarily the states of Michigan, Minnesota, and Wisconsin. More recently, several western states have also been receiving notoriety for this hatch, namely California and Oregon.

What about northern New England, you ask? Hold on to the gunnels, folks. I will get to those hallowed spots in Maine, New Hampshire, and Vermont later in this book.

3. Intro – Hexology 101

The Trout Lily, sometimes called Adder's Tongue or Dogtooth Violet, blossoms in the month of May. Because it grows for only a short time, it is referred to by botanists as a spring ephemeral. Don't be surprised to find tasty morels close by. PAINTING BY THE AUTHOR

Our star of the book owns the scientific name, *Hexagenia limbata*. It belongs to a large classification (an order) of mayflies called Ephemeroptera which are grouped together because they all share very short life spans. As an aside, there are many springtime flowers like trillium, spring beauty, and trout lily that are referred to as "spring ephemerals", because…you guessed it, they all have a very short growth span restricted to early spring.

This order of mayflies is further divided into several scientific families, one of which, Ephemeridae, includes all mayflies that burrow in their nymphal stage, including our 5-star stud, *Hexagenia limbata*. This mayfly has a magnificent life cycle that usually spans two years. One can start of course anywhere in a cycle, but I chose to start with the adult duns, the stage immediately following nymphs, since duns are the phase we probably most often see, and most likely imitate when fishing with Hex flies. (I suppose that could be arguable since there are a lot of nymph and spinner imitations out there.)

Exactly how large is a Hex dun mayfly? No definitive answer here. Just as body sizes vary in all other living things, mayflies tend to follow suit. Most biologists use metric measures and Celsius temperatures, but I am going with the antiquated English system. My measurements of a few female duns show a body length a tad in excess of an inch, and two tails of the same length. That means a female adult is about two-plus inches in total length, while male

Litobrancha recurvata, sometimes called the Dark Green Drake, is of similar size as Hexagenia limbata, although much more darkly hued so that the duns almost appear black on the water. The author likes to use the name "Recurve Hatch" when this mayfly is hatching.

3. Intro — Hexology 101

As one can tell from the smile on Sean Fowler's face, he's more than pleased with the results of this Hex Hatch.

duns have been measured at several tenths of an inch shorter. This is one huge mayfly.

Is this our largest mayfly? Depends. Some venerable biologists believe that *H. limbata* is still not the largest mayfly out there. They like *Litobrancha recurvata* (formerly of the *Hexagenia* genus) as top dog, finding it to be .118 inches longer. But I just have to get this in. I have fished over this latter-named mayfly hatch, called by some the Dark Green Drake Hatch, many times and would actually like to take credit for giving it an alternative name, the "Recurve Hatch", after its scientific species name, *recurvata*. There just isn't any green on these mayflies folks. None. And yes, I have measured a few of these mayfly insects, too. True, *L. recurvata* is one very large mayfly and truly on a par with *H. limbata*, but I have found some Hexes to be a little larger overall. And to throw a spanner in the whole works, I have found that some ponds and lakes seem to produce larger-sized Hex mayflies than other

3. Intro – Hexology 101

waters, which could account for some of the variations in measurements.

The coloration of my favorite mayfly, the Hex, includes colors ranging and blending from whitish to yellowish and shades of brown. No green. So why are they so endearingly called a *green drake* in much of Maine? See chapter 11.

To summarize, male and female Hex duns (and Recurve duns) are ginormous mayflies, and as a result, bring big ole bastid fish to the surface – for our pleasure.

4. Heavy Panting – Hexology 102

The first adult mayfly stage, called the dun, is the phase that immediately follows the molting of a nymphal shuck on the water's surface. They are fragile, gorgeous, and vulnerable all at once. These duns, while resting on the surface and contemplating when to take flight, have their four wings folded together above their bodies, somewhat reminiscent of the inactive World War II planes. That shape is the primary identifying trait of almost all mayflies.

But how about this? In the waning minutes of evenings, when large caddisflies are hatching, I have foolishly misidentified the *adult caddis* as a Hex mayfly. Here's why. As the adult caddis first emerges from its exoskeleton on the water's surface, the wings are folded vertically just like a mayfly dun, but it is very brief – maybe 2-3 seconds. The caddis then quickly folds its wings in a tent-like trifold along its dorsal side in typical caddis-style, no longer mimicking a mayfly.

This caddis fly has already gone through the "it could be a mayfly stage," and settled its wings along the dorsal side in typical tent-shaped caddis style.

But in near darkness, an experienced fly fisher can easily be fooled. Almost immediately after folding its wings, the caddis does its crazy dance, skittering and zig-zagging across the surface before liftoff (unless chomped on first by an aggressive fish) giving away its identification.

The best way to avoid this mistake is to remember that *Hexagenia* mayflies don't usually skitter across the surface after hatching. Instead, they will pose like a sitting duck for a bit, maybe flutter a little, and take off if not crippled. Fortunately for this crusty ole fisherman, I was alone when I made this misidentification and had nary a soul to listen to my flimsy rationalization for the embarrassing error.

After a Hex nymph molts to an adult dun (called a subimago) producing what anglers call "the hatch", the weak-flying duns fly and flutter like moths to nearby trees, shrubs, and other structures. Within 1-3 days, the duns will molt for the very last time into what anglers call spinners and biologists call imagoes. It's interesting to note that mayflies are the only insects that shed their skins (shucks) *after* developing wings that enable them to fly. Neither

A dun (subimago) Hexagenia mayfly is on the left and a spinner (imago) on the right. The wings of duns are almost opaque while the spinners' wings are glass-like or translucent.

adult stage has mouthparts so they do not feed. The physical appearance of the dun and spinner wings differs dramatically; the wings of the dun are opaque and dull in appearance whereas the spinner's wings are translucent and glass-like. This is the time in its life cycle when areas near the Great Lakes are inundated with mayflies, affecting radar screens as mentioned earlier. In Northern New England, it's not quite the dramatic scenario of snowplows and shovels needed to rid accumulations of mayflies, but it can still be somewhat impressive. For example, Vermont fly-fishing friends Terry and Mary Van Veghten have reported seeing the **Brassua Dam** (on the Moose River in Maine) fairly thickly coated with Hex duns and spinners.

This Hexagenia mayfly has just molted, shedding its outer exoskeleton to become a spinner. Typically, that is "dun" on the leaves of shoreline vegetation.

After several days as duns and then molting to spinners, both male and female adult spinners take to the air and mate. These copulating flights, more generally called spinner flights, almost always happen at dusk and after dark. Once mating has occurred, the females either drop their payload of eggs while flying close to the water's surface or, in the case of an audience, can perform 9.9-rated belly-flops to release their eggs. Lying on the surface the female's body quivers to unfetter the egg packets that will propagate a new generation of Hex mayflies.

I have never witnessed what I would call a real Hex spinner flight, but I do often see the remains of a previous night's "orgy", including just wings (from avian predation) and "spent" male and female spinners laying prostrate on the water's surface. That, sadly, is the ephemeral life cycle of the adult Hex mayfly coming to an end; however, it is also the beginning of a whole new generation of *Hexagenia* mayflies.

After settling to the bottom, most of the eggs will soon hatch into the first larval stage and then go through a few molts before settling in for the winter months. Some sources report that a few eggs may overwinter before developing further, and I suppose they would be the eggs that were last deposited, late in the year. (It's not unusual to see Hex mayflies in September and even October.) It's now time for our Hex nymph to take the podium.

5. Domiciles for Naiads — Hexology 103

As might be expected, there is typically little nymphal growth of the Hexagenia mayfly during the winter months, but once the warmth of spring temperatures arrives, any overwintered eggs and young nymphs will begin the molting process and grow in size with each shedding. This is very similar to that which takes place with crayfish, lobsters, and other crustaceans as they outgrow their exoskeletons.

The nymphs will pass through as many as 30 instars (time between molts) over two years before achieving the size needed to swim to the surface in June and July when they cast off their ugly duckling exterior to become swan-like adults and perpetuate the species. Thirty or so molts is amazing in itself and is the most of any mayfly species.

Hex nymphs (also biologically referred to as naiads) require silty, muddy, or somewhat sandy substrates for habitat. The bottom material must be soft enough to burrow through, but yet firm enough so their u-shaped

The Hexagenia nymph (naiad) lives in a u-shaped burrow constructed in muddy or silty bottoms of ponds and lakes and some rivers. DIAGRAM BY THE AUTHOR.

"digs" don't collapse. Typically, that specific habitat is located in ponds and lakes, although some silty, slow-moving stream sections fit the requirements as well. The average depth of sediment needed by these benthic naiads is around four to five inches. For

The Hexagenia nymph has three tails although the dun and spinner stages have only two. These beastly-looking critters live in the mud for around two years before swimming to the top and metamorphosing into an adult dun.

the most part in northern New England, stream bottoms are too stony and lacking the depth of silt needed to support Hex nymphs.

The uncomely nymphs cannot hold a candle to the graceful, handsome adults. The yellowish/brownish/blackish naiads develop two rows of gills along their abdomen, and their heads are fitted with tusks. Unlike the duns, these nymphs sport three tails instead of two. Their toughened tusks are used to move sediment around while tidying up their silty abodes (called "plowers" for this reason), and the external, feathery gills undulate to bring oxygen and food particles to them. They are detritivores, meaning that they consume fine organic matter as well as phytoplankton (microscopic algae and bacteria) for nutrition.

The shape of the nymphs' tusks is one way biologists can differentiate *limbata* from *recurvata* nymphs. When I was teaching and had access to microscopes, I sometimes collected undigested nymphs from the stomachs of trout that inhabited a local pond. Looking at some of those dead, three-tailed nymphs under the microscope, I could see the tusks clearly for identification purposes. Using published photographs for comparison, I was able

5. Domiciles for Naiads — Hexology 103

I doubt many fly anglers will dispute that this is a trophy brook trout. This wild, slab-sided squaretail came from a tiny, remote pond in the Deboullie region of northern Maine and was released. COURTESY RED RIVER CAMPS

to identify some nymphs as being *Litobrancha recurvata*, the close cousin to *Hexagenia limbata*. As far as I know, I was the first to positively identify that nymph in my favorite Vermont trout spot, **Seyon Pond** (pronounced Say-on, and sometimes called **Noyes Pond**) in Groton State Forest. That mayfly is the cornerstone of a beloved Seyon Pond "Recurve Hatch".

How about the water depths in which Hex nymphs live? Here again, there is a variable. One scientific study found ten feet to be the average, and that seems about right to me. But the actual range of depths can be from several feet, or less, to as much as 40 feet, and sometimes deeper. In most lakes and ponds that I fish, the duns pop up to the surface quite frequently in 10-20 feet of water.

Some sources report nymphs rarely leaving their burrows based primarily on the artificiality of live laboratory conditions; however, a few studies show that nymphs may come out of their u-shaped tunnels to feed. Most scientific data support that

5. Domiciles for Naiads — Hexology 103

nymphs are primarily nocturnal and that they do leave their domiciles when molting.

The Recurve Hatch at Seyon Pond in Vermont happens around Memorial Day weekend. This mayfly is believed by some to be a bit larger than Hexagenia limbata. It provides one heckuva hatch to fish, and you don't have to worry about getting home late since the hatch typically commences around 2:30 PM and ends around 5:00 PM.

6. Scuba Gear and Ice Fishing

During the winter of 2018-19, I heard from a reliable source that Vermont state fishery biologist Jud Kratzer was catching lake trout while ice fishing at Vermont's **Caspian Lake** that had *Hexagenia* nymphs in their stomachs. I just had to follow up on it, so I emailed Kratzer, and here is part of his report to me, dated January 6, 2020:

*"Leighton, I've been noticing Hex nymphs in lake trout stomachs for several winters now. It seems to be a fairly common occurrence on **Caspian** and **Echo Lakes**, and we've also observed it at **Willoughby**, **Seymour**, and **Little Averill Lakes**."* [He continues to tell me that he started using homemade jigs that resembled Hex nymphs and that he has been successful catching lake trout in this manner.] *"As far as how the trout capture them (nymphs), I am pretty clueless. I've seen (winter-caught) lake trout stuffed with too many Hexagenia to count, but never seen sand or muck in their stomachs. That may suggest that they* [lake trout] *are not rooting through the lake bottom to find them."* [He continued to another theory.] *"Since suckers are well-adapted for sucking invertebrates up off the bottom, possibly they, or other fish, roust the nymphs from their burrows but don't capture them all. Then if the nymphs are up and about trying to find a new home, that could be when lake trout get them."*

Most interesting. And I suppose another possibility is that maybe some nymphs molt at times (maybe even more so than past evidence shows) during the winter, and then come out of their benthic abodes to accomplish that physiological change, but may not make it back in time before becoming a meal for a hungry-eyed laker.

6. Scuba Gear and Ice Fishing

Another report of this Hex-related oddity came from my hard-nosed ice fisherman son Andy Wass of Northfield, Vermont. Upon hearing about Jud Kratzer landing lake trout through the ice using a fly that resembled a Hex, he tried jigging a fly just off

This small lake trout caught by the author's son, Andy Wass, was fooled by jigging with a Hex nymph fly on the bottom. Fishery biologists have verified that lake trout eat Hex nymphs during the winter months. ANDY WASS PHOTO

the bottom in about 40 feet of water. A 16-inch laker was completely fooled into believing he had a Hex nymph in his mouth.

Yet Maine fishery biologist Tim Obrey of the Moosehead Lake region in Maine reports this, dated 1/13/2020:

"*We have done extensive stomach analysis on lake trout on* **Moosehead Lake** *for many years. I don't recall seeing any Hex nymphs (during the winter). We (do) see them a lot in the spring and summer. Nearly all of our lake trout are feeding on smelt in the winter.*"

And yes, for you doubting Thomases, there are *Hexagenia* in Moosehead Lake. To enhance Kratzer's findings, I was able to find some piscatorial reports from the Midwest that indicated a large number of fish species had Hex nymphs in their stomach contents when examined during the winter season.

So, there it is, a challenging unknown in the life cycle of *H. limbata*. *Do* the nymphs exit their u-shaped burrows to molt and thus get wolfed down by predatory fish, or, are these nymphs rooted out either directly or indirectly? Any of you who are fascinated by this seemingly "hexing" problem, please feel free to don a wetsuit with scuba gear, enter through an ice fisherman's enlarged hole and see what the hell is going on down there. Once accomplished, please report your findings to Jud, Tim, and me.

Once a Hex nymph reaches about 30 molts, usually over a two-year period, they are ready to leave their subterranean home to explore another world. This typically happens during June and July (sometimes as late as August and September) and near or after dusk. The naiad swims rapidly to the surface. At the waterline, their exoskeleton/case/shuck splits, and thereupon emerges a beautiful sight to fly fishers, adult Hex male and female duns proudly looking like so many delicate Lilliputian sailboats. You are

Big Black Pond in the Deboullie region of northern Maine is a gorgeous place to fish and as a bonus has a Hex Hatch.

6. Scuba Gear and Ice Fishing

witnessing the true fairy tale of "frogs turning into princes". Interestingly, all *Hexagenia* don't seem to emerge from their shucks at the same rate. The first time I learned of that was at Red River Camps in the Debouille region of northern Maine. The owners at that time were Rhonda and Mike Brophy, and Mike reported to my brother Stan and me that there was indeed a Hex Hatch on **Big Black Pond**, but that they linger a bit longer after emerging from their cases than the Hex on **Island Pond**, where their camps are located. I'm sure that was a direct observation on Brophy's part, and I don't take it lightly, as I have found many written accounts to verify this pond to pond variation.

7. Onset Temperatures & Journals

When do *Hexagenia* nymphs sense it's time to rise to the occasion and grab some air? One particular report I found stated that the number of daylight hours was a factor. Maybe. Another source I found stated that the "water temperature must reach 68 degrees F" for nymphs to swim to the surface. Does that mean surface temperatures or bottom temperatures? Since lakes and ponds are relatively shallow where Hex nymphs exit their burrows, I'm guessing that this measurement was at the surface. But some nymphs hatch from depths of 20-40 or more feet. What's the chance that the surface temperature (ST) is the same as the temperature at the bottom of those water columns? I'd say slim to none. The thermocline has probably started to set up in most lakes by Hex-hatching time, but

Hexagenia nymphs leave their burrows and ascend the water column in an undulating motion to reach the surface. DRAWING BY THE AUTHOR

it's likely to be of little depth at this time of year. So, yes, water may be 68 F degrees at the surface on July 4th, but it's going to be colder at 20 to 40-plus feet in depth. Those deeper nymphs are definitely not starting their journey to the top when the ST reaches 68 F. I have noticed that Hex tend to hatch from deeper and deeper water as the hatch moves along from the day of onset to the last days of the hatch. I'm betting the reason for that sort of rolling hatch from shallow to deep water is because it takes longer for the water surrounding the nymphs in deeper water to reach that magic temperature of 68 F.

Since most of us won't be using bottom temperatures as an indicator, it's the STs we anglers want to know and can measure easily. My religiously-kept fishing journals of Hex hatches for about 30 years I think is worthy of mention here.

I enjoy keeping journals, all kinds of journals. They include but are not limited to fresh-water fishing, salt-water fishing, firewood gathering, duck hunting, terrorizing rabbits and hares, moose shed hunting, and morel mushroom gathering.

Journals kept by the author over a period of 65 years. They run the gamut from fishing to firewood. The fishing journals have been a most important source while writing this book.

One body of water where I have regularly fished the Hex Hatch in Vermont is **Caspian Lake** in Greensboro, and recording STs for this lake has been a part of my records. When the ST on this lake reaches 60 Degrees F, this kid greases his fly lines, feverishly ties a few last flies, and cancels all appointments for the next three weeks…or actually, more like a month just to be on the safe side. On this very deep and clear lake, the ST at the hatch onset (the first day I see more than one adult dun) has ranged from 65 to 70 degrees F over a few years, for an average of 66 degrees F. That's not too far off from what scientists have recorded. I am not quite willing to say that an onset hatching ST of 66 F will be the same on every body of water that has a Hex Hatch, but I do believe, though, that this average temperature is a fair representation of what it might be like throughout Northern New England on similar bodies of water.

A very nice rainbow trout caught during the Hex Hatch at Caspian Lake by Terry Van Veghten of Calais, Vermont. The surface temperature was right in the ballpark at 70 degrees F.

I believe that surface temperature is the most important fact when trying to determine the time to start looking for Hex hatches and is much more accurate than going by dates of previous years' hatches. But here is something you need to realize. Most serious Hex anglers (especially the grizzled ones) can be very taciturn when it comes to sharing specific details about the whens, wheres,

7. Onset Temperatures & Journals

and whats of a hatch. So, don't expect these vital temperatures to fall into your lap while watching the nightly news. You will be on your own. Just grab a thermometer, drive to your Hex-water locale, and take the water's temperature.

8. Five Steps to Heaven

To be as effective as possible fishing the Hex Hatch, I want to be there on the day the hatch begins. Of course, that's not always an easy feat, especially if your pot-of-gold pond is some distance away, but I have accomplished it a number of times. I typically verify the hatch onset in four ways: talking to other fly anglers, measuring surface temperatures, checking for the presence or absence of shucks (which can be done most anytime), and

Karen Sikorsky of Bradford Camps in northern Maine displays the kind of fish most anglers wish to land during a Hex Hatch. This handsome 19-inch squaretail came to a Stimulator dry fly. The author's suggestion for similar success is to...follow the "Five Steps to Heaven". PHOTO COURTESY BRADFORD CAMPS

of course, investigating for the presence or absence of adult duns. I'm also fine with being at the Hex Hatch earlier than the onset and actually do that quite often while checking up on the little buggers and the STs. You *can* get some action before a hatch begins, especially when using nymphs, and I have also "pounded them up" (no fish rising) with surface imitations as well when there are no duns on the water. My overall success at arriving during a hatch onset, or in the early days of the hatch, comes down to what amounts to a 5-step, somewhat fishy, but productive process.

Here is Sage Wass's 5-Step system for determining when a Hex Hatch will begin. Though it is intended to be lighthearted, there are also several slivers of truth to it. I have named it, "Five Steps to Heaven".

STEP ONE: Daytime temperatures are reaching the upper 60s with a lot of 70s, and it's early June. This is accompanied by an indescribable itch. Others are noticing that you seem more forgetful for your age group. It is now time to move to LOW ALERT STATUS. Locate all fly-fishing gear. Gas the truck. Gather together all bottles of Geritol and 5-Hour Energy that you can find. Review past Hex Hatch journals.

The author and his fishing partner Sean Fowler of Plainfield, Vermont, found that spruce gum is at best a temporary patch for a leaking aluminum canoe in the North Woods of Maine.

STEP TWO: Air temperatures finally reach the 70s several days in a row with possibly some scary 80s thrown in. It may be early to mid-June. This will surely be accompanied by nerve-racking thoughts such as, "OMG, what if I have already missed the hatch!". Status becomes RED-ORANGE ALERT. You should locate a working thermometer, preferably digital if you are over 50. Rig three fly rods. Patch any canoe leaks. (From experience, spruce gum is only a very temporary fix.)

STEP THREE: Air temperatures are consistently in the 70s and 80s. It may be mid to late June. This stage is accompanied by so many nervous tics that your family urges a trip to the ER. STATUS IS NOW **RED** ALERT! You *must* take the pond or lake's *surface temperature!* You should be looking for onset STs of 65 to 70 degrees. Look for cast-off shucks from the evening before and *pray* you don't see any. (You don't want to miss the first day of the hatch if possible.) If you are there come dusk, look for

RED ALERT. It's mid to late June and air temperatures are in the 70s and low 80s. Take your go-to pond's temperature. Look for shucks and Hex duns. THE HATCH is about to begin. It's time to make the doughnuts.

8. Five Steps to Heaven

avian or bat activity and scan the surface for duns. Okay. It's not on. Close but no congratulatory cigar. Go home. No brooding necessary. *You haven't missed it.*

STEP FOUR: Air temperatures are 70s with more 80s. You are a nervous wreck at this stage and extremely touchy. You tend to ruminate at work. "Just *how* early is early retirement?" Status remains at RED ALERT with emphasis on **RED**! The key now is to compare the temperatures you measured the last time at the pond with upcoming weather. If the last measurement was close to the onset temps *and* the next several days are going to be warmer than normal, *you need to be there every day.* Easy for you retirees to say, as the whispers go. So, what to do? Geez, folks, this is fly fishing at its apex. It's life. My suggestion is this. Complain to co-workers and family of an ill-feeling, a…bug…coming…on. Be sure to mumble the word Hexitis so that your "illness" sounds grave. Stagger a little bit. Then when out of sight, *beeline* it to the pond of your choice. (Of course, all your fishing gear has already been appropriately stashed out of sight in your vehicle.) *But*, if there's no imminent warm-up predicted, and maybe just the opposite, a cold spell, you can *try* to skip a day before testing the waters once more. This does come with severe, adverse side effects, though. Nightmares rear their ugly heads where you imagine everyone else is hitting the hatch like gangbusters and you have been detained by the local game warden for forgetting your damned license. Worth it to skip a day you ask? You decide.

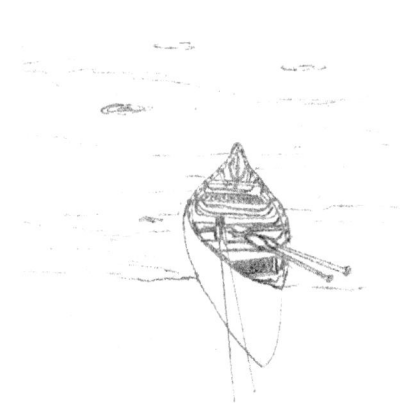

It's 8 PM and the fish are rising. LET'S GO!

STEP FIVE: NOTHING HAS CHANGED. **RED** ALERT STATUS remains. Should I go again to check on the hatch and see if I can hit the onset? Is Hexitis debilitating? COME HELL OR HIGH WATER GO! You are into the Hex Hatch!

Believe it or not, folks, humor aside, this 5-step technique works for me. So much so that I have hit the beginning of the hatch a number of times. Try it. (Just go easy on the Geritol.)

9. Who Shops at the Hexagenia Supermarket?

As might be expected, *H. limbata* enters into many food chains with fish near the top of that energy pyramid. Almost every species of fish living in the same habitat as Hex mayflies use at least one stage of the mayfly as a food source. In many instances, fish like trout and salmon feed on both transformations of their life cycle, the nymph, and adult. As mentioned earlier, lake trout make use of the nymphs as food, apparently all year-round to some degree. But do lakers come to the surface for duns? On occasion. June 16, 2004, saw me land my first lake trout ever on a dry fly, a

Beautiful Willoughby Lake in Vermont at Hex Hatch time. Willoughby is known for its salmon, rainbow trout and huge lake trout.

9. Who Shops at the Hexagenia Supermarket?

Hex emerger, although it was during a brown drake hatch. It stretched the tape to 14 inches. In 2018 a Hex fly-fisherman told me that he had landed two lakers on dry flies while fishing the Hex Hatch the previous year. It happens, but not with regularity. It does add a little spice to the mystique of what species you may catch on the next cast, though.

The following experience that I had on **Willoughby Lake** in Westmore, Vermont, some years ago is an example of the aforementioned mystique. It was getting into that "twilight zone" of Hex fishing when the fading light starts to become a detriment. I could just make out a decent-sized fish cruising and gulping duns a bit too far for my casting distance, although the fish was slowly working its way towards me. Knowing that my time was getting squeezed for the last chance to score on a rainbow or salmon, I impatiently waited and waited for the fish to come closer, determining its direction of travel after each rise. When it got into my casting wheelhouse, I laid a Compara-dun-style fly smack-dab in its path. Slurp. I hooked the fish and it felt like a really good one.

The author was handed this photo from friend Terry Van Veghten after a Hex fishing trip. Suckers feed on Hexagenia mayfly nymphs and they ALSO take Hex dry flies from the surface. This white sucker was caught just prior to a Hex Hatch on a Hex nymph fished with sinking line. TERRY VAN VEGHTEN PHOTO

9. Who Shops at the Hexagenia Supermarket?

I was ecstatic. As I played the fish, though, something didn't seem quite right about the way it was fighting. There were no jumps or real zings as I would have expected from a rainbow or salmon. I played it carefully for some time until I could slide my net under it at boatside. In the 9 PM darkness, my headlamp didn't show the pinkish-red stripe of a rainbow, nor the black-dotted silvery side of a salmon. Nope. There it was. A gorgeous 21-inch... *sucker* lying there with my fly in the corner of its puckered mouth. Ay-Yi-Yi. After unhooking then releasing the fish, and with a sigh heard round-the-lake, I called it a night and motored back to the launch. And did I ever hate to end the evening on that puckered note.

I have also caught lake trout and suckers up to 19 inches just before an evening Hex Hatch by using sinking fly lines and nymphs. These results, coupled with jigged lakers that spit out Hex nymphs when netted, have led me to believe that suckers, lake trout, and other non-target species collect in the vicinity of Hex Hatches to feed on the nymphs. Often, when I have had a fish-finder aboard, I have marked large fish hunkered near the bottom in depths of 20 or so feet, adjacent to where *Hexagenia* hatches occur. No question in my mind that those fish are lakers, suckers, and large yellow perch making use of the Hex smorgasbord.

The list is quite long when I recall other species of fish that I have "fooled" during a Hex Hatch. It includes brown trout,

Yellow perch are mighty good eating but when you are targeting salmonids during a Hex Hatch, they do nothing but gum up your fly.

9. Who Shops at the Hexagenia Supermarket?

smallmouth bass, yellow perch, chub, rock bass, sunfish, bullpout, and even smelt. Yes, I once caught a 5-inch smelt on a Hex nymph. Friend Terry Van Veghten has also caught smelt during the hatch but on dry flies. Other than the brown trout, I typically show severe disdain for distractions caused by non-target species during a hatch. The time to fish during an active Hex Hatch is finite. Read, a *very* small window. I certainly do not want to waste time bothering with fish that aren't trout or salmon. I must say, though, that there's nothing better out of a frying pan than a yellow perch…well, maybe bacon. But when zeroing in on a honker trout, even fried perch fillets get the snubbed nose from me. Besides, non-focused species invariably gum up your fly so much that you need to dry and "re-grease" it before casting again, so much so that even a little Fly-Agra won't help. As an alternative, though, you *can* grab fly rod #2 and put the #1 rod away.

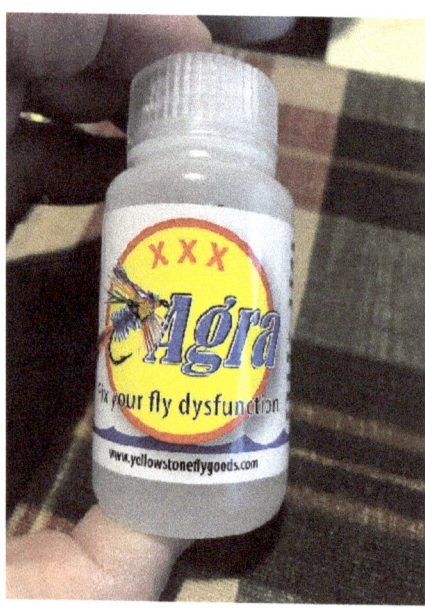

When non-target fish species gum up your dry fly during the Hex Hatch, even some Fly-Agra might not help much to…stiffen the bristles.

Vermont lays claim to a fisherman who is like no other. His name is Drew Price and calls Charlotte his hometown. To my knowledge, Drew is the only person who has landed at least one trophy-sized fish of all 33 eligible fish species that are part of the Vermont Fish & Wildlife Department's relatively new Master Angler Program. It took him eight years to accomplish this astonishing feat.

When Price launched his plan in 2010, he was strictly a fly angler and told the program's administrator, State Fisheries

9. Who Shops at the Hexagenia Supermarket?

Biologist Shawn Good, that he planned to catch all 33 species by fly fishing. By the end of that year, he had landed 12 species, all

Drew Price of Colchester, Vermont, with a nice pike-pickerel hybrid taken from Lake Champlain. According to fishery biologist Shawn Good, this hybrid fish occurs inadvertently from male pickerel milt and female pike eggs. Price catches other species on Champlain during its Hex Hatch. VT F&W

with a fly rod. Two seasons later, he was up to 24 out of 33 listed fish, again, all on a fly rod.

This wasn't done in a pell-mell manner at all. He researched each fish to learn it inside-out, and he talked to fishery biologists and other anglers. But by 2014, it was becoming more of a challenge for Price. The last few species were tight-lipped to his fly-fishing gear, and he realized that he had gone as far as he could with his choice of "weapon". So, he decided to give an inch, but take a mile, and switched to other fishing tactics like ice fishing and spinning rods. He was totally new to both of these strategies, but they worked. One by one he moved up the species list to 32, and then became stuck on third base with a real toughie, the pike-pickerel hybrid. It took him three more years, but he eventually filled that last slot.

9. Who Shops at the Hexagenia Supermarket?

I'm not sure how many of the 33 species Price caught on home-tied flies, but I suspect many of them. I also don't know if any of the record fish were caught during a Hex Hatch, but I do know that he has landed carp, smallmouth bass, and sheepshead (freshwater drum) on **Lake Champlain** during the period of Hex hatches. Price says that carp are "suckers" for Hex nymphs at Hex Hatch time and he's pretty sure it's just a matter of time before he lands one on a dry fly. Bass can also become very focused on the Hex, according to Price, and he loves to sight-fish them on a flat with calm water using Hex nymphs. What about the bottom-loving cusk or burbot? I bet this tasty fish also swallows its fair share of Hex nymphs. The list goes on.

Another fish species worth mentioning that feeds on Hex nymphs is the northern pike. In the Midwest and Canada, these toothy critters, as well as other predatory fish, are so enamored with the availability of nymphs during the Hex hatches, that they are likely to pass on eating young-of-the-year walleyes. Acting as a buffer, that in turn allows the populations of young walleyes to "catch their breath" and grow.

I have never fished the Hex Hatch where only brown trout are the quarry, but they have come at times, like lakers,

Nice brown trout like this one can be caught during a Hex Hatch. They may be a surprise incidental species, or in some lakes and ponds the main target species.
ANDY WASS PHOTO

9. Who Shops at the Hexagenia Supermarket?

unexpectedly. One Vermont lake that I have spent more time on than any other (**Caspian Lake**, in Greensboro) has a few wild brown trout, although it is considered primarily a rainbow lake for Hex Hatch fishing. A few of these pretty browns are landed during the Hex Hatch, including one boated by fellow fly-fisher Dave Oles of Barre, Vermont, back in July of 2000. Dave hooked the fish on a Hex dry fly and it really gave him a tussle, but without jumping at all and that befuddled us. Deftly played, he guided the trout into my waiting net where we could see the reason for no aerial jumps. It was a gorgeous brown of about 17 inches and fat as a football. And in this same Vermont lake, a young fly angler at the time in the early '90s, Willie Brown of Woodbury landed a nice 16-inch brown trout fishing the evening Hex Hatch. No sir, we do not snub our noses at brown trout when targeting salmon, rainbows, or brook trout.

You may have noticed that walleyes are missing from my rather extensive list of fish caught during a Hex Hatch. As much of a wild trout and salmon fisherman that I am, I still have had a real jonesing to hook a tasty, white-fleshed walleye during a Hex Hatch. So, what's the problem? Me. Would I need to take a side trip to the land of 10,000 lakes? Nope. I just can't seem to relinquish a trout/salmon Hex-fishing trip to fish a place I know that both *Hexagenia* and walleyes exist. And there are a few of those locations within a two-hour drive of my home.

A reliable source once told me that he had a relative who owned a camp on **Lake Carmi** in Franklin, Vermont, and the camper claims there are great Hex hatches on that small lake. Salmonids are non-existent in Carmi, but it has an excellent warm-water fishery, especially for walleyes and perch. The camp owner reported that ole marble-eyes cruise the surface during these Hex Hatches gulping down adult mayflies. Unseen by the camper, of course, are the many nymphs also tucked away by the walleyes. And I'm sure that the bass, northern pike, and huge yellow perch in this piece of water do the same. Unfortunately, the lake has been overwhelmed with blue-green algae (Cyanobacteria) blooms in recent years. The State of Vermont developed and enacted a

9. Who Shops at the Hexagenia Supermarket?

"crisis response plan" in 2018 to help control the primary instigator, phosphates, predominately from agricultural runoff. The walleyes are still there. Not so sure about the mayflies.

Lake Champlain also has extensive Hex hatches during the summer, *and*, the lake is full of walleyes, salmon, lake trout, a few steelhead, and brown trout. I'm going to crawl out on a dead limb here, but I am willing to bet a bamboo fly rod (luckily, I own no complete ones) that someone has fly-fished the Hex Hatch on this huge lake and has caught walleyes on the surface, and probably salmon, too. There is a lot of after-dark fishing on Lake Champlain and you have to wonder, just what are they up to? From experience, I know one favorite nighttime activity on Champlain is trolling for walleyes, as they come to the surface; I've done it myself during the awesome Perseid Showers in August. But how many fly anglers make use of the Lake Champlain Hex hatches by challenging themselves to fly fishing for walleyes? (I'm betting Drew Price will be all over it this summer.) There is one more species in Maine that I would just love to catch on a dry fly during the Hex Hatch, and that is the magnificent blueback trout. Bluebacks, or Arctic charr (char) if you wish, are found in only a very few Maine water bodies—14 the last time I heard. They prefer deep, cold oxygenated waters and no doubt uncommonly come to the surface to feed on adult mayflies, although I'd bet that same bamboo fly rod I don't have, that they often feed on Hex nymphs. Bob Mallard, the author of *Squaretail*, reported he once caught a blueback with a small mayfly spinner pattern on the surface at **Big Black Pond** in the Deboullie area of northern Maine, and in one other instance, I read that a fly fisherman landed a blueback of over 23 inches on a green drake dry fly. No other reliable sources of this feat came to my attention, although there may be some.

I have fished Big Black Pond many times and fooled some large brook trout from that beautiful spot, as well as some bluebacks. But all the bluebacks were caught on streamers fished deep. Most were small (9-12 inches) although, in July of 2013, I did net

9. Who Shops at the Hexagenia Supermarket?

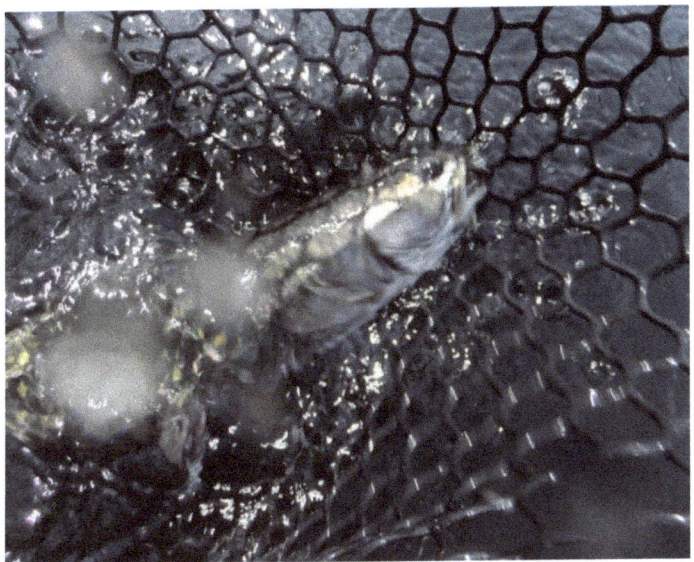

A pretty, Big Black Pond brookie coming to net.

one gorgeous male specimen that measured 15 inches with an orange-peel-colored belly. Big Black does have a Hex Hatch as mentioned earlier and it would seem that early in that hatch, soon after its onset when the ST is still relatively cool, would be the best possible time to nail a hungry blueback on the surface. But, due to the fairly extensive walk out in the dark, and geezer-type knees and hips, I have never stayed to fish that hatch until dark. Maybe next time. (Be aware that bluebacks are rare in Maine and when caught should be released.)

There are of course many other predators of Hex mayflies in addition to fish. Feeding primarily on underwater nymphs are voracious dragonfly larvae, loons, various water beetles, crayfish, leeches, and some amphibians. As the 2-tailed duns make their stately appearance from their 3-tailed shucks at the surface, they also become food for avian predators. Included are a variety of birds such as grackles, swallows, cedar waxwings, ducks, and gulls, as well as bats.

9. Who Shops at the Hexagenia Supermarket?

Blueback trout are found in only a few of Maine's ponds and lakes. This pretty 15-inch male came from Big Black Pond in Northern Maine.

It's worth mentioning how some of these natural predators can influence Hex anglers. I have oftentimes verified the existence of a hatch simply by watching bird activity. In particular, grackles seem to key in on feeble-flying mayfly duns (and caddis) after hatching. The birds will sit on a branch along the shoreline until spotting one, then fly out to grab the unsuspecting insect, often leaving just the wings behind.

One last try.

My journals indicate a large number of bats in past years showing up at the very last squiggles of light, picking adult Hex out of midair using ace pilot loop-de-loops and also plucking them from the

9. Who Shops at the Hexagenia Supermarket?

water surface. That was a much more common sight 15-20 years ago before the white-nose syndrome fungus attacked many of our native bats. Back then, bats were so common during hatches that I would stop fishing once they "took over". Bats would often mistake your fly for the real thing and try to take it from the water, and in some instances would acrobatically home in on your fly during the cast, only to be hooked.

10. Ducks, Duns and a Grumpy Fisherman

And what about ducks? Let me tell you about those wascally waddlers. Not too many years in the past, I stayed at a set of sporting camps in northern Maine. It was Hex Hatch time and my brother Stan and I were flailing fly rods and flies over waters next to an underwater reef each evening. The first night out, just when things got to a pee-your-pants pitch with super-sized *Hexagenia limbata* shucking their shucks, along came a horde of ducks. Oh, boy. Right into the center of our fishing living room, they came, chuckling like the imps they were. Ge*t out of here*, I hoarsely growled with gritted teeth. No dice. Not only did they chase natural mayfly duns within our casting range by skedaddling across the surface, but they also zeroed in on our artificials. They put the kibosh to fishing that evening – and the next – and the next.

I finally decided that it was time to man up and complain. But to whom? The ducklings' mothers? Other fly fishers? It seems that these ducks were being hand-fed regularly from the sporting camp dock by well-intentioned duck lovers. Okay. Guilty party identified. Naturally, the ducks hung around that area for a good part of the day, but our prime Hex-fishing spot was close enough to the dock so it was nothing for them to paddle their little butts over to "our" area where there was some delicious natural protein available. "Phooey to bread", they said.

10. Ducks, Duns and a Grumpy Fisherman

Timing is everything in the world of Hex fishing. GET OUTTA HERE!!

So, I dutifully complained to the camp owner pleasantly, and she completely understood the conundrum: fun-loving campers who pay for a stay and like to feed the web-footers, and the hard-nosed Hex anglers who pay for a stay and like to catch wild trout. There wasn't much she could do that year lest she hire some early-season duck poachers. She did promise her best to stop the duck feeding and would post signs, "Please Don't Feed the Ducks!" (I suggested something a tad more ominous, "Please Don't Feed the Ducks – Grumpy Geezer Fishing") Of course, the hope was if patrons didn't feed the wild ducks at the camp's dock, the ducks would spend more time at the other end of the pond, and then not be as easily drawn to the Hex-fishing area.

Some might suggest fishing elsewhere on the pond. The problem is that this particular Maine pond is very small and the reef mentioned is undoubtedly the best spot on the entire pond to fish the hatch.

10. Ducks, Duns and a Grumpy Fisherman

The duck problem is by no means unique to this Maine fishing destination. **Echo Lake**, in northern Vermont has a nice Hex Hatch and robust rainbows pass Echo Lake water through their gills. A number of years ago, there was an Echo Lake heyday when large numbers of 16 to 24-inch rainbow trout were caught with regularity during its Hex Hatch, although that great fishing "era" has since seriously abated to something a tad less than normal. But Echo Lake also owns a duck problem. I have chatted with several anglers over the years who told me that ducks ("camp ducks" that are hand-fed) spoiled their fly fishing on many a night during Echo's Hex Hatch. Ducks *love* mayflies.

Rainbows like this 22-inch specimen were once common fare on Vermont's Echo Lake during the Hex Hatch. There are still a few fish like this in Echo, but watch out for the ducks. (Note the Comparadun dry fly in its mouth.)

Let me goad you with one last question. Do trout consume more Hex in the nymphal stage or as an adult mayfly? By far, fish prefer the nymphs. After examining the stomach contents by microscope from several fish caught during mayfly hatches, I estimated that as much as 90% of their food intake came from nymphs. The rest consisted of cripples (wings malformed), and of course duns. Understand that this was not a scientific approach

10. Ducks, Duns and a Grumpy Fisherman

by any means but merely an eyeball estimate made under a microscope. Nevertheless, when it comes to fly choices during a Hex Hatch it seems my microscopic analysis should tell us something about fly choices. But no. Instead we listen to our "love-to-see-a-fish-come-to-the-surface" hearts. And to be sure, it's the rewarding splash or slurp to a dry fly that ultimately brings the Izaak Walton out in most of us.

Many of the swirls you see during a Hex Hatch are fish taking the nymph just before reaching the surface. I'd even go as far as

This giant Recurve mayfly didn't quite make the author's hat, but close enough.

to say *most*. If a nymph makes it to the surface *en tout*, it typically doesn't take but a few seconds to break out of its exoskeleton unless it is damaged or deformed in some way. Generally, after a

10. Ducks, Duns and a Grumpy Fisherman

few more seconds they become airborne. Most splashy, noisy rises that you might hear or see during a hatch are likely fish keying in on adults, often just as the dun starts to flutter a bit before heading for greenery...or your hat.

And where does all this lead us? Right back to where we started this life cycle. I have often wondered if I could capture, and then transport, a sufficient number of adult duns to a pond that doesn't own a Hex Hatch, and if they might propagate to start a new population of Hex mayflies. Theoretically, I think it could be "dun". From a philosophical standpoint, though, I keep coming back to the phrase, "Don't fool with Mother Nature".

11. What's in a Name

Brother Stan and I were fishing out of Nahmakanta Lake Wilderness Camps in northern Maine and eyed a nearby Heritage pond that owner Don Hibbs had recommended since we would have only a short window of fishing before dark. It looked promising. It harbored only wild brookies and although the pond was very small and shallow (9-foot maximum), it boasted of 16-inch two-pound squaretails and a lot of them.

This shallow Heritage pond in the Nahmakanta region of Maine not only supported a moose population, but two-pound wild brook trout, as well. When not feeding, the trout hunker down in the muddy substrate that is cold and well-supplied with oxygen.

11. What's in a Name

We carried our gear into the fly-fishing-only pond on a trail that took only 15 minutes and found the small boat right where Hibbs said it would be. It was our first day fishing on this trip, so we were primed to land some nice speckled trout. We stayed till dark and landed only two trout, a 9-incher and one 12 inches long. We never saw a rise that appeared to be made from an Eastern brook trout that would have been larger than what we caught.

Back at the lodge on beautiful **Nahmakanta Lake**, we queried Don about the trout haven that we had just fished. He said that you wouldn't believe the number of good-sized trout in that pond *if* you hit it just right. He also related an amusing story regarding the native trout in the pond. Canadians would call them mud trout, he said, because that's where they stay when not feeding and when the water column is too warm. At that time, we were in the middle of one of those wicked July hot spells, and a measurement of the surface temperature proved to be 78 degrees when we fished it the following day. No wonder trout weren't rising. Hibbs continued to say that he had once watched some trout be-

A nice Nahmakanta wild brook trout.

ing stocked in a similar shallow pond and that they all darted right for the bottom *into* the soft mud and weeds when released. Of course, the mud is almost always colder because of springs in

11. What's in a Name

these shallow ponds. (Think of wading while swimming and the cold mud oozing up between your toes.) And in the mud these trout stay until hunger pangs send them darting toward the top but then rifling it right back into the mud. That's how squaretails survive in many shallow ponds, and I have seen it in other places, as well. Thus, the designation mud trout...a name surely not befitting the most beautiful fish in North America.

I'm hoping that you picked up on my use of the many common names for "trout" in this chapter's opening paragraphs. Nope, not done to baffle you. Done to illustrate the potential confusion of using common names.

In the 1700s a Swedish botanist by the name of Carl Linnaeus devised a system to classify organisms based on similarities of physical traits. He's the guy to blame if you dislike the use of scientific jargon. But on the other hand, he is also the mastermind to

Two sea-run trout, or salters, caught on a Silver Doctor Bucktail fly by the author on Mount Desert Island as a high school senior. In late spring, when salters first arrive in fresh water, they have a silvery-purplish hue to them and are as scrappy as brook trout can be.

award credit for the basis of our modern-day scientific classification system called taxonomy.

Common names, the bane of scientists' conversations, tend to be geographical in nature. Take my favorite species of fish the brook trout. In parts of Ontario, they lovingly refer to them as "specks". Many Mainers, especially old-timers, love to call them "squaretails". Downeasters near the coast of Maine use the names "sea-run trout" or "salters" for those trout that migrate to the ocean and back. Lake Superior has a population of potamodromous (those that migrate from freshwater lakes up streams to spawn) brook trout called "coaster trout", or "rock trout". And in parts of Canada the name "mud trout" is used as a common name.

Linnaeus wanted to avoid this ambiguity by assigning every living organism a special (scientific) name made up of two parts that *no other* organism would share - its genus and species. He also expected this name to be universally accepted by the world's scientific community. His classification system, with a few tweaks over the years, is pretty much intact and internationally used

Ephemera guttulata is the scientific name for the Eastern Green Drake mayfly. It is almost as large as a Hexagenia mayfly and its common name, Green Drake, is often confused with Hexagenia's common name. The Eastern Green Drake dun has three tails, whereas Hexagenia has two. PHOTO TROUTNUT.COM

11. What's in a Name

today. So, what's in a name? An Eastern Brook Trout, a salter, a sea-run trout, a spec, a coaster, a squaretail, and a mud trout are all *Salvelinus fontinalis* everywhere in the world.

And so, what about mayflies? Same problem. More common names and more confusion. Let's start with our star of the book, *Hexagenia limbata*. Some of its common names in the Midwest are Michigan Caddis, Fish Fly, Great Lead-winged Drake, Canadian Soldiers, Shadflies, Giant Burrowing Mayfly, Sandfly, Michigan Wiggler, and Green Drake. And there are more. We are a bit more exacting in the Northeast since the only common names I have ever heard are Hex, Drakes, Green Drakes, and Damned Big Mayfly. Therein lies a problem. Admittedly, some could give a rat's ass about this common name discussion, but because of my science background, I feel that fly anglers should at least be aware of the issue. It's interesting to note, by the way, that because of multiple common names for some mayfly species, a few biologists/authors use *only* scientific names when referring to mayflies in their books to avoid all the confusion of common names.

A gorgeous mayfly owning the scientific name, *Ephemera guttulata*, a second cousin to *Hexagenia limbata* is also called a Green Drake, as is the Hex. As you can see, confusion reigns supreme here. And it goes by several aliases as well. Other common names for this very large mayfly (anglers' hands-down favorite on Pennsylvania's Penn's Creek) are Shadfly, Green May, Eastern Green Drake, and the most widely used and commonly accepted anglers' handle, Green Drake.

Confusing the matter more, this mayfly hatches nearly at the same time as Hex mayflies, and both are often found inhabiting the same water body. Also, these two mayflies are similar in size, with *E. guttulata* being a tad smaller than the Hex. But there are distinct differences between these two beautiful insects. The easiest way to distinguish the two, with an adult mayfly in hand, is to count the tails. Hex adults have two and *E. guttulata* (herein to be called the Eastern Green Drake, EGD) have three. Easy peasy. Also, if this mayfly you are eyeing has *any* hint of light green to it at all it's an Eastern Green Drake. The Hex mayfly sometimes

Hexagenia limbata.

appears to be greenish to an observer and in photos, as well, but it's the faint yellowish hue of the wings that gives it that apparent shade. The EGD duns do vary in color somewhat, depending on the area in which they live. Water with a limestone base produces EGD mayflies that are more likely to have wings and bodies that are suffused with a yellowish-green, especially noticeable when flying. Other EGDs may be a grayish color with dull brown markings. One other difference is the spinner. The EGD mayfly spinner, called a Coffin Fly, has blackish and white body markings. Hex spinners do not.

In summary, if a giant mayfly has three tails, a greenish hue, and mottled wings, it is no doubt the EGD, *Ephemera guttulata*. If

No matter which "Green Drake" hatch we are fishing over, the goal is to land trout like this handsome Maine beauty. MARY VAN VEGHTEN PHOTO

a galdarned big mayfly has two tails, no green coloration, and a networked wing design, it's our megastar, our big cheese, *Hexagenia limbata*.

There is another huge mayfly that can be thrown into this mix and that is *Litobrancha recurvata*, often called the Dark Green Drake. This species was once named *Hexagenia recurvata* until some

Litobrancha recurvata

astute biologists found structures that they believed were lacking in similarity to Hexagenia as previously thought, so they changed its genus name to *Litobrancha*. (Yes, biologists can do that.) That may well be the reason that so many anglers refer to it as a "Hex" mayfly, other than examining the color differences between the two. These two mayflies, *L. recurvata* and *H. limbata* are about the same size and both adults have two long tails. But *L. recurvata* is a much darker adult mayfly, appearing black at any distance. Does it have any green tint to it? Nope. None. They have no yellowish-white wing coloration either, as do Hex mayflies. *L. recurvata* does have similar yellowish segmental stripes on the abdomen, but again, the base abdominal color is much darker than *H. limbata*.

And what about the frequently used term, "drake"? My gosh, there are Green Drakes, Gray Drakes, Black Drakes, Brown Drakes, Yellow Drakes, Slate Drakes, ad infinitum. What's up with that? From my research, it appears that the term "drake" is always used in reference to a mayfly species. Okay. Good so far. But let's not leave it there. What might be the *origin* of this "mayflyish" word? The best that I can determine is that it is Middle English in nature and initially might have come from the word

Nice fat brookie caught during the Dark Green Drake Hatch (Recurve Hatch) on a nymph.

"drako" meaning "the chief duck", as in a male duck. It appears that around 1400-1450, the English, while constructing artificial flies to resemble mayfly insects, dressed them in feathers from a male duck (drake), producing a "drake flye". So, there is a piece of trivia to delight all your fishing friends at the next Neighborhood (Social Distancing) Block Party or Trout Unlimited zoom meeting.

A beauty of a brown trout fooled by Doug Lyons. Was this trout sipping Eastern Green Drakes? Lyons is working on a book about Battenkill fishing. COURTESY DOUG LYONS

After talking with state biologists from all three states (Vermont, New Hampshire, Maine), it appears that *E. guttulata*, the Eastern Green Drake, has not been biologically documented in Vermont, although has been in New Hampshire and Maine waters. I did find one fly angler, Doug Lyons, who as a long-time student of the **Battenkill River** in southern Vermont, has seen a few EGD (*Ephemera guttulata*) mayflies on that river. He clarifies that statement by adding that the mayfly's appearance is more of

11. What's in a Name

a curiosity than really a fishable hatch. Lyons further added that he has identified a few *Hexagenia* on the 'Kill' as well.

Andy Schafermeyer, a fisheries biologist for the New Hampshire Fish and Game Department agrees, that the Eastern Green Drake and Hex overlap in both geography and time of year for hatching in parts of the Granite State, and that it leads to some confusion with anglers. He reports seeing the EGD mayfly throughout Northern New Hampshire and has witnessed blizzard-like hatches on the **Connecticut River** in Colebrook. Those Connecticut River blanket hatches have been verified by Maine State Fisheries Biologist, Scott Davis, as well.

Maine has some verified hatches in its northernmost regions and a few have been reported by anglers in Western Maine. Lou Zambello, the author of *In Pursuit of Trophy Brook Trout*, tells me that there are some EGD mayflies in the Rangeley Region of Western Maine. He cited the **Upper Magalloway** near Rump Pond, a small portion of the upper **Kennebago River**, and **Kennebago Lake** as having sporadic hatches.

Let me exit this chapter by saying that I actually *like* the common name, Green Drake, for *Hexagenia limbata*, and that it's perfectly fine with me for anyone to call them that. Just saying.

12. Doughnuts Make it Special

I like to think that much of the excitement of fishing the Hex Hatch comes before the casting. For example, choosing the "perfect" destination, organizing the gear, talking up pre-trip chatter with friends, and patronizing treasured stops along the way. Take my excursions to water bodies in Vermont's Northeast Kingdom that are rife with *Hexagenia* and have wild rainbows that produce blubbering fools out of sane men and women. My pre-trip planning always involves checking up on Mother Nature first. There's nothing worse than arriving at your lake or pond, only to be turned away by wind that wouldn't allow an amphibious barge to

One more cast.

launch, let alone to cast a dry fly. And since the Hex Hatch centers right around the 4th of July, thunderstorms can be a huge safety issue. It happens—sometimes thwarted before you even uncase your fly rods. When I have incorrectly interpreted the weather gods, it's nothing but sulking from there on in, although it doesn't take but a few minutes on the return trip home to plan for the next attempt.

On one Hex fishing gamble quite a few years ago, my friend Terry Van Veghten and I wagered that despite the prediction of thunderstorms around our lake, we could hit the hatch and just get off the lake in time before being slammed broadside by the storms. (Hexitis is a wicked tease.) As we started to cast, a last look at the lowery skies scudding upon us indicated it was time to fish or cut bait. Exit and run it was…or get fried. And guess what? The trout were just starting to rise. (I have witnessed this phenomenon many times.) I got in a few quick casts and had a wicked rise from a large trout, but missed it. My cohort was some proud

Tom Beauregard was some pleased with this nice rainbow landed during a Hex Hatch, and he didn't need to dodge any thunderstorms in the process.

12. Doughnuts Make it Special

to be using his brand new "secret killer" Hex dry fly. He managed two casts.

With lightning chasing our behinds, I was puttin' the boots to that outboard across the lake. We *just* barely got all our gear into the truck when all hell broke loose. Winds that straightened flags. Gushes of rain that created washouts. Bolts of lightning that stood the hair on our backs. On the drive home, we had to detour several times to dirt roads because of fallen trees. Driving along one sketchy section on a dirt road, we found it was also blocked by a fallen tree, so I had no choice but to take the best of the worst options in that downpour and cut across a farmer's field trailering the boat. A glance at my copilot verified his state of mind…absolute terror. We made it but weather is always an important factor to consider.

Toller and Widgie were great Hex fishing partners.

If the weather looks promising, I next decide on a companion. We all have our favorites. My choice comes from a long list of anglers…and non-anglers…who I know will enjoy a Hex safari to the hilt. Among the non-anglers are one or two of my closest friends who don't even want to fish, but just love the excitement and all the aromas (donuts included) associated with the evening…my Labrador Retrievers.

Choosing the "perfect" body of water to fish is sometimes as easy as explaining to your significant other that, no… four nights of fishing in a row *isn't* really enough. The easy route is to live with past success and go to a familiar haunt, even though sometimes you might feel the urge to explore a pond that has been on your list for many years and that you've never tried. It can be a tough call. Some other factors you might want to consider when choosing the Eden of Hex waters include: whether you prefer to fish from shore rather than using some kind of watercraft, the species of fish you are targeting, the abundance of non-targeted fish species, how popular it is with the Hex- fishing community (I don't relish rubbing elbows with a lot of other anglers), the size of fish you hope to catch and if they are wild fish, the ease of launching your watercraft, and how far you have to drive. And it may be wise to ask this question. Are you working the next day? If so, you may want to see the clock hands in front of midnight before you crawl into bed.

Lawrence Pyne enjoys some strawberry shortcake on July 4th while awaiting the Hex Hatch. His lab Willow is keeping an eye out for rises.

12. Doughnuts Make it Special

I sometimes choose a place that allows me to fish for lake trout before the evening hatch, especially if I'm not short on time. Casting hardware and jigging for lakers prior to a Hex Hatch is a fun preliminary to the real reason I am there. And, since Hex hatches in Northern New England happen at strawberry pickin' time, it's a special treat for me to bring along the makings for a sumptuous strawberry shortcake. I'm *almost* convinced that these pre-hatch, fun activities lay the groundwork for excellence in the soon-to-begin Hex Hatch.

What about the solunar tables and charts to determine when to fish? Simple. I don't even look at them for Hex fishing. I haven't found that these tables make a big difference when fishing the hatch. I could be wrong, but it's important to remember, that the time available to fish is at a premium. My mantra is, *go when you can*. I will add, though, that I *do* use the solunar tables for other types of fishing and believe in them…up to about 70% accuracy.

My last but certainly not the least important aspect to embrace when selecting a place to fish would be valuable stops along the way. I know what you are thinking. Fly shops. Nope. If you are worth your salt, all your gear will be with you. The answer is bakeries or doughnut shops. I have been known to drive more than a few miles out of my way to be sure I hit a cherished bakery and spend a few dollars. These fried morsels of delight wondrously tickle the taste buds if you arrive at your location early, or even better, they more than fill an empty angler's tank on the late-night drive home.

If you ever fish lakes or ponds in the north central part of the Green Mountain State you *must* be sure to stop for doughnuts (and more) at Connie's Kitchen in Hardwick. I was introduced to these large, flavorful, *crunchy* doughnuts by partner-in-crime, Terry "Donut Authority" Van Veghten. And OMG are these snacks (plain or sugared) the cat's meow. I can almost say that they are the best doughnuts on the planet. Yup, that good. But just a bit of a warning. The word has spread far and wide, so they are likely to be gone by noon. And, no, Connie is no relation.

12. Doughnuts Make it Special

As the sign indicates, you should stop at Connie's Kitchen in Hardwick, Vermont, on your way fishing...or anytime. They make the world's best doughnuts. TERRY VAN VEGHTEN PHOTO

13. Secret Ponds

I can find only four secret ponds in Maine, New Hampshire, and Vermont... at least according to state directories. How much you wanna bet that's a glaring error and that there are closer to several hundred, or even thousands. Doesn't *everyone* have at least *one* "secret pond"? And therein lies a huge problem for me as an author.

Exactly which ponds in this state triad do I name without stepping on some wader-calloused toes? Probably very few. So, what to do when we all want to know *where* to fish? As a writer, I am torn between disseminating worthwhile information for Hex-thirsty readers but at the same time not revealing everyone's so-called "secret pond". It's a dilemma of the biggest proportions. But if I'm going to go as far as to tell readers *how* to catch fish, I would be far amiss not to name some of each state's most prospective waters of *where* to catch fish.

Listening to my inner fishing soul, I am honoring the few requests that I have received not to name certain bodies of water. In addition, when I sense the importance of not listing particular waters because of what I feel might be a sensitive fishery, I have not included them. In general, these few ponds are small, typically harbor wild brook trout, and see little fishing pressure. A whole lot of us want these precious settings protected in as many ways as possible for years to come. But believe me when I say that you will still have plenty of choices to fish a *Hexagenia* heaven.

We also have to give some credit to those who have discovered their own "secret pond" by good old-fashioned determinedness, laborious research, and in some instances a lot of energy to get there. We all would love to have fishing holes like that, and how much more priceless it is when we have earned it.

Sometimes we are treated to more than just fishing at Hex Hatch time. Here, Mike Scott hopes for a rise with this sun-setting backdrop on a "secret" pond in Vermont.

    Several easy observations may help you locate your own secret Hex pond, such as examining the windward shoreline for Hex cases. If a hatch of some dimension has occurred an evening or two before, the pond or lake will likely have some cases floating in the wash, or at the edge of the shore. I once verified the existence of a hatch this way...in the middle of the day. Remember that these remnants of the molting process will have *three* tails and be about two inches long. Another tell-tale giveaway can involve a midday jaunt by boat, or even swimming, at a body of water you may be curious about. While boating, I always try to check out any "carm" slicks for floating shucks, as most flotsam and debris ends up there.

Years ago, when Hex hatches were unknown to me, our family went to a Vermont State Park for a picnic and swim at **Lake Groton** in Vermont. While showing off my Mark Spitz swimming strokes to the kids, I kept seeing a lot of insect-like "things" floating on the water. I don't believe that I ever quite figured it out back then, but today I know they were Hex exoskeletons (shucks). Lake Groton has no trout or salmon but is full of largemouth and smallmouth bass. That hatch is probably still happening today and might be worth a bass angler's effort to ply the waters with a dry fly or nymph.

Sporting a Hexitis smile, Mary Van Veghten shows a handsome brookie that she landed on a secret pond in Maine. TERRY VAN VEGHTEN PHOTO

13. Secret Ponds

Maine fishery biologist Frank Frost displays an impressive blueback (char) from **Big Reed Pond**. *Frost was one of the many fishery biologists to help the author in writing this book. MDIFW*

So, which ponds and lakes is this author ready to give up? I am willing to spill the beans on most waters that I have successfully fished the Hex Hatch in the last three decades, and that is about 30 different ponds and lakes. I am also listing Hex waters that I have heard of, or read about, realizing that there may be a shade of inaccuracy, so I have chosen carefully. The third source comes from state fishery biologists. Some of these biologists are fly fishers and some are not. But they do offer a good source of

13. Secret Ponds

valuable information for anglers who are interested in knowledge about specific ponds and lakes located in that biologist's district.

Other than naming the general region of each state, or in a few instances naming of a town where a pond is located, you will not find directions on how to get to Hex waters listed in this book. Today there are so many ways to locate a body of water (Google Earth, Delorme's Gazetteers, GPS, etc.) that I decided to leave that part up to you, the anglers.

Comparing the three states…VT, NH, and ME…it is clear that different species of fish are more commonly caught in one state than in another. In Vermont's Hex waters, you are most likely to be fishing over rainbow trout, both wild and stocked. In a few ponds and lakes, wild brookies and brown trout can be expected to rise to a fly as well. New Hampshire's fishing will be mostly for brookies and rainbows, both wild and stocked, with a few locations also giving up brown trout. Of the three states, Maine is by far the squaretail's promised land. This is the state to fish if *Salvelinus fontinalis* is your fancy. Landlocked salmon also rise to the occasion on some of Maine's fishing destinations, and a very special treat is in store when you are not sure if a rise is from a gorgeous wild trout or acrobatic salmon.

14. Skinny on Vermont

So, you want to land a fish over a Hex Hatch in the Green Mountains of Vermont? Most of the Hex notoriety in this state goes to the ponds and lakes in the northeast sector, an area endearingly called the Northeast Kingdom. Important common denominators these water bodies enjoy are water clarity, lack of pollution, ample silty substrate, and of course our celebrity of the book, *Hexagenia limbata*. Among the lakes and ponds that I rate near the top for feisty rainbows are **Echo, Caspian, Willoughby, Maidstone, Crystal,** and **Holland Pond.** Two other options to consider are **Big Averill Lake** and **Little Averill**, although one of my sources says the Hex Hatch is a tad on the spotty side there. If wild fish are your meat and taters, then spend your time at 789-acre Caspian or 1,692-acre Willoughby, but expect slower fishing. A pretty little pond tucked in close to the Canadian border, Holland Pond has recently bumped some of the traditionally well-known Hex ponds down a few pegs. Holland, at 334 acres, has always been a decent pond to fish, and although nothing to sneeze at, the fish size was typically a fat 13-15 inches. But I am now beginning to pick up whispers of much larger fish, and I believe that is primarily due to a change in the stocking regimen. Biologist Jud Kratzer told me that initially yearling rainbows were put in Holland, but that they were mostly being used for fodder by predators such as loons and pickerel. So, since 2014, the state has initiated a change by stocking 2-year-old trout instead, averaging about 15-16 inches, and that predation on these larger rainbows has decreased, allowing the fish to put on some length and weight. He said that yearling browns are also being stocked, and they are doing fairly well. How about a pickerel contest? Everyone gets prizes for catching and taking pickerel from Holland. Maybe even a grand prize for the largest and the most. Jud?

Former guide, David Smith, of the Newport area, smiles when he chats about fishing the Hex Hatch for rainbows at Crystal (778

This great photo by DeLora Reardon shows a good-sized brookie about to be swallowed whole by a loon. Loons are a picturesque part of the fishing environment but they do get their fair share of trout. DELORA REARDON PHOTO

acres) and Echo Lake (530 acres) that occurred a few years back. He and his son Francis cast over the waters of these two lakes often during the "rainbow heydays". David admiringly recalls a six-pounder netted from Echo and six rainbows, 20-24 inches, landed at Crystal by son Francis. Both of these lakes have been somewhat on the skids in recent years, but hatches still occur and both water bodies still support rainbow trout.

Fly tier Ken Grimes of Columbia, New Hampshire, is another pro from that Echo Lake prime fishing period. Most fly fishers in northern New England, whether trollers or casters need no introduction to this 80-year-old master fly tier. His flies have fooled thousands of fish over the years…flies that seem to last forever. Grimes started tying in high school, and by his senior year was already selling flies in three NH stores. After his college years, things really took off according to Grimes, and he has been at the vise ever since and loves doing it. His wife, Mary, used to tie the venerable gray ghost for him, her specialty, although she is now retired from that job. I might add that this genial, former teacher, with a crushing handshake, is still tying thousands of flies today. In my last phone conversation with him, he said he was working on an order of 177 *dozen* flies. Go get-um, Ken. "Don't Let the Old Man In", as Toby Keith sings.

Not surprisingly, Grimes is a darned good fisherman to boot.

Echo Lake and Crystal Lake in the Northeast Kingdom used to produce some serious rainbow trout during the Hex Hatch. This honker of a rainbow was landed by Ken Grimes at Echo Lake in 1999. It measured 27 inches and weighed 8 lbs. And...he caught it on a dry fly. COURTESY KEN GRIMES

I'd have to say that his favorite water for chasing fish over the years has been Echo Lake in Charleston, VT. A few Echo Lake facts may help support that supposition. How about 92 rainbows, 20 inches or over, between him and his fishing partner, Ted Burns, in one year? Or, how about 15-17 fish in just two evenings...that's *each* evening of fly fishing at Echo? In addition to fly fishing for rainbow trout, Grimes has one heck of a trolling history landing big lake trout, including a huge laker from Echo at 40 ¼ inches and 30 pounds. This great fly-tier can also put fish in his boat.

Grimes says he and his friend, Burns (a former student) of North Stratford, would put his boat in at Echo about two dozen evenings in a row when the Hex Hatch was on, and that they did that for two years when the fly fishing was at its peak. In the best year (1999), only two of the 92 rainbows landed were kept, one a 5 ½ pound fish that they couldn't revive and a 27-inch, 8-pound beast that he decided to have mounted.

The best fishing lasted for about four years (I *still* wonder how I missed out on that…) and the average fish they landed were 20-23 inches. He said that other anglers were not doing as well because they were "spending too much time flailing the water and putting fish down, catching smaller fish and not knowing the tricks." So, why was this northern NH team (it sometimes included Burn's two sons, Bill and Dan) so successful at netting the largest fish? Both he and I think it came down to three strategies and he unabashedly admits that he kept them on a tight rein at the time. These tricks of the trade will be explained in detail in chapter 21.

A rainbow is putting a nice bend in the author's fly rod and producing Hexitis smiles, as well.

Their "good luck" was obvious to other boating anglers so that by the next evening there would be two to three boats right where they had fished the previous night. They had to keep changing their fishing location because of the increasing number of "land grabbers", as Grimes called them, but he said with a chuckle, "We still caught fish." As for the dreaded ducks bothering during a hatch, he reports that they did indeed interfere to some degree while they fished. Another observation he made was the countless number of bats at dusk. They were so common back then, gobbling up adult mayflies, that they'd leave a mat of hex wings

Rainbows of this size were once common on Lake Willoughby. This wild, 19-inch 'bow was fooled with a dry fly during a Hex Hatch, and released.

among the thousands of shucked Hex cases on the water.

After the hatch slowed at Echo, they would then head to 1,692-acre Willoughby Lake for its evening Hex Hatch. Because of Willoughby's colder water temperatures, the hatch started towards the end of Echo Lake's hatch, yet these two lakes are only eight miles apart. And there they continued their unbridled success, albeit not quite as productive as Echo…only three to four fish a night! These fish averaged 17-25 inches and the evening's take might have also included a landlocked salmon…if they didn't break them off, said Grimes. The wind at Willoughby (a much larger lake) was more of a factor than at Echo and limited the fishing to some degree. At Echo, he always preferred just a ripple when fishing, believing that it made his fly look more realistic.

Grimes did fly-fish two other Northeast Kingdom lakes, **Seymour Lake** and **Shadow Lake**, but didn't do well because "they hit the hatch wrong."

You should have noticed my mention of Caspian Lake quite frequently throughout the book. A primary reason for fishing this deep, clear, camp-lined lake so much is its proximity to my home, a leisurely 35-minute drive. Another motive has been the hefty numbers of wild rainbow trout and lake trout. But as a heads-up, the number of rainbows seems to have significantly dropped in recent years, yet there are still a few 2-4-pounders swimming its waters that will put a substantial bend in your fly rod.

Do brook trout ring your bell? Yup, mine too, and my absolute first choice in Vermont would be beautiful **Jobs Pond** in Westmore. Brookies were once stocked there and with some naturally occurring trout, Jobs produced a decent fishery with an occasional lunker. Today it is not stocked. All the trout are bred within its waters and it is still a go-to fishery. Jobs is small at 31 acres, but man-o-man, it holds some first-class wild trout and has a very nice Hex Hatch. The fishing is no pushover and will test

A trophy squaretail from Jobs that was trapped by fishery biologists and released. VTF&W

your self-control since these wild fish do not come easily to net. As you can tell from the accompanying photograph, a Jobs excursion could produce a trophy trout for you. Have patience. They are there. Even if you shouldn't happen to land a wild brookie, the scenery is rewarding in itself.

Other squaretail waters with Hexagenia hatches that are worth investigating include **Long Pond** in Westmore and **Lewis Pond**. According to fishery biologist Kratzer, Long Pond, at 76 acres, has both wild and stocked brook trout, and even though they aren't abundant, some big ones are coursing Long Pond water through their gills. Lewis Pond (69 acres) isn't the brookie retreat it once was but still has a few wild fish. Be advised, though, smallmouth bass now outnumber the trout two to one, and some of these bass swimming the waters of Lewis manage to reach three pounds or more.

Seymour Lake is a large (1,769 acres) Northeast Kingdom lake that has a healthy population of wild brown trout, as well as some stocked landlocked salmon. It also has huge Hex hatches. With some persistence (and willingness to put up with 3–6-pound smallmouth bass) I would bet a dozen of Connie's doughnuts that a brown trout or salmon could be enticed to a fly during its Hex Hatch. Another brown trout water not too far distant is 626-acre **Island Pond**, and taxidermist Walt Driscoll of Island Pond says that he has seen big Hex Hatches right into September on that pond. Driscoll reported that four to five years ago, brown trout in the four to six-pound range were fairly common at Island Pond but he feels that they are lower in numbers today. I can tell you, there's not much discussion needed regarding whether or not a 5-pound brown trout on a Hex fly would light my fire.

Eligo Lake, Nichol's Pond, and **Nelson Pond** offer an opportunity to fool rainbows with a fly rod and dry fly during a Hex Hatch. These three ponds have coughed up very large fish in the past, although primarily lured to trollers' hardware and bait, and at Nelson… using corn under lights at night! Nelson also has a population of brown trout, and a few grow to massive size.

14. Skinny on Vermont

Vermont has a number of remote trout ponds, such as Little Rock Pond, that harbor very nice brookies similar to this 16-inch fish. Throw in a Hex Hatch and you could be in business.

One pond I've had on my "must-try list" for a good ten years is **Peacham Pond** near Groton State Forest… brown trout water. The trout are stocked but can grow to mammoth proportions, up to ten pounds and over, because of an abundant smelt supply. Reliable reports also place *Hexagenia* mayflies in the pond, although I'm afraid that their numbers are limited. Peacham is one of the few ponds I know of that has a winter drawdown related to a hydro dam (Aziscohos in Maine is another), and this drawdown undoubtedly kills a large number of silt-burrowing Hex nymphs. But, again, I'm willing to bet my favorite Hex fly that under ideal conditions (stay away from July 4th) a handsome brown trout could be enticed to take the perfect dry fly on Peacham waters.

As for the southern parts of the state, I must admit mostly ignorance. Finding specific information about Hex waters in that region has been as hard as holding on to a wriggling eel, although I was clued on to one small brook trout/rainbow trout water, 63-acre **Miller pond** in Stratford. It not only has a Hex Hatch but is stocked with trophy rainbow trout and brook trout. One other

14. Skinny on Vermont

Lawrence Pyne displays a beautiful rainbow trout from Caspian Lake that came to a Hex dry fly. SEAN FOWLER PHOTO

lead I got was from Vermont resident and author, Peter Shea. He reminded me that quite a few years ago he led VPT's "Outdoor Journal" host, Lawrence Pyne, on an overnight camping-fishing trip to **Little Rock Pond** in the Green Mountain National Forest near Wallingford. The fishing video produced from this trip was after any mayfly hatch, but Shea coughed up the fact that this pretty, 20-acre pond on the Long Trail's doorstep does indeed have a Hex Hatch… which he has successfully fished. Shea reported that he has fooled trout up to 13 inches in this 39-foot-deep pond and that back then, the 4th of July weekend was his time frame for experiencing what he calls a "good Hex Hatch".

And in Shea's book, *Long Trail Trout*, he declares that 16-inch plus bruisers are swimming there as well. Shea says to look for cedar waxwings flying out from shoreline trees and nabbing mayflies in flight to indicate a hatch is on. Sounds like a super destination for all you hiker-anglers out there who also cherish coming down with a little Hexitis.

The Clyde River in Newport, Vermont, has built its reputation on landlocked salmon. Josh Adams, owner/guide of Great Drake Angling, illustrates why. The salmon was released and stretched the tape to 30 ½ inches. BLAKE HACKERSON PHOTO

And then there is Lawrence Pyne, the host of the award-winning show, "Outdoor Journal", who lives in Weybridge, VT. I think I can safely call Pyne a friend and confidant, but trying to elicit the names of Hex ponds from him for my book was about the same as trying to find hens' teeth. Pyne told me that, yes, there are a couple of walk-in ponds with a Hex Hatch "somewhere" in the Green Mountains of VT.

As an anomaly to Vermont Hex locations, there is a river with a stretch of slow-moving water that once harbored Hex mayflies - the **Clyde River**. The Clyde is famous for its landlocked salmon runs near Newport where it enters Lake Memphremagog, but

14. Skinny on Vermont

taxidermist/fly angler Walt Driscoll, who lives near the Clyde, once told me many years ago that its upper reaches had a Hex Hatch. According to biologist Kratzer, the very upper end of this stretch has good numbers of decent-sized brook trout, where they inhabit only the

Serious competition.

colder water. Most of this 4-to-5 mile stretch of river, known as Buck's Flats, is too warm for trout though, and is rife with warm-water species of fish. It can only be fished by canoe but it is a nice float based on my past duck hunting adventures. Are the Hex still there? I'm not sure, but I would guess so. The trout are there. Anyone up for some exploring? Are there other Hex Shangri-las in Vermont? You betcha. This time, I bet some tasty morel mushrooms that with some intrepid exploration, a lot of question-asking, and some hard-nosed determination some can be found.

15. Granite-Lined Waters of New Hampshire

For a small chunk of New England, the hard-rock granite state owns a lot of lakes and ponds where Hex mayflies call home. A lot of the ponds, though, are very small and at relatively high elevations that require a hike to fish. Almost 50 remote trout ponds in New Hampshire are stocked by helicopter or brought in by backpacking with fingerling brook trout which in many cases grow to eight inches by the second growing season. These same fish can reach the middle teens after three growing seasons. Are these fingerlings then considered "wild" trout once they have lived in a remote pond for enough years to attain foot-long dimensions or even "trophy" size? It comes down to a matter of semantics and what your definition is for wild, native, and stocked trout. I admit that I am drawn to ponds and lakes where I have the potential to catch what I term "wild trout", that is, trout that were born in situ and not released by any kind of stockings. Would I enjoy fishing for and catching large trout that grew from stocked fingerlings? Does Swiss Cheese have holes?

I have fished only two New Hampshire ponds during a Hex Hatch so most of my data for the "Live Free or Die" state comes from NH's fishery biologists, and one of them, Andy Schafermeyer, was a huge help to me regarding the North Country waters. I'm going to begin with two very special northern NH ponds, **Big and Little Greenough**, which are the only two public water bodies over 10 acres that support brook trout at sustainable levels without the assistance of stocking…in the entire state. These ponds, located in Wentworth's Location, were last stocked in the early 1980s. Not too far from the mighty Androscoggin River,

15. Granite-Lined Waters of New Hampshire

both Greenoughs are special for the scenery and the brook trout that they produce, says Schafermeyer. And indeed, I can verify his account of the picturesque surroundings based on my two fishing trips to these ponds. Both ponds breed gorgeous brook trout of

Big Greenough Pond located in Wentworth's Location, New Hampshire, has three ingredients to make a good day of fishing. It has a Hex Hatch, a few trophy brook trout, and offers breathtaking scenery.

trophy size, and although Big Greenough has a smaller trout population, perhaps as low as 100 (plus or minus) fish, they tend to be larger on average than those in the smaller pond. Schafermeyer believes the low density of trout in Big Greenough (234 acres with a maximum depth of 103') could be a result of two populations of predator-fish (brook trout and lake trout competing with one another), or possibly related to habitat limitations and a weak forage base. There are no rainbow smelt present and that would seem to me to be a possible future consideration for NHFG. Stocking smelts has been relatively successful in many areas of New England and a smelt population in Big Greenough could decrease lake trout competition with the squaretails by adding a new forage base.

To support the fact that Big Greenough coughs up some sizeable trout, I noticed that a state record brook trout of over four pounds was caught there in July of 2005, and Schafermyer told me that while survey-netting in the fall, they have encountered strapping trout of over four pounds. He believes, and I wholeheartedly concur, that even if you aren't successful at landing a wild trout there, the solitude and landscape make it a very worthwhile trip.

Little Greenough, at 42 acres and a maximum depth of only 10 feet, has "tons of feed" for its brookie population, especially chubs, says Schafermeyer. The wild trout grow fast and 12-14-inch brookies are relatively common, with some much larger fish. My one trip there only produced several 8-9-inch trout, but I did

Little Greenough Pond is small and relatively shallow, but it grows some awesome wild trout. Terry Van Veghten can vouch for that fact with this handsome trout that he nailed on a dry fly. MARY VAN VEGHTEN PHOTO

see huge female Hex duns starting to hatch around four PM, which is a little unusual. Nevertheless, I just didn't seem to have the Van Veghten mystique, and couldn't come up with a larger fish, even though I did see one very nice fish rise…of course, three casts away. And yes, like a fool, I didn't play it out until dark.

I have made the three-hour trip from my Vermont home to both of these waters when I was a tad sprier, and after perusing my fishing journal from those bygone days, I found an interesting

15. Granite-Lined Waters of New Hampshire

summation written after my last trip in 2008, that I called the Big Greenough Pond Rating Game.

**Big Greenough Pond Rating Game
Note: Ten is GOOD & one is BAD...very bad**

Anticipation...Scores a Ten... What with rumors of 5-pound native brook trout coming from this remote pond and a reputed Hex Hatch to boot, it was a no-brainer to assimilate the two into a potential fishing love fest.

Trip...Scores a Five... No pre-dawn wake-up (departed at 10:30 AM) coupled with maps and notations that were on the money proved akin to taking candy from a baby. However, the late-night return to my comfy Adamant home at 11:30 PM was an expected downside to the trip. In addition, to stop at "Mickey D's" specifically for a cool, coffee milkshake at 10:00 PM only to find that the milkshake machine had been shaken beyond repair was enough to bring tears to my eyes. And, without seeing a single moose, deer, or bison over and back, the three-hour drive had few flowers to smell. Although, a book tape about explorer Ernest Shackleton's trip on the Endurance in Antarctica was more than entertaining while handling the wheel of my Toyota. The lack of real people to share in the exploration of Big Greenough Pond (there were three "gotta do something else" potential riders) ...sucked.

Walk-In... Scores a Seven... With at least three different sites to approach Big Greenough, I had to check each one of them out before unloading. Choice #1 was a walk of about 420 yards down a camp road with just a minor uphill grade coming back. No rocks, no roots, and some Hex shucks along the shoreline made this seem possible, but the length was stretching it a tad for a 66-year-old with all his gear, and a gate that seemed to say, "I'd rather you didn't walk down this road." Choice #2 was just up the dirt road a bit farther. I could even drive a short distance down this trail, but huge puddles, glacial erratics (boulders), and

15. Granite-Lined Waters of New Hampshire

The Poke Boat at 27 pounds was just the ticket for carrying to the lake and back but lacked creature comforts for a long day of fishing.

pythonic root wads, along with what I assumed to be at least a 430-yard distance put this option at the very bottom of my list. Choice #3 at the north end of the pond was paced at 225 yards, down a camp road, with the pond visible from the road. Although it had its share of boulders and a hellish steep return to the truck for about one-third of the trail, the relatively short lugging distance won me over. Plus, there was a place to park and... Hex shucks along the shoreline. With everything tucked into my Poke Boat, the carry to the pond was an easy task, and even the slide back uphill to my truck required only one trip - and three stops for pulse checks.

Pond Esthetics...Scores a Ten... Big Greenough is indeed a remote and beautiful destination. Much of the shoreline is strewn with both large and small granite rocks. Many of the boulders created a scene reminiscent of Shackleford's icebergs...groups of huge granite megaliths sticking above the waterline with most of their mass below water. In a paddle around the pond, I could find only three camps, and only one was visible from the pond itself, but it was a beauty...showing evidence that

15. Granite-Lined Waters of New Hampshire

it was a log cabin constructed in years gone by. In addition to the above, I was the only human to use this body of water for the entire five hours.

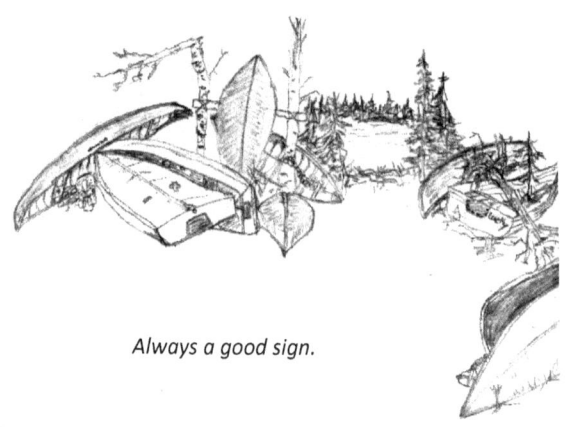

Always a good sign.

Fishing…Scores a disappointing Zero… I never caught a trout, never saw a trout, and never saw a trout rise. I dredged the bottom with sinking lines and plied the surface with floaters. What's up with that? I did notice that there were about a dozen boats pulled up on the shoreline where one trail ends at the pond, and in remote country, that is always a tell-tale sign of…something.

Hex Hatch…Scores a Seven…Sporadic Hex mayflies were hatching from about 4:30 PM on, more so when I left at 8:30 PM. There were *plenty* of them to entice a trout to the surface (albeit briefly, as the surface temperature was a *horrid* 76 degrees) but not one fell victim to the gaping jaws of a 4-pound trout, let alone a ten-incher in my part of the pond. I did not see a "blizzard" of mayflies, but of course, I didn't stay right up to the final bewitching hour. The proverbial writing seemed to be written on those hallowed camp walls… "It ain't gonna happen. Go home."

Bugs…Scores an Eight…I was rarely bothered by flying insects to warrant a lathering of Ben's finest, or use of a bug net.

There were a few skeeters, a few deer flies, and a few blackflies towards dark. Even the lug out was mostly free of biting pests.

Poke Boat...Scores a sore Four...Lack of room, difficulty stumbling in and out of it, and lack of comforts of home make this craft a big loser as a fishing craft. But, at 27 pounds and for ease of putting on and taking off a vehicle, as well as dragging to the water's edge, it is unsurpassed.

Food...Scores an Eight...If not for the sandwich that soaked up melted ice cubes in the bottom of the cooler, this would have been a Ten. The strawberry shortcake served on granite at Big Greenough is superb.

Another strawberry shortcake bites the dust and saves the day. Big Greenough Hex were hatching but no trout were rising because of torrid surface temperatures.

15. Granite-Lined Waters of New Hampshire

Wildlife...Scores a Five...Although an eagle, six hares, a bevy of mergansers (that surprised the poop out of me AND them), a kingfisher, and bloodsuckers are nothing to scoff at, the lack of moose, deer, and bison killed this rating.

Decisions...Scores a Four...Here I have to take into account the unknown versus the known. In the search for pain-free paths to the pond, I stumbled upon a *much* better way to carry into Little Greenough. It's on the backside of the pond and a mere 25-30 yards (of course with accompanying root wads and boulders) from the road. After discovering this trail, I was tempted to forego the Big Greenough experiment and instead fish the smaller pond, what with those beautiful trout that the Van Veghtens caught there several years back, and with a trail that teased like the aroma of baking bread. I thought it over for a few minutes, but the lure of the unknown (and four-pound trout) won over the bouquet of baking bread. Btw, while driving out, I noticed a car parked at Little Greenough, and with a sliver of light still available, I stopped

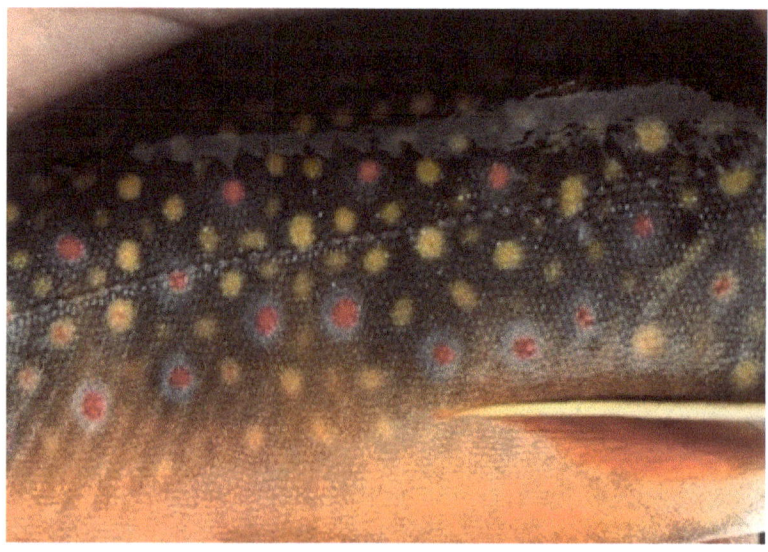

Slab-sided brookies with a mosaic like this are sulking in the waters of Big Greenough, but you won't see them with surface temperatures at 76 degrees. TERRY VAN VEGHTEN PHOTO

15. Granite-Lined Waters of New Hampshire

to walk the enticing 25-yard path again. Be damned. Trout were dotting the surface of the small pond like so many raindrops, including a huge, gulping 'bloop' from a very nice trout within throwing distance of shore. Wouldn't you know…

Overall Experience…Scores a Ten…I am glad that I went, but I'll bet my shortcake on Little Greenough Pond with its beckoning finger next time.

In retrospect, after gaining more knowledge about this glorious hatch, I have to say that my rating of a zero for the fishing on that trip wasn't really fair to the fish. Who wants to rise to the occasion when surface temperatures are flirting with the ambient climate found in a sauna? Although I have seen brook trout rise for a mayfly with STs that warm, I'm guessing it must be more of an instinctive reaction in most of those instances. In addition, playing and releasing a brook trout at those temperatures can easily result in a dead fish. Rainbow trout are a tad more tolerant of high STs, but I have found that even they are very reluctant to come to the surface for food under those conditions. So, I'm going to bump up my "fish rating" for that memorable adventure to a Score of Five, post-factum, but no higher. After all, I did give the brookies a chance to show themselves by going to their cellar with a sinking line.

Would I return to Big Greenough someday? Absolutely. Would I do it alone? Probably not. Would I go earlier in the season? Right on. Would I take my 27-pound Poke Boat? Absolutely not. (I sold it to a duck hunter.) And, would I take the makings for strawberry shortcake? You be the judge of that.

Where else in NH's North Country might you find water and Hex mayflies? With Schafermeyer's help, I came up with the following list: **Munn Pond**, **Mirror Lake** in Whitefield, **Back Lake**, **Nathan Pond**, **Upper Trio Pond**, **Lower Trio Pond**, **Mountain Pond** in Chatham, **South Pond**, **Christine Lake**, **Profile Pond**, Echo in Franconia, and both **Diamonds, Big and Little**. Are there others? For sure, but that's a helluva start for someone with a little time on their hands.

15. Granite-Lined Waters of New Hampshire

If squaretails are your fancy, Munn, Nathan, Profile, Echo, Mountain Pond, Lower Trio, and Upper Trio each get a vote. Profile in Franconia is probably the best known of the group. Like Upper Trio, it is FFO (fly fishing only) and is a pretty little pond with a maximum depth of 15 feet. Three-year-old brookies are stocked there making it quite possible to hook a three to four-pound Eastern brook trout. On the downside, there are some yellow perch present and the roar from passing vehicles on nearby I-93 can be an unwanted distraction.

Remote Nathan Pond in Dixville is aerially stocked like a lot of secluded ponds, but the trout do very well there, says Schafermeyer. This small pond maxes out at 21 feet and holds some very nice

Brookies like this can be had in NH's remote ponds.

brook trout. Steve Angers, owner of North Country Angler in North Conway, has fished many of NH's walk-in ponds, and in his book, *Fly Fishing New Hampshire's Secret Waters*, he likes both Nathan and Lower Trio for large brook trout. He writes about Nathan Pond, "At 22 acres and more than 20 feet deep, this is a habitat that holds big trout." And when talking about the Trio Ponds, he says both receive aerial stockings and that there is some natural reproduction as well. "We have fished Upper Trio Pond several times, but Lower Trio Pond is the one that calls to us", says Angers. "It is bigger and deeper and has larger trout available to the fly fisher. We have caught trout larger than 16 inches there."

If you enjoy seeing a "leaping leopard" at the end of your line, Little Diamond, South Pond, Mirror Lake, Back, and Big

15. Granite-Lined Waters of New Hampshire

Diamond all have rainbow trout, with the Diamonds and South also supporting brookies. Of special note is Big Diamond in Stewartstown. In February of 2020, a new state record lake trout was iced from that water body weighing a whopping 37.65 lbs. Tom Knight of Center Harbor, NH, used a size XXXL sucker to fool the 42-inch laker with a mind-boggling 27-inch girth. I know, that's not exactly fly fishing, but it surely could be an excuse to get out a trolling or jigging rod to pass the time while waiting for an evening Hex Hatch. It's more than interesting to note that when I asked Schafermeyer how a fish like that reached such gargantuan dimensions in a relatively small body of water (181 acres and maximum depth 100 feet), he said, "They (lake trout) are growing big eating our hatchery-stocked rainbow trout!" Schafermeyer said he *also* handled another behemoth laker caught there this winter by Cory Stillings that pushed the scale to 27.84 pounds. I can hear the chorus now from all the hard-core laker anglers, "Keep stocking those rainbows!"

Are you a mixed-species Hex angler? A few fly fishers fit into a group that I'll call "conglomerate anglers"; that is, they relish the unknown and instead of targeting a particular species, they prefer to fish where a variety of quarry may come to a fly. If you are of that ilk, Mirror and Back Lake fit the bill perfectly. Both of these waters are stocked with all three species of trout—brookies, browns, and rainbows, and if you don't mind a bass with its aerial displays, they are also part of the mix.

It's hard to beat the hues of a fall-colored brown trout and 197-acre Christine Lake in Stark owns a few of those beauties. With a maximum depth of 65 feet, this accessible pond also has a population of rainbow smelt, and that forage fish no doubt accounts for some of the very large browns finning its waters.

Moving further south in the state I relied on NH state fishery biologist Ben Nugent and department volunteer Scott Biron for my Hex information. Mid-state NH includes an area known as the Upper Valley and Biron reports that **Simmons Pond, White Pond** in Wilmot, **Solitude Lake**, and probably **Chapin, Cole, and Butterfield Ponds** all support a Hex Hatch and offer brook

15. Granite-Lined Waters of New Hampshire

trout for an angler. Simmons, Solitude, Cole, and Butterfield Ponds are all walk-ins and several of them are very remote if that's what paddles your canoe. Cole at an ungodly 59 feet deep, and only 17 acres, is FFO, as is Chapin.

The Lakes Region of NH is probably best known for its largest lake, **Winnipesauke**, and the accompanying Laconia Motor-

A fishery biologist who was of great help in writing this book was NHFG biologist, Andy Schafermeyer. Brown trout like this fish that was electroshocked in the Upper Connecticut River are also swimming in other NH waters, such as Christine Lake in Stark. Schafermeyer is the author of a book titled, "Three Idiots with Fly Rods". NHFG

cycle Week on the grand lake's shores. But **Big Squam Lake** has its own well-known identity. It was the location for some of the filming of the Academy Award-winning film "On Golden Pond" in 1981. And yes, Henry (Fonda), you no doubt missed the large hatch of Hexagenia mayflies that occurs there.

Go-to waters in the Lakes Region for Hex anglers that brag of 1000 acres or more include **Winnipesauke, Big Squam, Winnisquam,** and probably **Newfound, Waukewan,** and **Wentworth Lakes.** They are all stocked with rainbow trout and all but

Wentworth and Waukewan are stocked with one of my favorite salmonids, *Salmo salar Sebago*, the landlocked salmon. Ben Nugent reports that Lake Winnipesauke salmon are low in numbers right now because of hatchery issues, but NHFG has addressed those problems and is expecting a good fishery to return to this well-known lake by 2023. In the meantime, there are still some very nice salmon and rainbows in Lake Winnie to tease a fly. But Nugent feels if Hex-fishers are interested in targeting salmon, Big Squam might be the place to go.

What about mid-sized to small waters in or near the Lakes

Perfect Landing.

Region? Again, with much-needed help from Ben Nugent, I can safely list the following NH puddles as having Hex Hatches so thick that they will block light emanating from a full moon. (slight hyperbole) These include **Little Squam, Spectacle** in Groton, **Upper Hall, Sky,** and probably **Sunapee** and **Lake Winona**. Brook trout inhabit Spectacle, Upper Hall, Sky, and Winona, while rainbows are found in Spectacle, Little Squam, and Winona. Sunapee is the lone member of this list to have salmon.

15. Granite-Lined Waters of New Hampshire

Nugent said that salmon are doing very well in both Big Squam and Sunapee Lakes right now, and salmon stocked the 'COVID-19 spring' of 2020 (from 2018 eggs) should be very close to the "target size". And if this accompanying photo of a Sunapee Lake salmon caught in April of 2020 by Andy Schafermeyer is any indication, they will be robust as well. But don't expect to catch a wild landlocked salmon, as it's pretty rare to see a wild fish in any of the Lakes Region Waters.

Landlocked salmon are doing well in NH's Lake Sunapee. They would be a fun fish to catch during its Hex Hatch. ANDY SCHAFERMEYER PHOTO

All these brook trout waters rely on hatchery-raised fish although a few small, wild trout live in Upper Hall Pond and probably a few others. Sky Pond at 14 acres and Upper Hall Pond are FFO, and a check of trophy trout results shows a nearly 18-inch brookie landed in Sky Pond during 2018. Angers also mentions in his book of catching brookies more than 16 inches out of Hall.

Okay, folks, how many of you are going to test the igneous-rock waters of New Hampshire during its Hex "season"? And how many of you are going to use the "Five Steps to Heaven" to locate new ponds which can then be added to the Hex-waters list? See you there.

16. Pine Tree State Has It All

Introduction

It was a first. My brother Stan and I were about to fish our inaugural Hex Hatch. Here's how it all fell into place. We both had been itching for a trip to Maine's North Woods to catch some squaretails. Remembering our father talking about **Sourdnahunk Lake** (also **Nesowadnehunk**) as a revered fishing destination, this "trout factory" didn't require much discussion. Done deal. With all our gear stowed in giant garbage bags in the back of my brother's pick-up, we left Southwest Harbor on June 28, 1988, with all the excitement of teenagers on their first date.

Our trip to Sourdnahunk took us through the heart of Greenville on beautiful Moosehead Lake and within a few tempting feet of the Maine Guide Fly Shop. Of course, it was impossible not to make a stop...and impossible to leave without a wallet that looked like it had been on a Keto diet. Talk about a candy store. Dan Legere, the affable owner, set us up with "the flies we should have at Sourdnahunk because of a huge mayfly, the Green Drake, that was hatching". Huh, we thought. Sounds interesting. We left his store with bags of flies, leaders, and ...anything else that looked like it would add to our success. Included were White Wulffs, mayfly imitations with two long tails curving upwards like scimitar swords, and our introduction to a new fly that Dan called a **Wiggle Nymph**. This underwater fly was essentially two small nymphs tied on separate hooks joined by some monofilament. I remembered Ken Allen giving this fly lots of accolades in *The Maine Sportsman*, especially for, as he called it, "dredging the bottom" of

16. Pine Tree State Has It All

ANY SECOND NOW! "Dredging the bottom" is very effective with flies like the Wiggle Nymph while using sinking fly lines. The fly resembles the Hexagenia nymph.

a trout pond. We had already gone to school, K through 12, and hadn't yet cast a fly.

After settling into our cabin at Nesowadnehunk Wilderness Campground, we headed out for the evening fishing in high spirits. After paddling down the shoreline a short distance, and poking the canoe's bow out around a point, our first college-level Hex class came to light, "How to Get Along with Other Anglers 101". We were shocked to see anchored boats lined up along a shoreline resembling a flotilla of tugs waiting to guide an ocean liner. Depending on the evening, the number of boats and canoes ranged from 8 to 14, all armed with two fly rods…sometimes three.

16. Pine Tree State Has It All

Neither of us enjoyed fishing in the middle of an armada, but we decided it was best to do as the "Soudyhunkers" do when in Nesowadnehunk Country. We joined in. And we caught fish. Mind you nothing huge, but 9 to about 14 inches in length and as pretty as the scenery.

We did our best to learn by observation without being rudely obvious, and couldn't help but notice an elderly couple anchored inside of us who quietly, and without fanfare, caught trout after trout. Their tactic was simple. Cast a dry fly out not too far, and let it sit...and sit...and sit...until bloop, a fish would take it. The one without the fish would reel in, net the other's trout and then they'd do it all over again. Since that trip, and after many years of fishing the Hex Hatch, I have learned that this strategy *does* work, but it takes the patience of Job.

The author "cut his teeth" on this first ever fishing trip over a Hex Hatch on Nesowadnehunk Lake in northern Maine. The spunky brookies averaged 9-14 inches and rose for dry flies with reckless abandon.

After several more days of fishing at Sourdnahunk, another realization came to us. Most anglers were using a dropper along with a dry fly or another nymph. When questioning the store proprietor about it we were then introduced to what he called the best nymph going. Drum roll. THE Maple Syrup. We looked at it in the display case quietly asking ourselves "really?", but thinking, "Come on, a piece of pipe cleaner with a few sprigs of yellow calf tail on a hook?" You *gotta* be kidding! Of course, as with all "killer flies", we ended up buying a few, probably more to placate the owner than feeling that this was going to be our next red-letter fly. Zoom forward to today. I now admit that easy-to-tie fly called the Maple Syrup (sometimes with my modifications) has duped more brookies, bar one, than any other fly I carry. At first, Stan and I referred to this Alvin

Theriault-designed fly as a "Sugar Nymph" because, be darned if we could remember its real name, which of course was totally embarrassing to me as a resident of sacred maple syrup country…Vermont.

One memorable day during this trip, Stan was having trouble catching fish, while I, the elder brother was a tad more successful. I should add that my brother was a lobsterman, fishing out of Bass Harbor, Maine, and the tough "farmer's regimen" that work is never done, coupled with a few hours after midnight wake-up call, left him few precious minutes to fly fish, if any. So, there was some rust. That evening we had paddled right into the middle of a Hex Hatch and every time a fish rose, we'd flail our flies as quickly as possible towards the rise. Stan hadn't landed a trout all day, so I

Stan Wass, of Southwest Harbor, Maine, uses his lobster-fisherman ingenuity when caught without a canoe paddle on a remote pond in northern Maine.

could sense a cloud of annoyance hovering over him. On one of his flails to a rise, he cast forward way too soon (trying to beat my cast to the rise) and hooked his nose with a gorgeous, new White

Wulff fly. As a responsible elder brother, I laid down my fly rod (and man did that hurt with fish still rising) and extracted the Wulff from his schnozzola. Be damned if he didn't catch the biggest trout of the day on the very next cast. That was my introduction to Hex fishing and I've been…"hooked" ever since.

So where else in Maine can you find a Hex Hatch besides Nesowadnehunk Lake? The BIGGER question is *where* to start since Maine boasts around 3,400 "lakes" and 100s of small ponds. It looked to be a daunting task for this writer. Showing some unusual perception, I decided to divide the state into the same regions that the MDIFW labels as their working districts, naming some Hex ponds/lakes in each, while adding a little bit of drivel (as well as some facts) about a few of them. Hold onto your seats. This is gonna be a ride and a half. Maine is one large state.

A display at the Outdoor Heritage Museum in Oquossoc of this skin-mounted Squaretail Trout symbolizes the heart and soul of Maine's ponds and lakes.

16. Pine Tree State Has It All

Maine State Heritage Fish Law

Before I get into the risky business of naming some specific Maine waters that offer a Hex Hatch, I need to explain a relatively new term used to describe many Maine lakes and ponds, and that is State Heritage Fish waters. In 2005, the Maine State Legislature enacted a law known as the Maine State Heritage Fish law (SHF) with the ultimate purpose of protecting the brook trout in lakes and ponds that had never been stocked. This new law was initiated by the Sportsman Alliance of Maine (SAM), directed by George Smith, and brook trout advocates such as Maine Guide Gary Corson and writer/activist Bob Mallard, as well as other stewards of Maine's wild trout. Since then, the law has been amended several times, once to also include Arctic char and in 2013 to include waters not stocked in the last 25 years.

In 2017, an organization known as the Native Fish Coalition (NFC) was formed by Bob Mallard, Emily Bastian, Ted Williams, and Tom Dickens to conserve, preserve, and restore the wild native fish in Maine. Since then, NFC has expanded into New Hampshire, Vermont, and Massachusetts, and has plans to push out even further. NFC has had a laser focus on the ponds and lakes that harbor these wild native fish and are named State Heritage Fish waters. Many of these ponds and lakes (close to 600 in total) have never been stocked...ever. New ponds are being added to this distinguished list every year, and as I write this, each pond is being posted with signage to identify them as such and to warn anglers of the number one threat to brook trout and arctic char found therein...introduction of invasive fish. (There are maps on the NFC website, *NativeFishCoalition.org*, which identify these unique and valuable water bodies.) Under the State Heritage Fish law, the use or possession of live bait is prohibited. I would urge readers to go to NFC's website, read what they have done and are doing, and if possible, volunteer your services or donate money to the organization. Many volunteers have given freely of their time to be on the governing boards as well as to post signs on these (mostly) remote waters. Each of these important places deserves our utmost care and reverence when fishing them.

The author's Great Uncle, Stan Walden, from Greenville, Maine, was responsible for this effective trout bait, the Chub Sandwich.

Moosehead-Allagash Region - Region E

Sitting a tad west of the middle of Maine is one wicked big puddle called **Moosehead Lake**. It is the focal point of what the MDIFW labels as Region E, and it's going to be my launching point for Maine Hex waters. I can still recall the first time that I saw Moosehead Lake as a teenager, topping that last hill going into Greenville. I was awestruck after hearing so much about it from my father over the years. That was in 1955 and our family was on a week's outing at **Upper Wilson Pond** where we stayed in a gorgeous old camp that had walls plastered with outlines and shellacked wooden cutouts of large trout and salmon. We fished for squaretails in Upper Wilson Pond and drove the short distance to Moosehead to troll for togue. I was absolutely in heaven. One hallowed spot on Upper Wilson was known as the "lava beds", and my Uncle Stan Walden from Greenville knew the crosshairs for that fishy spot. Back then, worms were part of our fishing repertoire, and my uncle's go-to bait was a… "chub sandwich". True story. This delightful sounding fish bait consisted of a worm, a piece of chub then another worm all threaded onto a number 6 hook, fished near the bottom in about 25 feet of water. And yes, this bait actually caught brook trout.

Since those teenage years I have fished the Moosehead area off and on right up through 2019, and for that reason, it seems appropriate that I start Maine's Hex ponds and lakes with this cherished Maine region. Every story written about Moosehead Lake seems to start by detailing the lake's scopic dimensions. If you don't know those measurements by now, I suggest taking a trip there to see for yourself. It's huge. How huge? Its length is equal to 17% of the distance from northern Maine to mid-coastal Maine. While Moosehead is just one fishable location in Region E, it is worthy of mention in this book since it does support a *Hexagenia limbata* hatch. Renowned Maine fishery biologist for Region E, Tim Obrey, keyed me onto this fact. I should mention that he is a Hex fisherman and ties a doozy of a Hex dry fly called a Sexy Hexy. He kindly shared the fly with me which you will find in chapter 21.

Landlocked salmon are abundant in Moosehead Lake, and if you can find a Hex Hatch, the salmon for sure will be there and hankering to check out your Hex imitation.
PHOTO COURTESY BRADFORD CAMPS

Obrey is well-known for his fisheries work in this region, especially with squaretail trout. When I asked if there was a Hex Hatch on Moosehead, he said, "There are a few (mayflies) around but I've never found any real concentration to fish over." He has seen a few on the lake side of **East Outlet Dam**, and I have read

16. Pine Tree State Has It All

that the biologists can sometimes see fish gulping Hex mayflies right in front of their office windows in downtown Greenville. My dollars are also betting there are silty-bottomed coves in this huge expanse of water (74,890 acres) that produce a good hatch. One other source, biologist Scott Davis from Region D, told me that he once had a most memorable Hex event on Moosehead Lake. Davis said the lake is so large and windy that it is difficult to get ideal conditions for an evening hatch when there is little to no wind. But, when karma is on your side and all the stars line up, you are in for one Hex of a time. Davis referred to an evening like that off Hardscrabble Point a few years back during which he landed nine landlocked salmon, including some "pounders". So, the opportunities are there. You just have to find them. In addition to possibly catching some very nice salmon as Davis did, Moosehead's waters have also been producing goliath squaretails in recent years. The majority of these gorgeous, crimson-spotted trout with azure-blue halos are pulled through the ice but Obrey says enough big fellas are patrolling the shorelines for casters to get into the action, as well. Is a 3-6-pound brookie possible on the working end of a fly line at Moosehead Lake? Omigod yes. As a side note, smallmouth bass have unfortunately become established in Moosehead from illegal stockings, so they well could be in the mix, too.

I read in one of Dan Legere's fishing blurbs that there are something like 40 brook trout ponds within a one hour drive of Greenville, and only five of them are stocked. That is a big *whoa* for wild trout anglers. A few of these nearby bodies of water that support a Hex Hatch include **Rum Pond, Brown Pond, Secret Pond, Indian Pond,** and **Brassua Lake**. Obrey says that there aren't many trophy ponds in the immediate area of Greenville, but plenty of places to fool 12-16-inch brook trout. Both 14-acre Secret Pond and 245-acre Rum Pond grow decent trout and Obrey

16. Pine Tree State Has It All

especially likes Rum Pond. He says, "The hatch there is not overwhelming so it tends to create competition and active searching for food. The fish work the surface like a dolphin, sucking down everything in their path. Just lay the Hex pattern about 10 feet in front of them and get ready," he adds. Because of a harvest slot limit at Rum, big fish must be released, and that has resulted in good numbers of wild fish over 14 inches. **Salmon Pond** at 12 acres (which I'm guessing also has a Hex Hatch), produces an occasional big trout too, says Obrey, but tends to be a little slower fishing. All these ponds have hungry brook trout and Brassua also has salmon. Rum, Secret, and Salmon ponds are all Heritage ponds.

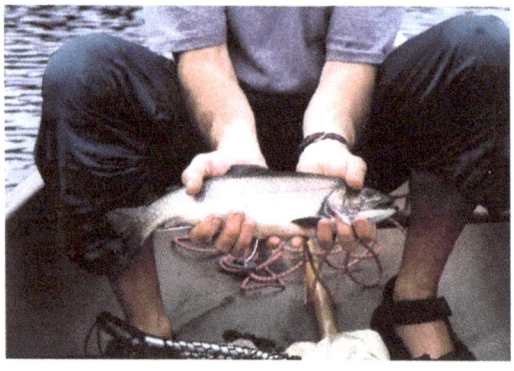

This Salmon Pond brookie shows the capability of large trout growing in miniscule waters. MARY VAN VEGHTEN PHOTO

Looking a little to the west of Greenville is a large tract of land encompassing more than 15,000 acres called Little Moose Public Land Unit. This popular piece of land is spiderwebbed with hiking trails and has camping areas with ponds in a remote setting. Obrey says that some of these outlying ponds "make good trout", although he didn't mention if they have Hex Hatches. My Social Security check is betting that they do.

While rummaging through information about the Greenville area, I kept reading about the name of a local fly tier and Hex fisherman named Bobby Shufelt. I imagine some readers recognize the name as he is the originator of the Shufelt Special streamer fly. Shufelt developed this fly around 40 years ago and it is an absolute killer in the Maine North Woods. It's interesting to note that he kept it a secret for ten years or so before putting it on the market to sell. Initially, he didn't paint eyes on the streamer but today he does, believing (as I do) that it increases the number of strikes from fish. I've also heard that he catches salmon with this fly right off the piers in downtown Greenville.

Not too far distant from the Little Moose Public Land Unit (about 15 miles NE as the crow flies) is a wonderful jumble of ponds in the West Forks/Forks/Johnson Mt. area that places you right back into wild trout country again. One cluster of ponds, due west of Moosehead and about eight miles north of West Forks is smack dab in the middle of a recent collaborative land purchase by the Trust for Public Land and Trout Unlimited. This 8,160-

David and Kathy Scott cast for wild brookies in a remote pond in the Forks region of Maine. PHOTO BY DELORA REARDON

acre tract of land named Cold Stream Forest (CSF) was purchased by the aforementioned groups in 2016 and is now a Maine Public Reserve Land boasting nine ponds, most swimming with wild squaretails. This area was also Dud Dean's playground, a fictitious, quintessential Maine guide dreamed up by Maine writer, Arthur MacDougall. I guarantee you that Dud Dean's spirit is all smiles about this land purchase.

16. Pine Tree State Has It All

Most, if not all, of the CSF ponds support a Hex Hatch, including **Lone Jack, Lang, Little Lang**, **Durgin**, **Big Berry,** and **Little Berry** ponds. This group of Heritage trout ponds ranges in size from 11 acres (Lone Jack) to 37 acres (Lang) and all but one of the nine total ponds are FFO. (**Fernald Pond** is the ugly duckling in CSF. It is thought to be barren of trout.) Some of these ponds require a short walk and are suitable for carrying a canoe (Lone Jack and Big Berry) while the rest are hike-ins requiring a bit more expenditure of energy. Float tubes are recommended.

Sitting a-plunk the CSF border lies another exceptional trout water, 205-acre **Cold Stream Pond**. It is a 62-foot-deep Heritage pond that sports a Hex Hatch and is "full of wild brook trout" according to Tim Obrey. Obrey reported that they trap-netted (live trapping) this pond a few years ago and caught over a hundred trout the first night. All the trout were given a fin clip and nets were reset. The following day the trap-nets gave up another 100 trout, and not one with a clipped fin! See you there next Hex Hatch.

Many western Maine ponds grow trophy brook trout as displayed by Mary Van Veghten. This magnificent fish was 19 ½ inches and weighed 3 ¾ lbs. It was fooled with a Hex Nymph fished on a floating line. The whereabouts? Van Veghten reports it was in the "Moosehead region". TERRY VAN VEGHTEN PHOTO

16. Pine Tree State Has It All

Just west of the Kennebec River Gorge and southwest of Cold Stream Forest sits another cluster of trout-rich waters, including **Ellis Pond**, **Round Pond,** and **Chase Stream Pond**. Ellis is the largest of this triad at 85 acres and is relatively deep at 38 feet. It is a productive pond that is capable of producing trophy brook trout. Round Pond is small at 30 acres and brags of 38-foot water depth. The brook trout are reportedly fast-growing in Round and

Some of western Maine's trout ponds produce exceptionally-colored brook trout.
MARY VAN VEGHTEN PHOTO

gorgeously colored. Chase Stream Pond is a typical Maine trout pond at 31 acres large and 12 feet deep, but according to Al Raychard in his book, *Remote Trout Ponds in Maine (1984)*, that's where the commonality ends. Raychard speaks of this pond in glowing terms as "one of the finest trout waters in Western Maine", one that is also blessed with drop-dead scenery. (Since Raychard's account (1984), I'm guessing that the scenery may not have changed much, although I'm not certain if the fishery is still that good.) Round Pond produces a Hex Hatch, and should I have Hexagenia frass rained upon me if Chase Stream and Ellis don't, as well. All three are Heritage ponds with Round and Ellis being FFO. It is possible to drive to each of these ponds but a heads up for Round Pond. Be *sure* your directions are up to snuff as there are at least 20 other Round Ponds in Maine.

Another area of fine trout ponds can be found yet further west and several are well-known in the fly anglers world. Included in this strung out-group of enticing trout waters are **Grace, Little Enchanted, Rock, and Iron Ponds**, all FFO, and all Heritage waters. Grace Pond is the largest and probably the best known at 150 acres and 41 feet deep. It is a consistent trout producer for average-sized brookies but not known for its trophy fish. It's a pretty pond with a rocky bottom and boulder-strewn shoreline. One sporting camp is located at the north end of this western

A few of western Maine's remote ponds have an abundance of trout of this size and are a ball to catch on a dry fly. DELORA REARDON PHOTO

pond, Browne's Grace Pond Camps. Even though Grace sits at a relatively high altitude, spring holes are needed to sustain trout through the summer months.

Little Enchanted is probably the next best known of this quartet, and even though it is only 35 acres in size, it is a whopping 55 feet deep. This remote, soft-wood-surrounded pond is noted for its quality fishing, picture-postcard environs, and large trout that it can pony up.

Rock and Iron Ponds are separated by a little less than ¼ mile and both have dirt road access for launching a canoe. Rock is the larger of the two at 124 acres with a maximum depth of 30 feet. I have seen reports that rate this pond anywhere from good to excellent for squaretail fishing. Iron Pond is shallow with a depth up to nine feet and reportedly proffers classic Maine tea-colored water.

I have verified that Hex mayflies can be found on Iron, Rock, and Grace ponds and my seventh sense tells me that those three are not unique and that Little Enchanted has them as well. All are FFO and all are Heritage ponds.

The Jackman area of Maine is known as a hub for logging and snowmobiling in the winter months. Come summer, though, it's renowned as a squaretail trout fishery in its many remote ponds. Jeff Reardon says the orange muddler seen in this nice trout's jaw is a great attractor fly for any western Maine trout pond.
DELORA REARDON PHOTO

About a dozen miles north of this last group of ponds, nestled in among mountains and just 16 miles from the Quebec border sits proud Jackman village. The 2018 census shows Jackman's population to be 686 spirited folks. Jackman is probably best known for being part of Maine's northwestern timber country with a working forest that allows the public to recreate with few restrictions. Jackman is also known for the Moose River, white water rafting, 200-plus-pound deer, snowmobiling, and an abundance of high-quality trout ponds. In a past issue of *The Maine Sportsman*, William Sheldon wrote that there are around 125 Heritage waters in this neck of Maine's woods which includes those I have already listed. And one of my trusted informants told me "the whole area has *Hexagenia* hatches". Want to discover some

The AMC tract, Jo-Mary locale, and Nahmakanta sections of Maine offer brook trout such as this 18-inch centerfold trout. DAVE OLES PHOTO

more? Then get out your *Maine Atlas & Gazetteer* and a map of Maine's Heritage Ponds. Mark a couple of ponds that are saying to you, "Hex waters, fish me if you can." Then reserve a cabin at one of the area's sporting camps or pitch a tent at a local campground around the first week in July. In addition to searching on your own, most sporting camp owners are free with fishing information if you stay with them.

Moving east from Moosehead in Region E, another concentration of Hex waters can be found in the Appalachian Mountain Club tract consisting of 66,000 acres and also in the Jo-Mary Lakes locale. The AMC Little Lyford Lodge & Cabins and several other AMC Lodges offer a nice base of operations to fish local ponds during the Hex Hatch. Tom Seymour, in an article for *The Maine Sportsman*, wrote that the fishing can be fast for trout on 21-acre **Little Lyford** and 160-acre **Horseshoe Pond** using dry flies and that larger trout are typically found in **Big Lyford** listed at 152 acres. The **West Branch Ponds** southeast of Kokadjo also have Hex mayflies and are all Heritage ponds. All of the aforementioned are FFO. It appears that there are 14 Heritage ponds in this AMC designated land, all walk-ins

Debsconeag Pond in the Nahmakanta area of Maine is only one of many remote ponds that has plenty of brookies to rise to a fly during a Hex Hatch.

16. Pine Tree State Has It All

except for the West Branch Ponds. The Jo-Mary country further east also has abundant Hex hatches and word has it that **Jo-Mary Pond**, at 40 acres, has nice brook trout…if you can catch them.

A little further north is the 11,000-acre Nahmakanta Public Lands expanse and the 46,000-acre Debsconeag Lakes Wilderness Area that are riddled with remote trout ponds and lakes. Most are home to excellent brook trout fishing and prolific Hex hatches. One example is remote **Debsconeag Pond** which is aerially stocked but grows very nice trout. There are also many Heritage

Dave Oles of Barre, Vermont, is all smiles with this pretty 18-inch trout caught in the Nahmakanta region of Maine. TOM ALDRICH PHOTO

waters here that will tempt those who prefer to duke it out with wild trout. As is true in many Maine locations, a majority of these waters are walk-ins and are a special treat to the hiker/camper gang. If this locale intrigues you, there is a set of sporting camps called Nahmakanta Lake Wilderness Camps situated on gorgeous Nahmakanta Lake that provides all the essentials for a home away from home. Owners Don and Angel Hibbs run a classy business situated on a beautiful lake, and Don loves to send sports to his favorite fishing areas for both trout and salmon. My brother and I stayed at these camps a few years ago and landed some very nice trout during the Hex Hatch. Don also clued us into one of his favorite flies to use during the hatch, and I've been using it ever since. See chapter 21.

A short distance northwest of Nahmakanta, embraced by **Chesuncook Lake** and the North Maine Woods' Golden Road, is a relatively small area that showcases another group of Hex ponds, including **Kelly Pond, 1040 Pond (Unnamed Pond), Blood (Duck) Pond,** and **Otter Pond**. I'll also include **Slaughter Pond** (although it's not close to the others), a remote, well-known FFO water that's situated at the southwest corner of Baxter State Park that also produces a nice Hex Hatch. All of these except 1040 Pond are Heritage waters.

Chesuncook-Ripogenus-Caribou Lake, the huge lake formed by the famed Ripogenus (Rip) Dam, takes the white ribbon for third place for size in the state of Maine. And like all large lakes,

Uh-oh. Looks like moving water. This hefty salmon was indeed taken from the West Branch of the Penobscot River in Maine, by Mary Van Veghten, but those waters come from Ripogenus Lake just a short distance upstream. TERRY VAN VEGHTEN PHOTO

16. Pine Tree State Has It All

it can get dangerously windy in a hurry and requires knowledge ahead of time about incoming weather, especially for small craft like canoes. This body of water is full of landlocked salmon produced from prime spawning grounds, but there are way too many for the amount of forage (rainbow smelt) and they have been eating themselves out of "house and home". Efforts are underway to remedy that problem including a very liberal harvest regulation that allows anglers to keep as many salmon as they want under 16 inches. Also, an annual Chesuncook Memorial (or Labor Day) Weekend fishing derby was initiated in 2018 with the primary purpose to cull small salmon from the lake's population and therefore increase the growth rate of remaining fish.

A key player in all this, fishery biologist Tim Obrey believes the approach will work after a few years. "There is reason to be optimistic about the future of salmon at Chesuncook," Obrey says. "The derby helps to spread the word that it's okay to keep the small fish, and the quicker those fish are thinned, the quicker the smelt will recover and the larger salmon will be seen. We are still seeing some good runs of smelt in the lake's tributaries, so I think that helps put us in a good situation," he continued. This fishery approach isn't without precedent. Obrey has led a similar study on Moosehead Lake to reduce its population of togue, allowing the smelt numbers to increase for salmon and trout forage.

Biologists in Region D have also instituted a similar strategy on another Maine body of water, **Aziscohos Lake** in the Rangeley Region. The attempt at Aziscohos is much like that at Chesuncook, to reduce the population of small salmon and thereby reduce the pressure on smelt so that salmon will have a better chance to grow to a larger size. Fishery biologist Elizabeth Thorndike, from Region D, says "It's honestly too early to tell if it's working on Aziscohos. We conducted a creel survey in 2018 (the first year the new regulation was in effect) to monitor lake use by anglers, and documented a nearly 60% increase over the previous survey, demonstrating that anglers were receptive to the new regs. We'll be conducting a creel survey again in 2021 as well as some trap-netting. We are hoping to see some improvement." As in all these cases, anglers need to *keep* fish for it to work. Moosehead is already showing signs of success with its togue reduction.

Yes, I certainly did digress, but I think it's important for anglers to be aware of new programs that are meant to increase fishing opportunities for us all. So, what about the Hex at Chesuncook? They are there along with plenty of salmon, a few brook trout and unfortunately, yes, there are plenty of yellow perch and chubs to befoul your dry fly, too. My feeling is that despite its size Chesuncook has a good Hex potential, especially for salmon. If you give this monster lake a try, though, you *must* know about incoming weather ahead of time, wear a life jacket if in a canoe and be on full alert for approaching angry weather.

I became somewhat familiar with this area back in 1992 when I fly-fished its ponds with a longtime friend, Jay Boomer while staying at Allagash Gateway Campground on Ripogenus Lake. It was one of those spur-of-the-moment trips, mostly prompted by

Friends, Erland Coombs (left) and Jay Boomer, discuss the merits of fishing trout in nearby waters. Coombs gave the author and Boomer a tour of local ponds in the Chesuncook area.

16. Pine Tree State Has It All

Jay's friendship with Erland Coombs who spent his summers at the campground and promised to show us some good trout fishing. Turned out that Erland was a gold mine from the Golden

This 14-inch wild trout from Kelly Pond took a Caspian Wulff around 9 PM, just as the Hex Hatch was becoming close to a blanket hatch. This trout ended up in a frying pan for a late-night meal. JAY BOOMER PHOTO **Author's Note: You will see some photos in this book where the angler is holding a fish by the gill cover, as the author is here. It is a hard habit to break, but if a fish is to be released, it is not a proper way of fish handling.**

Road. He drove us around in his truck to point out ponds that we should fish while camping there. One nice gentleman.

We arrived rather late in the afternoon on July 20, and Erland said, "You have a half-hour to get your gear ready!" So, the heck with setting up the tent. We wanted to fish! We followed Erland to 30-acre 1040 Pond (named for its elevation) for some evening fishing. The pond had a huge growth of lily pads and a resident moose population. We managed to boat several small trout but a couple who were camping at the Big Eddy on the West Branch of the Penobscot River landed a beauty of a trout that stretched their tape to 18 inches, and we estimated was a solid 3 ¼ to 3 ½ pounds. That fish set the tone for the rest of the stay.

Back at camp, it was raining and pitch-black dark, so we decided to sleep in the back of Jay's truck instead of setting up our tent in the rain. The truck's cover (a slab of plywood) was only as high as the sideboards. Talk about rain on the roof and claustrophobia.

The next day, Erland thought we should go to 64-acre Kelly Pond to fish what he called the "Drake Hatch". He told us this pond was known for giving up large trout, and indeed, even though we never caught any of those large trophy trout we did manage to see swirls and had missed takes from some very nice fish that would be measured in pounds instead of inches. We caught a few trout in the 13-14-inch range and saw Hex ("Drake") mayflies galore. We started to see fish rises around 7:30 PM and the Hex duns began coming off around 8:00 PM, earlier than what I was used to in Vermont and other places in Maine. By 9:00 PM, it was a blanket hatch with little space to land a fly. There is a remedy for this, but remember, this was in my early years of learning about the Hex Hatch.

Otter Pond saw our canoe as well. Erland told us that a 6 ¼ pound behemoth squaretail had been landed there the year before, which surprised us since this pond is only 25 acres with a maximum depth of 15 feet. Alas, we were skunked.

A little southwest of Otter sits Blood (Duck) Pond, one of the prettiest bodies of water in this part of the state. This spruce-bog

16. Pine Tree State Has It All

pond boasts a towering view of Big Spencer Mountain to its west, and it's been suggested to me that the view is so awe-inspiring that you will have trouble keeping an eye on your dry fly. Despite its *extremely* shallow water (three feet max) it supports a healthy population of wild trout and is classified as a Heritage pond. With those depths, spring holes are of course the critical factor for keeping these trout alive during the summer months. I can't confirm the existence of a Hex Hatch at Blood Pond as we didn't fish

Many Hex waters are kind of bland when it comes to scenery. On the other hand, there are some that will provide knockout vistas.

it, but with Hex Hatches in nearby **Ragged Lake**, I'm betting a free book to anyone who can prove there isn't one.

Of special note for this trip to Allagash Gateway Campground, was the date on which these *Hexagenia* mayflies were hatching…July 20, 21, and 23. That is much later than most years and the latest I have ever witnessed a full-fledged Hex Hatch. My journal notes for that year, 1992, indicate several reasons for this late hatch. At the beginning of the 1992 fishing season in Vermont, I had recorded "late spring with late ice-outs", and the Recurve Hatch at a local pond I often fish was more than a week later than usual. Also, I had fished at Red River Camps in

16. Pine Tree State Has It All

the Deboullie region earlier in the summer. That entire area of Maine had received five inches of rain towards the end of June, and although we fished until June 30th at RRC, there was no evidence at all of a Hex Hatch by that time. All this leads me to believe that colder than normal water temperatures had delayed the hatch throughout the state and accounted for the very late hatch near Chesuncook.

As a final aside to this trip, our host and friend Erland Coombs passed away in 2014 and although my fishing friend Jay Boomer is still alive at 88 as I write this book, the demons of dementia have taken his innate abilities to the point where his wife Cindy says, "It's left me with a man I don't recognize". Jay, ole pal, I am remembering the good times for both of us.

Tucked in between huge **Chamberlain Lake** (many 5-pound trout) and **Eagle Lake** is a much smaller but very productive **Indian Pond**, at a little over 1200 acres. This Heritage pond has no history of ever being stocked and quite often is passed up by fly fishers who are drawn to the nearby historic Allagash Waterway, which could be a mistake since this is trophy trout water. Three to five-pound trout are not out of the question here. Hex? Most of the lakes and ponds in the Allagash region support Hexagenia mayflies, including expansive **Churchill Lake**. So, with the chance of seeming a bit brassy, I am guessing that Indian Pond produces the mayfly, as well.

Bringing up the rear of Hex waters for Region E is a large, well-known lake northwest of Baxter State Park and west of Chamberlain Lake, known as **Allagash Lake**. It is considered by most who know the Allagash Wilderness Waterway as the wildest and most scenic of all its headwater lakes, and at least partly responsible for that description would be the restrictions attached to the usage of this 4,210-acre lake. The closest dirt road is about four miles distant and only kayaks or canoes (no float tubes) are allowed on this pristine body of water. No motors of any kind are allowed on the lake, including ice augers during the winter ice fishing season. There are generally two ways to access this Heritage water, paddling from upper **Allagash Stream** or **Johnson Pond** on its northwest side, or by mile-long Carry Trail at its south end. There are monitored campsites on the shores of Allagash Lake and no fee is charged.

The lake has historically been well-known for its brook trout that commonly reached 18 inches and abundant lake trout (togue) that had no problem attaining ten pounds or better. But in recent years these fish have been running smaller and less robust than the lake's historical pattern. It is believed by state fishery biologists that this is caused by an overabundance of predator-fish (primarily togue) and an under abundance of forage fish (rainbow smelt). So, during the winter of 2020, ice fishing regulations were relaxed to facilitate the reduction of togue numbers, but it will be a few years before the results of this experiment are known. I have read that the Hex Hatch at this lake often occurs around mid-July.

Allagash Lake, from all accounts, is a beautiful spot to fish, and does indeed have a Hex Hatch.

Penobscot Region – Region F

Sitting proudly in north-central Maine is 5,267-foot Mt. Katahdin, the centerpiece of Baxter State Park (BSP). This area of the Penobscot Region warrants too many adjectives and superlatives to give it justice in just a few sentences, so I'll whittle it down to a phrase I found and like… "an outdoor paradise". It is probably best known for being the northern terminus of the Appalachian Mountain Trail and the vast network of hiking trails interlacing its boundaries. Anglers love this wild area of Maine too for its many trout ponds…about one hundred, give or take a few. No one seems to know exactly how many of BSP's ponds support a Hex Hatch, but I would bet the recipe for my favorite trout fly

Mt Katahdin looms in the background over this BSP trout pond. DELORA REARDON PHOTO

that it's all of them. Jeff Reardon of Maine's Trout Unlimited has fished the *Hexagenia* hatches in these ponds for many years and he says you need a heads-up towards the end of June, because "BSP's mayflies can start hatching as early as the third week in June, but on most ponds, the hatch is concentrated at the end of June/beginning of July."

16. Pine Tree State Has It All

A state fisheries biologist for Region F, Kevin Dunham, told me that **Kidney, Daicey, Celia** and **Foss-Knowlton** ponds in BSP all have very strong *Hexagenia* hatches.

Using a map titled "Brook Trout Heritage Lakes of Maine", I identified 49 of the park's waters as being Heritage waters. Native trout (never been stocked) are found in 33 of them, whereas 16

According to Jeff Reardon, large trophy trout are rare in BSP's ponds, but most will give up a 16-inch fish on occasion. BSP ponds are renowned for their Hex Hatches. DELORA REARDON PHOTO

have wild trout but have not been stocked in the last 25 years. Only seven BSP ponds are stocked including **Lower South Branch, Upper South Branch, Rocky,** and **Round Pond.** Rocky and Round require little to no hiking and there seems to be a buzz on the internet regarding Rocky Pond. Nine ponds are fly-fishing-only (FFO) and one, **Wassataquoik Lake**, has a population of Arctic char. If you decide to fish Wassataquoik, be prepared for a lengthy hike and a beautiful lake that is riddled with boulders both above and below the lake's surface.

16. Pine Tree State Has It All

Dark Green Drakes (Litobrancha recurvata) also hatch in some BSP ponds.

How many of these waters offer a chance to net a trophy squaretail, say 16 inches or better? Experienced BSP trout angler Reardon believes that there are at least a few of these fish in most ponds, except for the small, very shallow, and very high elevation waters. He can cite at least a dozen of these mountain gems that have given up trout of that size to his flies. Reardon says, "They (16-inch or larger trout) are not common except in a few waters, but most of the ponds will cough one up on occasion."

One huge plus for fishing these hike-in ponds is that many of them offer camping facilities and have canoes stored along the shoreline that can be rented by using BSP's first come, first serve sign-up system. The most remote of all these trout ponds with a campground offered by BSP is 20-acre **Russell Pond.** This pond is highly rated for its aesthetics with a rocky bottom and exceptionally clear water. Even though it has a high trout catchability, it isn't known for producing trophy trout. Float tubes and personal canoes are acceptable in the park, and there are a few ponds that don't require any hiking, such as 38-acre Daicey, 96-acre Kidney, and 93-acre South Branch.

Sitting on BSP's western boundary is a Hex spot mentioned at the beginning of this chapter, **Sourdnahunk Lake,** also called

16. Pine Tree State Has It All

Nesourdnehunk. This brook trout haven is very large at 1394 acres and is the second largest lake in Maine with an FFO regulation.

Regarding FFO waters, it is interesting to note that Maine has 165-170 ponds and lakes with this regulation, New Hampshire owns far fewer at 30, and the Green Mountain State can claim only one, Seyon Pond.

Sourdnahunk was last stocked in the 1950s, so all trout are wild. Even though it hasn't earned a reputation as a trophy trout lake, George Smith, who owns a "Phoenix" camp on

A small 10 1/4-inch trout from Little Sourdnahunk, had its stomach crammed full of caddis pupae. Unlike the Hex mayfly, it is the pupal stage of this caddis fly that swims to the top of water to hatch into an adult.

Sourdnahunk, tells me that his family and/or guests have caught trout up to 16 ½ inches and he believes others have landed fish a little larger. I have also heard of a few 17–18-inch trout coming from this lake in the past ten years or so. Don't get me wrong, those are trophy trout in my book, but what the lake may lack for huge trophy trout is made up for in quantity. Fishery biologists say that Sourdnahunk has one of the highest "fish caught per hour" ratios in this region of Maine, and as a result, the fishing can be awesome during its annual Hex Hatch.

Only about one-half mile north lies its junior-sized compatriot, **Little Sourdnahunk.** Even though this 102-acre FFO pond is considered to be a part of Region E, I'm including it in the discussion of Region F because of its proximity to Baxter and Big Sourdnahunk. This pond has never been stocked so it is classified as a Heritage pond and is managed as a trophy brook trout water. A bonus for fly anglers is the panoramic view of Mt. Katahdin from the pond.

I did fish Little Sourdnahunk back in the late 1980s with my brother Stan when we were initiated to our first Maine caddis hatch. This large tan caddis with mottled wings and a green abdomen gave us fits. Trout were rising in the middle of the afternoon, obviously keying on this large caddis fly, but being ill-prepared, we could not match what they were taking. It appeared to us as time went by that the trout were feeding on pupae as they ascended the water column, not the adults. My 1989 journal tells me that I finally landed a 10 ¼-inch trout on a Green Drake nymph and the trout was chock full of caddis larvae and pupae. It was a humbling experience to have so many decent trout (no trophies) rising within casting distance and being unable to unlock the door to success. My notes indicate that we didn't stay late enough to check on the Hex Hatch, which you can bet was a mistake. We did count 25 snowshoe hares on the way back to camp, though, something of a consolation prize.

Straddling the border between Maine and New Brunswick, Canada, southeast of BSP, sits a large sprawling body of water named **East Grand Lake.** Landlocked salmon have always been the primary calling card for this 16,000+ acre lake, although togue have played a dandy second fiddle. In recent years, though, smallmouth bass have probably bumped togue from their red ribbon second spot to the white ribbon third. I fished East Grand as a teenager and young adult and caught both salmon and togue. During one trip early in the season, the salmon were right on top thrashing and slashing as stripers do in saltwater, but their targets were smelt, not mayflies. Trolling through the surface chaos with a streamer assured us of a salmon to net. We also spent a lot of time trolling for togue during those halcyon days, using monel wireline with a large 5-inch copper spoon, a lot of weight, and sewed on shiners or smelts. We bumped the bottom with these rigs, especially in the area of Greenland Cove and we were very successful, landing

East Grand Lake is known for its landlocked salmon fishing.

Henry Wass, the author's father, hefts two East Grand Lake salmon, taken back in the early 1950s.

togue up to 12 pounds. I recall one day that we had a spent 20-pounder next to the boat...which we were unable to net before the leader broke.

As mentioned earlier, I remember that during one of those East Grand trips with my father, our car was besieged by mayflies one evening while driving, so much so that windshield wipers were needed. I'm guessing that those were Hex mayflies. I also can recall several June evenings on East Grand Lake seeing some kind of large insect on the surface that fish loved, but we couldn't catch. (We were casting Mepps spinners.) Again, I suspect those were Hex mayflies that were attracting salmon and trout. Kevin Dunham, the fishery biologist for Region F, which includes East Grand, told me, "I can only assume there is some Hex activity on East Grand, but I am unsure how widespread it might be and do not know that for certain." There are some brook trout in East Grand, but the excitement would be if landlocked salmon got into Hex hatches on this lake.

Fish River Lakes Region – Region G

This region of Maine is known far and wide as "The County" but on most maps, it's called Aroostook County. What about Hex Hatches this far north? According to the regional fishery biologist Frank Frost, "This hatch is very common and widespread in Aroostook." He adds, "That said, there are only a small number of actual fisheries where anglers target fish that are feeding on *Hexagenia* mayflies. All the Fish River Lakes (**Mud Pond, Cross, Square**, and **Eagle lake**) have the hatch." Square Lake is best known for a relatively large number of anglers who fly fish for trout and salmon

Salmon are a primary target in the Fish River Region of Maine. COURTESY BRADFORD CAMPS

16. Pine Tree State Has It All

THE hatch is on. Postpone all activities other than fishing for the next two weeks.

during this hatch. Frost says that some anglers have tried to fish the hatch at 6,000-acre **Long Lake** but with little success. Mud Pond is a large but shallow pond at a little over 1,000 acres but its maximum depth is only 11 feet. Cross Lake (2,515 acres) and Eagle Lake (5,581 acres) are much larger and have a history of giving up large trout and salmon. It seems like I am forever reading about trophy fish being caught from those ponds. So, what's wrong with trying to persuade one of those girthy salmonids to rise to the occasion and gulp down your favorite Hex fly? As Frost says, "We (biologists) see this mayfly in almost all waters we sample in our region but few of them are actually fished."

Bill Graves, an outdoor writer from this same region of Maine, concurs with Frost that "Green Drake" (Hex) mayflies are common throughout the area, although he speaks of them as "randomly hatching in the Fish River Chain of Lakes". According to Graves, the hatches here are "advantage-lakeshore owners" since they can keep their eyes on the evening conditions much more easily. He says, "For the rest of us, it's a guessing game unless someone calls with the hot tip that Green Drakes are hatching, but even then, the hatch may end before we arrive." I see an answer to the Hex-angler problem in The County. Find a reliable source living on one of the lakes who will call you as *soon as they see a single mayfly*.

Another outdoor writer from The County, Mike Maynard, tells me something similar. Hex are up there but they are hard to pin down. I like his glass half-full summary about chasing the Hex Hatch, though. "If nothing else, just chasing the rumor of a Hex Hatch can lead you into waters that you've never seen and still offer spectacular fly fishing just using generic patterns," Maynard adds good-naturedly.

Probably one of the best-known areas for Hex Hatches in the "Crown of Maine" is the 21, 871-acre Deboullie Public Reserve. Infused with many trout ponds, miles of hiking trails, and numerous camping sites it sits only 30 miles from the Canadian border. I have spent many hours over the years fishing out of Red River Camps located in this area and can attest to the great trout fishing.

Jen Brophy is the owner of Red River Camps in the Deboullie region of northern Maine, and not only can she handle carpentry and plumbing jobs at the camps, she is also a great fly angler. COURTESY RED RIVER CAMPS

16. Pine Tree State Has It All

Hex hatches are abundant in **Upper Pond, Denny's Pond, Island Pond, Big Black Pond,** and others. Upper, Denny, and Island ponds are all under 35 acres in size and FFO. Big Black is an absolutely gorgeous hike-in spot at 147 acres. Not only do trophy trout populate these ponds but it is a wild trout paradise for those who enjoy the prospect of fooling, playing, netting, and usually releasing wild, self-sustaining squaretails as I do. All four of the aforementioned waters are Heritage ponds and there are others in this isolated wilderness.

Red River Camps are situated on Island Pond and offer a classic north woods experience for anglers. Jen Brophy is a second-generation owner of the camps and with her right-hand lady, and chef, Gloria Curtis, there seems to be nothing they can't and won't do to make your stay enjoyable. Like most Maine sporting camps, they have canoes stashed on a variety of the good trout ponds for use by patrons. For those who prefer roughing it, the Deboullie Region has over 20 primitive campsites that are available on a first-come-first-serve basis.

Stan Wass was mighty happy with this Deboullie Reserve 17-inch wild trout. He duped the fish on a Wiggle Nymph and it was released.

An added attraction to the Deboullie area is the chance to land a blueback trout (Arctic Char). No less than four Deboullie ponds are home to this rare Maine fish, one of which, 64-acre **Pushineer**, produced the state record (5.24 lbs. and 25in.) in 2008. The others that offer a chance of catching a blueback are **Deboullie, Big Black,** and **Gardner Pond**. These last three blueback waters range from about 147 to 283 acres in size. Mind you, these chars aren't especially easy to catch and rarely come to the surface during a Hex Hatch, but there is always hope. I believe the best time to entice a blueback to a Hex dry fly is at the very onset of the Hex Hatch when surface temperatures are usually the coldest during the roughly two-week hatching period. I have caught a fairly large number of bluebacks from Big Black but the majority of them have been less than 13 inches. I do confess that all were taken with a sinking fly line and streamers. The largest was a stunning, tangerine-colored male that reached 15 inches.

A little south of Aroostook County, in Piscataquis County, but still a part of Region G, you can find the **Currier Ponds,** although not easily. One of my sources for the book, Superintendent of the

A male blueback trout can be a sight to behold. This gorgeous 15-inch male was caught and released on Big Black Pond in the Deboullie Reserve.

Allagash Waterway Matt LaRoche mentioned the small but productive FFO Currier Ponds as having a Hex Hatch. If you enjoy staying at sporting camps, Bradford's on Munsungan Lake owned by Igor and Karen Sikorsky has a great reputation for making customers happy, and word has it that they can lead you to the Curriers for an evening Hex Hatch.

Somewhat south of the Curriers sits **Little Pillsbury Pond**. It's very shallow with only eight feet of water at its deepest but spring holes sustain the trout in warm weather. At 45 acres and regulated by general fishing laws, why am I listing this pond? In Al Raychard's book mentioned earlier, he says that despite no huge numbers nor a prosperous trout population, it does have one asset. "The chances of hooking a large-sized trout are excellent.", says Raychard. Apparently, the minnow and shiner populations are large enough for trout to use as a forage base and therefore grow to excellent size, and when *Hexagenia* mayflies hatch, I'm willing to bet that these trout switch diets and take advantage of those giant duns. There is a primitive campsite for use along its shoreline.

Rangeley Lakes Region – Region D

Is there anything that hasn't been said or written about fishing in the Rangeley Lakes Region of Maine? With such a rich fishing history that goes back to the late 1800s, and with local celebrities

The Outdoor Sporting Heritage Museum in Oquossoc is a fantastic place to spend several hours looking over the legacy of the Rangeley area. OUTDOOR HERITAGE MUSEUM

such as Cornelia "Fly Rod" Crosby and Herbie Welch, not much. The area is replete with fishing lore. Visit the Outdoor Heritage Museum in Oquossoc to see for yourself and be prepared to spend no less than two hours while there. The displays and artifacts will place you back in time when sporting camps and hotels were so common it was called Rangeley's "Golden Age". The museum shows you bonafide reasons why the area was considered an angler's paradise, with plentiful photographs and fish mounts. I'm guessing what you read in the next few pages of this book is a first account of the *Hexagenia* Hatch for this hallowed area of Maine. If there's another chronicle out there, I couldn't find it.

Depending on who I talked to, opinions about the Hex Hatch in the Rangeley Region ranged from, "is not that common", to "they occur in all lakes and ponds in western Maine that don't have extreme water level fluctuations", to "they are common throughout the summer in western Maine on almost all medium and large waters." I decided to list the names of places where I have been told, or read, that there are Hex Hatches, and you can take it from there. Tom Rideout owner of Sturtevant Pond Camps in Magalloway was instrumental in helping me with the following list, as was Brett Damm, owner of Rangeley Region Sport Shop in Rangeley.

Hex hatches occur on **Kennebago, Parmachenee, Rangeley** (yes, I said Rangeley), **Upper and Lower Richardson (East Richardson),** and **Mooselookmeguntic** lakes. Smaller bodies of water that have the hatch include **Big Jim, Little Jim, Tim**, and **West Richardson** ponds. (Kennebago, Parmachenee, Mooselookmeguntic, and Tim Pond are all listed as Heritage waters.) Are there other Hex ponds? For sure, but famed **Quimby Pond** is apparently not one of them according to Rangeley Region fishery biologist, David Howatt. Quimby (165 acres) is instead known for its legendary caddis hatch, and if you want to switch Hex flies for caddis imitations, I won't hold you back, as it could be worth your while at Quimby. Both squaretails and smelt are listed as species for this pond yet the pond's depth maxes out at only 12 feet. Smelt? Maybe that's one reason why the pond produces some very nice trout. A significant problem at Quimby is that it can get very warm during the summer months, but fortunately, there are enough springs to bide the fish by those hot seasonal temperatures.

Rangeley Region Sport Shop in Rangeley is a fine place to catch up on the latest fishing news and buy some tantalizing flies. Owner Brett Damm also offers a guide service.

With no fly rods in hand, a friend and I stopped by Quimby just to check it out (2020). Walking around the shoreline we were able to see one of those springs at work. In a very small inlet of the pond, where a spring was located, there were close to 100 finning trout. Most were 9-10 inches, yet several approached 15-16 inches. I am guessing that every other spring in the pond was providing the same oxygen supply. Special restrictions at Quimby do not allow any fishing near these spring gathering spots. I couldn't help but notice the 26 boats, canoes, and kayaks pulled up on shore at the carry-on launch site. (No spoken words needed there.) Howatt says that the pond's weedy demeanor and shallow water are deceiving because "It grows some very nice trout." 'Nuff said.

16. Pine Tree State Has It All

Quimby Pond produces some very nice brook trout and is a popular fishing destination. The line-up of canoes, kayaks, and boats on the shore whispered sweet nothings into the author's ears.

You won't find blanket Hex Hatches on Aziscohos but there is some evening dry fly fishing that will put smallish salmon and possibly a trophy trout in your net. SEAN FOWLER PHOTO

The Rangeley's region **Aziscohos Lake** is an enjoyable water to fish and harbors trophy brook trout as well as a hefty salmon population, *but* there is essentially no real Hex Hatch there. I have heard from one angler that he has seen several Hex adults while trolling the lake in July but it appears to be a rare occurrence. A massive water drawdown on Aziscohos in the late summer and fall allows little chance for Hex nymphs (or other burrowing mayfly nymphs) to establish themselves, and those few that

16. Pine Tree State Has It All

might be present in the substrate at the time of the drawdown are usually left high and dry.

Parmachenee Lake is known across the country by fly anglers, just for its name. A wet fly, The Parmachenee Belle, was originated by a sport who fished there in the late 1800s. The brook trout fishing at Parmachenee was once superb, so I was sad to learn that it isn't the fishery it once was. Fishery biologist Dave Howatt says that the lake is very overrated today. "Due to its restricted/gated public access and excellent spawning areas, the lake has an overpopulation issue," says Howatt. He continued, "As a result of low angler harvest and excellent salmonid longevity, the size, quality, and condition of the lake's brookie and salmon populations are quite poor." A chart Howatt produced from the most recent sampling of Parmachenee in 2017 clearly illustrates his perspective on the legendary lake. The lake does produce Hex mayflies, and if you hit it right, the action should be excellent according to Howatt. As I understand it, you can hike the rather lengthy road in past the gate to fish Parmachenee (or stay at Bozebuck's

Sean Fowler plays a feisty salmon on Aziscohos Lake. It came to a dry fly late in the day.

16. Pine Tree State Has It All

Mountain Camps and get a key), but carrying a canoe to the lake might be more of a hassle than it's worth.

Bosebuck Mountain Camps, owned by Michael Yates and Wendy Silvia since 2007, are situated at the northern end of Aziscohos and provide a perfect place to stay while fishing the lake and surrounding waters. The home lake provides some decent dry fly fishing for salmon in the evenings but I found that most anglers troll the 6700-acre lake, and these trollers pick up some dandy wild squaretails. Of course, not too far distant from Bosebuck's are some other magnificent waters such as the **Magalloway River** as well as some prime Hex ponds.

A special look at the Richardson Lakes is in order here although it doesn't exactly dovetail with much of this book. Not only do these two lakes have *Hexagenia* mayflies but they produce some whale-sized togue. On July 2, 2020, firefighter Erik Poland of Andover, Maine, pulled a Brobdingnagian 39 pound 3-ounce togue from the ninety-foot depths of Lower Richardson Lake, and that whomped the old state record from Beech Hill Pond set in 1958 of 31 pounds 8 ounces by Hollis Grindle. And Poland did it all alone. Why mention that tremendous feat (an hour plus of playing time) in a Hex book? It all boils down to two items as I see it. 1) Poland's record fish should be of special interest to *any* angler. 2) It provides added information for a Hex topic later in the book - what anglers can do for fun before a Hex Hatch starts. Btw, remember the giant lake trout taken in NH's Big Diamond Lake the winter of 2020 by Thomas Knight? Poland's fish outweighs even that laker which was 37.65 pounds, making Poland's the largest ever caught in New England. Very impressive, guys.

16. Pine Tree State Has It All

Mark Dunton of Grant's Kennebago Camps holds a pretty Kennebago Lake brookie. SAMANTHA SPENCER PHOTO

Brett Damm says that Kennebago Lake, the largest FFO lake in the state at 1,700 acres, produces the best Hex Hatch in the area and is excellent fly fishing, although access to this trout and salmon lake is also limited. Gates prevented anglers for years from driving to Kennebago to fish unless you were lucky enough to know a camp owner, stayed at Grant's Kennebago Camps, or Reggie Hammond's Kennebago River Kamps, or hired the right guide who had access to the lake. But according to Damm, that has changed to some degree. Grant's Kennebago Camps, at the northwest end of the lake, is situated on state preserve land, and back in 1999, the state set up a "public use permit" system that allows public access to the lake as well as the use of a public parking lot at Grant's Kennebago Camps. By calling them ahead of time, you can get through the gate and will be issued a permit to park in the public parking lot. From there, public users must hand-carry their watercraft to the lake. (My understanding is that it's limited to no more than three groups a day.) Those who are issued a permit to fish the lake can rent a boat from Grant's if they wish and may even purchase a lunch from the lodge, as well.

16. Pine Tree State Has It All

Grant's Kennebago Camps have been around for eons (Ed Grant built the first camps in 1875) and have been owned by John and Carolyn Blunt since 1988. It is the ideal location to "set up camp" (18 cabins), ply the "Hexic" Kennebago waters for trout and salmon from a handmade cedar-planked Rangeley boat, and to enjoy fly fishing in other parts of this historic Maine region. The best bet is to call the Blunts for fishing information.

As you now know, *Hexagenia* hatches are pretty much restricted to the end of June and the first of July, but on occasion, a few adult Hex mayflies are seen in August, September, and even October. I added **Lower East Richardson Pond** to the Rangeley Region Hex-waters list based on some adult Hex duns seen there on Sept 19th of 2020. The Van Veghtens fished it on that date and these experienced Hex anglers counted five Hex duns. To me, that is indirect proof of a Hex Hatch earlier in June and July at Lower East Richardson. *Probably* the same can be said for **Upper East Richardson** since it sits just several whiskers away.

A spectacular Kennebago Region brook trout. COURTESY GRANT'S KENNEBAGO CAMPS

According to Damm, the Hex Hatch on Rangeley Lake is largely ignored by fly anglers. In a newsletter issued by Damm from his Rangeley Region Sport Shop on August 6, 2019, he said the following: "The Hex mayflies are still hatching on the area lakes. Fly fishermen hardly pay attention to this hatch on Rangeley Lake. Hex mayflies are a major hatch on the lake and could be a big draw if it were promoted." Many of these lakes also support salmon populations in addition to brook trout, so it's more than

Salmon like this 7 lb. 6 oz. specimen are possible fishing the Hex Hatch on Rangeley Lake.

possible that fishing during a Hex Hatch might produce either one of these salmonids, a surprise I fully enjoy.

On my last trip to Oquossoc in 2020, I saw a photo at River's Edge Sports of an extremely large salmon taken from the lake. Apparently, the fish had been cleaned before the official weighing, but even then, it came in over seven pounds and was 28 inches in length. Fishery biologist Liz Thorndike estimated the live weight very close to nine pounds. And based on a clipped fin, she said the landlocked salmon was seven years old. I'd say that salmon hunted down plenty of rainbow smelt over the years. The proprietor of River's Edge Sports, Jerry White, said it was the largest salmon he has heard of in 20 years from that lake. Imagine *that* fish on your 6-weight fly rod during a Hex Hatch.

The chart below is a summary of a few of the Rangeley area Hex waters, listing the acreage of each, whether it's a Heritage water or not, the species of salmonid fish you can expect during a Hex Hatch (togue populations are not included), and some special notes about each.

16. Pine Tree State Has It All

Pond/Lake	Size in Acres	Heritage Water	Salmonids	Special Notes
Jim, Big	320	No	BKT, LLS	Wild BKT. LLS stocked. Good growth.
Jim, Little	64	No	BKT	Limited natural reproduction. Stocked annually.
Kennebago	1,700	Yes	BKT, LLS, BRT	FFO (see write-up)
Mooselookmeguntic	16,300	Yes	BKT, LLS	Known for trophy BKT. LLS, alewife population present.
Parmachenee	912	Yes	BKT, LLS	Large populations of small fish (see write-up). Access road gated. Ike slept here.
Quimby	165	No	BKT	FFO. Some natural reproduction. Stocked (see write-up).

Rangeley	6,000	No	BKT, LLS	Some wild BKT. Is known for trophy salmon. Both species are stocked.
Richardson, Lower East	54	No	BKT	FFO. Stocked. Lightly developed.
Richardson, Upper and Lower	5,100	No	BKT, LLS	Some natural reproduction that needs augmenting by stocking. Alewife population present. Some quality BKT.
Richardson, West	423	No	BKT, LLS	Marginal water quality. BKT stocked. A few LLS. A few trophy BKT.
Tim	320	Yes	BKT	FFO. Good trout growth. Tim Pond Wilderness Camps with gated road.

16. Pine Tree State Has It All

Southeast of the Rangeley area, in the town of Industry, is 796-acre **Clearwater Lake.** I was told by a reliable source that this deep lake (129-foot maximum) has a *Hexagenia* hatch. It has ideal water quality for coldwater gamefish, and both landlocked salmon and brook trout are stocked in Clearwater to provide a decent salmonid fishery. (There is also a self-sustaining togue population.) On the downside for Hex anglers, the lake has a heavily developed shoreline and is very popular as a summer fun-in-the-sun destination so it might be difficult to fly fish an evening hatch. My suggestion? Try it on a rainy evening.

Traveling northeast of the Rangeley Lakes, and north of Bingham, you will find a remote, rocky, and beautiful place called **Pierce Pond**. This 1,650-acre body of water grows gold star squaretails and also boasts a Hex Hatch. One and one equals two. And in this case, "two" refers to the opportunity of landing a trophy squaretail on a dry fly.

As a kid, I remember reading Bud Leavitt's columns in the *Bangor Daily News* about behemoth brookies caught from Pierce Pond (five pounds and over) and even though it seemed a million

Squaretails like this 3-pounder are "relatively" common in Pierce Pond, but that doesn't mean that they are easy to catch.

16. Pine Tree State Has It All

miles away to a teenager, I always imagined going there someday to catch one of those trophy trout. I am one for two on that account. I have fished there on five different occasions over the years, and as of yet, I have not led one of its massive trout to an awaiting net. The closest I came was *almost* casting to a large swirl on Upper Pierce Pond on my very first trip. Instead, I offered the chance to my fishing partner, and as a result, a 19 ¼ inch brookie found our net. That fish was caught during the day and on an imitation caddis dry fly… a "greased-up" muddler that imitates an emerging Hex dun. It was a trout we all dream of catching on a dry fly.

The Hex Hatch at Pierce (called the Green Drake Hatch by locals) occurs on all three connecting parts… Upper, Middle, and Lower Pierce. In my mind, Pierce Pond offers the best chance in Maine to nail a three to five-pound brookie during a *Hexagenia*

R	6/11	Bob Anderson	Trout	3-6	20 × 11½
R	6/15	Chris Lehman	Trout	3-2	20½ × 11
R	6/17	Rick Wallace	Trout	3-4	20 × 11
R	6/17	Ryan Maguire	Trout	3-0	19½ × 11
R	6/18	Jim Fahey	Trout	3-2	21 × 10½
R	6/18	Jim Fahey	Trout	3-0	20 × 11
R	6/19	Pat Burns	Trout	3-1	20 × 10½
R	6/22	Ben Gale	Salmon	3-1	20½ × 11½
	7/4	Margaret Clark	Trout	3-11	20 × 12
	7/10	Chris Leo	Trout	5-12	21¾ × 15
R	7/10	Connor Lepore	Salmon	3-0	20 × 11
R	7/10	Peter Lepore	Trout	3-0	20 × 11
R	7/10	Patrick Lepore	Salmon	3-1	22 × 11
R	8/7	Paul Lepore	Trout	3-6	21 × 12
R	8/7	Michael Lepore	Trout	3-0	19½ × 13
				3-5	21½ × 12½

Cobb's Pierce Pond Camps has kept records of large trout and salmon, called "board fish", for many years. The "R" refers to the fish that were released.

hatch. All one has to do is to look at the revered "board fish" on the walls at Cobb's Pierce Pond Camps to become a believer. Each year, brook trout nineteen inches and over, or three pounds and larger, caught by Cobb's guests are listed on a lodge board with the angler's name, date caught, fish weight, and length. Salmon are also included on the annual board but it is the trout that take your breath away. It is a most impressive display. One year that I stayed at Cobb's, by the first week of August, a total of forty-six "board trout" had been registered. One was over five pounds, three were between four and five pounds and forty-two were between three and four pounds. About half of the board fish were released that year. (Andy Cobb, today's proprietor, says the percentage of released fish has crept upwards since then.) The majority of board fish are caught trolling since Pierce is not an FFO water. There is also this. More brook trout weighing five pounds or more have been entered into Maine's "One That Didn't Get Away" Club from Pierce Pond than from any other lake or pond. We are talking piscatorial facts here that should make any brook trout fanatic want to go there at least once. But it does come with a huge caveat. These beautiful trout do *not* come easily. (Recall my 0-5 stats.) I haven't accurately added up the time that I have spent casting on Pierce Pond in those five trips but a fair guess would be in the vicinity of 100+ hours, and how many casts does that represent? Oodles. For sure, I've had my chances. I can recall one trip in which I *broke off* three large fish during the Hex Hatch. **Inexcusable.**

    Friend, Lawrence Pyne can verify the ratio of time spent casting to rewarding results on Pierce, and this lefty is a corker of a fly fisherman. Fishing the lake in early June of 2017, Pyne estimates that he spent seven to eight hours of casting to come up with a gorgeous 18-inch Pierce Pond wild trout. The trout wasn't caught on a dry fly and wasn't caught during a Hex Hatch, but it does

16. Pine Tree State Has It All

A nice salmon hoodwinked by the author during one of Pierce Pond's mayfly hatches. This wild salmon came to a Hex Emerger and was released. LAWRENCE PYNE PHOTO

help to make my point, even though his ratio is not that bad for Pierce. Later that same month, Pyne and I made the trip from Vermont to try Pierce Pond once again. We missed the Hex Hatch

During evening mayfly hatches, Pierce Pond fly anglers line up along favorite shorelines awaiting rising squaretails and salmon.

but did have another large mayfly to fish over, what I believe was *Litobrancha recurvata* or the Recurve/Dark Green Drake mayfly. We fished hard and between the two of us, logged a total of 30 hours of casting flies. Yes, we caught a few really small trout and some very nice salmon, but not one of those Pierce Pond blue-ribbon trout came to net. And of course, it *should* be that way. Catching trophy squaretails should not be like a walk in the "pahk" or shelling peas. It's worth noting here that Pyne claimed our score of 0 trophy fish for 30 hours of fishing was the result of a phenomenon related to something entirely new to me. (See chapter 23.)

As on Sourdnahunk, boats and canoes line up along selected shorelines for the evening fishing at Pierce, and it's almost always on the Lower Pond. The majority of anglers stay at sporting camps that are located on the Lower Pond. It's just too much of a haul to fish the upper sections of the pond and then return to camp after dark, although there are limited camping opportunities on those sections of the lake for anyone who would like to stay overnight.

Experienced regulars at Pierce, aka "board fish members", say not to be afraid to blind cast during the evening hatch, letting the

A pair of mounted squaretail trout adorn the wall of Cobb's main lodge. Both were caught the same day on dry flies.

16. Pine Tree State Has It All

fly sit there as long as you can stand it since the fish are cruising, and a few anglers report that they catch most of their largest trout early on during an evening hatch. Large, wild trout are in there and they aren't leader-shy, but are still darned hard to put in a net.

Many flies work during a Hex Hatch at Pierce, and I will get into that in a later chapter, but

Lawrence Pyne forbade bananas on his boat while at Pierce, and then proved why with this nice salmon deked on a dry fly.

several local flies that were introduced to me while fishing there were the Haystack, the Campbell Fancy streamer, and a fly tied by one of the guides called a Huddler, which is a hybrid Muddler/Hornberg.

Some satellite ponds (all small) near Pierce, such as **Dixon, Fish, Grass, Helen, High, Kilgore**, and **Pickerel** also hold trout, and a few of them produce trophy trout, although I am not positive about Hex hatches. All but Kilgore are self-sustaining and all are FFO. Pickerel Pond is a catch-and-release trout pond.

In addition to the trophy squaretails at Pierce Pond, there is also a very good salmon fishery and the recent word is that even though salmon are stocked, the majority of salmon caught today are wild fish. It hasn't been difficult for a reader of this book to ascertain that my favorite fish to catch during a Hex hatch is *Salvelinus fontinalis,* alias squaretail, but I will be the first one to admit that there is an undercurrent of excitement when I don't know if the next rise will bring an acrobatic salmon or a bull-dogging brook trout. Both species mix in during a Hex Hatch at Pierce and you have to be prepared for the zipping "100-yard dash" of a salmon. Case in point. One wonderful evening at Pierce, I was anchored right where I like to be, a good cast from the rocky shallow water and a good cast from deep water. I had a rise early on during the hatch while casting out towards the main lake and *Salmo*

The casting looks okay. The weather looks prime. Big brookies are there. But this trip to Kilgore Pond was close to a bust. STAN WASS PHOTO

salar it was – and a nice one. After I set the hook, the salmon ran a short distance and then reached for the clouds to show off. The fish then headed for the far side of the lake in a screaming run that ended with a heart-rending…ping! I'm not sure what pound test my leader was that evening, but *standing on my loose fly line* was the surefire way to test the strongest of tippets.

I have since learned about an "old-timer" who has fished Pierce Pond for many years and likes to fish with bare feet so that he can tell when he's stepping on his fly line. Just keep in mind, once landlocked salmon are hooked, they almost always jump from the water to "give you the fin" and go on a tearing run. Do *not* be standing on loose coils of your fly line.

There are two sporting camps on Pierce Pond, Harrison's Pierce Pond Camps and Cobb's. The old-timer on the block is

16. Pine Tree State Has It All

A squaretail trout (shown by Mary Van Veghten) is hard to beat in the elegant looks department, and is the main reason the author would rather catch this fish more than any other during a Hex Hatch. TERRY VAN VEGHTEN PHOTO

Cobb's, which was purchased by 50-year-old Andy Cobb's grandparents in 1958. It is a very special place. I have stayed there five times and have never been disappointed. I was witness to a huge selling point during my very first visit there in 1989. My brother, Stan, and I are hard-core fishermen and went at it every hour we possibly could. One particular day it was raining and cold (the fireplace in the main lodge was, oh so tempting), but we had an outlying pond, Kilgore, on our minds and weren't about to change those plans. We left after breakfast, motored to the Upper Pond, hiked into Kilgore, fished hard much of the day, hiked out, and returned to Cobb's sometime in the afternoon. Soaked to the skin and more than a little perturbed that we couldn't land one of the big trout pulsing Kilgore's waters through its gills, and shivering like a chihuahua, we needed some TLC and fast. Staggering up the steps to our cabin you have no idea how we felt after opening the door and being greeted by…a roaring wood stove and *cabin that was toasty warm.* OMG. Someone had anticipated the type of day that we were having and made a special effort to have our woodstove going when we returned. That is taking care of your patrons, my friends, and it keeps them returning year after year.

16. Pine Tree State Has It All

The author had a great fishing relationship with his striped bass mentor, Harold Gassett, of Natick, Mass. Unfortunately, Harold is another fishing companion who has left earth for a fly-fishing pond in heaven. His smile was as contagious as his ability to catch fish, as this Upper Pierce Pond salmon shows.

Another memorable time at Cobb's was a trip with a friend Harold Gassett from Natick, Mass., and Stan in July of 1992. Harold was a striped bass fanatic and I was lucky to have him show me the" striper ropes" on Cape Cod over the years. (I once caught a 44 ¼ inch striper in the Cape Cod Canal using his gear, his 12-foot boat, and his striper know-how.)

Harold also loved raking cherrystone clams in Buttermilk Bay near The Cape, and always enjoyed sharing them with friends. He brought some of those tender clams to Pierce Pond on this, his only trip there before he passed away from asbestos-caused lung cancer, and we shared a delectable feast of Quahog Casino in between fishing trips one day. After we had finished fishing that afternoon and were heading to the main lodge for our supper meal, we could hear music of some sort emanating from the lodge. What the heck? Someone's birthday? As we entered the lodge a large group of guests awaiting their meal and someone with a "geetar"

16. Pine Tree State Has It All

were singing what ended up as a number one hit that summer, "Achy Breaky Heart" by Billy Ray Cyrus. And these folks were lifting the ceiling.

You can't drive directly to Cobbs Camps, but instead need a boat for the last half mile. (I love that aspect.) You can launch your boat (canoe) at the public landing or they will pick you up.

In my mind, there is a big advantage to using a boat while fishing Pierce Pond. I like to stand when casting and in something a helluva lot more stable than a canoe. I can also tolerate sore bones and muscles for a much longer time in a boat as opposed

Chet Remeson, one of America's best-known watercolorists of the outdoors sporting scene, has been a patron at Cobb's Camps for many years. Large fish that his family have caught at Pierce are outlined on the seats of his handsome cedar-planked boat.

to a canoe. (Advantage angler.) You can use your boat (canoe) or rent one, and access to Pierce Pond is possible even if you don't stay at a sporting camp. Boats can be launched at the public landing in Lindsey Cove by showing up at the gate on the road into Pierce or by calling Cobb's ahead of time and making arrangements.

And while talking boats, I have to throw this fun bit into the mix. On my last trip to Cobb's Camps, we were treated to sharing the same dining table as Chet Remeson, America's most popular sporting watercolorist. His watercolors of hunting and fishing have graced more magazines and sportspeople's homes than any other painter of his time. At 83 years young, and owner of several "board" fish at Cobbs, he was still plying the renowned waters of Pierce Pond with his wife, Penny. Of special interest was the boat which he trailered into Pierce Pond for use while fishing. Remeson had outlined on the bench seats of his gorgeously restored cedar-planked boat the largest fish that he and other family members have caught at Pierce Pond. One trout was over 4 ½ pounds. I believe that most of his "board/bench seat" fish were caught trolling, but still…

Sebago Lake Region – Region A

I once heard that there are no Hex hatches in Maine waters south and east of Bangor. I'm happy to report that just isn't true. Again, I had to rely primarily on Maine's fishery biologists for information. Sebago Region biologist Jim Pellerin reported that he has recently observed or heard of Hex Hatches on **Sebago Lake, Thompson Lake,** and **Hancock Pond,** and based on finding Hex nymphs in fish stomachs from other waters, that there are more. Sebago Lake gets a lot of attention in southern Maine, but not for its Hex hatches. *Salmo salar Sebago* is THE fish for this 28,771-acre monstrosity, Maine's second-largest lake. The salmon in this lake have had a checkered past, though, going through some population extremes, and what I hear from guide Tom Roth (Sebago Lake Guide Services), an outdoor writer who lives on the shores of this popular lake, the salmon are on a downward spiral

16. Pine Tree State Has It All

A very nice, 22-inch Sebago Lake landlocked salmon gets a smooch from Amy Blanchette before being released. Blanchette, who caught the salmon on a fly rod, was being guided by Tom Roth of Sebago Lake Guide Services. Photo courtesy Tom Roth.

as I write this in 2020. Pellerin supports that view but reminds me that these population swings are never static and that he expects the salmon fishery will gradually improve. He reports that during the years 2013-2014 the salmon fishery at Sebago was at an all-time high in terms of catch rates (Roth says 2010 was his best year for salmon fishing), but due to an increase in the lake trout (togue) population since then, more pressure has been put on forage fish (primarily smelt) for salmon, and the salmon fishery started to decline. But rumor has it that some very nice landlocks were landed during the late fall of 2020, pulling the scales down to five, seven, and nine pounds.

New liberalized fishing laws have been enacted on Sebago that encourage more angler harvest of lake trout in hopes of reducing competition for smelt. Pellerin reports that smelt populations are now being augmented with egg transfers from other waters and that other experimental efforts to reduce togue populations are being explored. "It won't turn around overnight but I believe we can reverse the situation (increase in salmon), especially if we can get anglers to harvest more of their legal (togue) catch," Pellerin

By stocking smelt eggs in tributaries of Sebago Lake, biologists hope to increase the smelt population. COURTESY MDIFW

reassuringly says. Why is all this important in light of the theme of this book? Salmon would be *the* target species when fishing the Hex Hatch on Sebago Lake...unless bass light your fire. And this is also true for 4,426-acre Thompson Lake, another well-known salmon fishery. Most of the salmon that come to net on this lake have been stocked, but there is also some natural reproduction according to Pellerin.

Want to put a nice brown trout in your camera's viewfinder? Hancock Pond at 858 acres could very well do the trick during its Hex Hatch. Brown trout are stocked annually at Hancock, and a smelt population in the pond is surely responsible for good brown trout growth. Pellerin passed along the results of a 2019 sampling at Hancock in which they found the average brown trout to weigh 2.5 lbs. and they had one fish that weighed 8.7 lbs.

State of Maine Fish & Game warden, Lucas Bellanceau, holds a tremendous brown trout netted in Hancock Pond, that tipped the scales to 8.7 pounds. COURTESY MDIFW

Pellerin says he is aware of one "hardcore Hex angler who is well-rewarded" when fishing the hatch at Hancock. A brown trout measured in pounds at the end of a fly rod adorned with a Hex imitation? Need I say more?

So how extensive and prolific is *Hexagenia limbata* in the Sebago Lake region? Maine Director of Fisheries and Hatcheries, Francis Brautigam, says that there has been some anecdotal evidence from lakefront property owners that *Hexagenia* hatches have become less frequent in southern Maine over the years although there is no scientific data yet to support that suspicion. But some research, footwork, and determination would no doubt repay a Sebago Region angler with a few more Hex ponds than what I have listed here.

Belgrade Lakes – Region B

There's nothing that gets my dander up more than learning about a body of water that has been corrupted by the purposeful, illegal stocking of fish. For example, it just kills me that smallmouth bass are now in **Moosehead Lake.** Another outrageous act was the illegal stocking of northern pike into the Belgrade Chain of Lakes in the 1970s. One water body seriously affected by that shameful stocking was beautiful **Long Pond**, once a nationally known destination fishery for landlocked salmon, with salmon reaching upwards of eight pounds. Brook trout were also an important fishery in that same watershed. Not anymore. With the illegal introduction of northern pike and later, either the illegal or inadvertent establishment of landlocked alewives (the 1990s), salmon, brook trout, and smelt are no longer existent in Long Pond. How sad, I say, that in a few minutes of personal greed/opinion/ideology the ecosystem of a watershed can be adulterated forever.

Due to the continued demise of 2,714-acre Long Pond, the MDIFW no longer stocks salmon and brook trout in that water body. To the credit of the fisheries biologists for Region B, a search was then on to look for a cold water, salmonid

16. Pine Tree State Has It All

replacement. Other states were having success managing rainbow trout in lakes that also had landlocked alewives. This was a light at the end of the tunnel. This prey-predator relationship was so fruitful that biologists in those states actually *depended* on alewives as the primary food source for supporting their rainbow trout populations.

Believing that this could also be done with Long Pond, the Maine Region B Fisheries Division, led by Jason Seiders, took a proposal of introducing rainbow trout into Long Pond to the public, including sporting camps and anglers. With substantial support, the decision was made to start stocking rainbow trout in the fall of 2016. That program is continuing and although it's still early to evaluate in 2020, Seiders offered this assessment: "The Long Pond rainbow program is still in its infancy, but reports from the last couple of years look promising. We've received accounts of several five-pound fish and the fishery at both the outlet and inlet dams have produced a lot of buzz." That's encouraging news for a new trout fishery at Long Pond.

So how do *Hexagenia* mayflies fit into this scenario? An interesting anecdote from Seiders is worthy of mention here. When asked if he knew of any lakes/ponds in his region with a Hex Hatch, he said, "We routinely receive calls regarding 'fish kills' every July. A great example is Long Pond in Belgrade. Every year we hear about thousands of dead fish washing up on its shores, and it's always the same outcome – Green Drake (Hex) casings mistaken for small dead fish." Hello! So, one part of the Hex

Oncorhynchus mykiss, is the rainbow trout's scientific name. The introduction of rainbows into Long Pond is already showing promise even though the program only started in 2016. PAINTING BY THE AUTHOR

equation is solved. The other side of the equation would be target fish during the Hex Hatch at Long Pond, and today that would be *Oncorhynchus mykiss,* the rainbow trout, although there are also a few drop-down brown trout from Great Pond that grow to trophy size. (Smallmouth bass are also abundant in Long Pond.)

Another interesting body of water in this region is **Little Pond,** the water supply for Damariscotta. A few Hex cases have been observed at this pond, according to Seiders. "But", he says, "the brook trout are highly focused on one particular food item, and they rarely stray from that, even during the Green Drake (Hex) season." Wait just a friggin' minute. Brook trout that don't feed on the largest, tastiest mayfly mouthful in Maine? This promoted some serious research by me although I must admit that I was first keyed into the idiosyncrasies of Little Pond in a *Maine Sportsman* article by Tom Seymore.

Seymore recently accompanied Seiders' team (fall 2019) on a trap net survey of the brook trout at 78-acre Little Pond and described the first trap netful of fish that he saw as "looking like footballs with fins". One of the brookies, measured at a robust 15+ inches, had just been stocked as a 10-inch trout the previous spring. "But that was the smallest fish of the lot," reported Seymore. "The rest of the fish were in the 16-18-inch category and weighed, on average, about three pounds." Thundering typhoons. What is going on in this 48-foot-deep Maine coastal pond anyway?

No, this is not photo-shopped folks! ***Little Pond*** *grows massive brook trout such as this 5 Lb. specimen in a few short years, but it would be a challenge to land one on a Hex dry fly. Is anyone up to the task? MDIFW*

16. Pine Tree State Has It All

Tiny midge larvae and pupae make up the bulk of Little Pond's trout diet. PHOTO EVAN KLAPSTEIN

To the rescue Jason Seiders. The trout growth in Little Pond is astounding, much faster than the pampered growth in a hatchery system. Even with some rainbow smelt in the pond, biologists find only insects when checking their stomachs, and unfortunately for Hex-anglers, these insects are not mayflies but instead, tiny *Chaborus* midge larvae. Managed as a trophy brook trout pond, the fish stocked in Little Pond are a special strain developed in the Maine State Hatchery system by hybridizing the Kennebago strain of brook trout with the Maine Hatchery strain. Seiders says, "Fish growth (with this new strain) is the fastest I have ever seen, and individual fish condition (length and weight) is closer to what we typically see in bass rather than trout." It appears that the prolific *Chaborus* midge is at least one cause of this phenomenal growth. Seiders and his team now stock all their better brook trout waters with this particular trout strain.

Would I recommend Little Pond as a Hex fishing destination? Man, with those deep-bellied brookies reaching pounds in such short order, I think it's definitely worth a cast or two despite the absence of large hatches. Just one mistake by a three to five-pound trout could certainly make it all worthwhile in my mind.

Caught during a trap-net survey in the fall, this Little Pond brook trout is enough to get a fly angler's blood flowing, even in the depth of winter. MDIFW

Scott Davis is another fisheries biologist who works in the Belgrade Region, and he reports that there are a lot of ponds and lakes in this area where "large mayflies" hatch and that some of them are probably Hex mayflies. But common use of the term "Green Drake" used by most people to describe any mayfly of size, leads to confusion as I have previously noted. Davis gave me a huge list of Region B waters that have "big mayflies", but with the qualification that he's not sure how many of these "big mayflies" are actually *Hexagenia*. So, I am listing these waters on a hunch that at least some of them have Hex Hatches, but it's up to you to do the fishing research.

Information in the accompanying chart will help you decide which pond/lake you would like to try. Those with an asterisk are the places I would cherry-pick if I lived nearby. (BKT=brook trout, BRT=brown trout, LLS=salmon)

16. Pine Tree State Has It All

Pond/Lake	Location	Size in Acres	Salmonids	Special Notes
Alford Lake*	Hope	577	BKT, BRT, LLS	BRT grow to a large size. Trophy BKT are stocked.
Bowler Pond	Palermo	34	BKT	Good trout growth.
Egypt Pond	Vienna	60	BKT	
Parker Pond*	Fayette	1,610	LLS, BKT	Large but relatively undeveloped.
Peters Pond	Waldoboro	10	BKT	59 feet deep.
Sanborn Pond	Brooks	98	BKT, BRT	
Sheepscot Pond	Palermo	1,215	BKT, LLS	Moderately developed shoreline. Some wild LLS
Spectacle Pond*	Vassalboro	139	BKT, BRT	Picturesque. BRT grow to trophy size.
St. George Lake*	Liberty	1,107	LLS, BKT	Picturesque. A good regional LLS water. BKT fishing has been excellent.

Recent news about highly invasive bluegill populations in the Sheepscot River Watershed is more than concerning. Sheepscot Pond, a deep oligotrophic lake that also has wild lake trout in addition to brookies and salmon, is now home to a large bluegill population. Fishery biologists have no idea when or where this population originated.

Grand Lake Region – Region C
This last region of Maine is the one I am most familiar with as it is where I grew up playing Pemetic High School basketball, swimming at The Bluffs on Echo Lake, catching sea-run trout in The Marsh, catching my first Atlantic Salmon on the Pleasant River, and giving my mother fits because of occasional buffoonery at school.

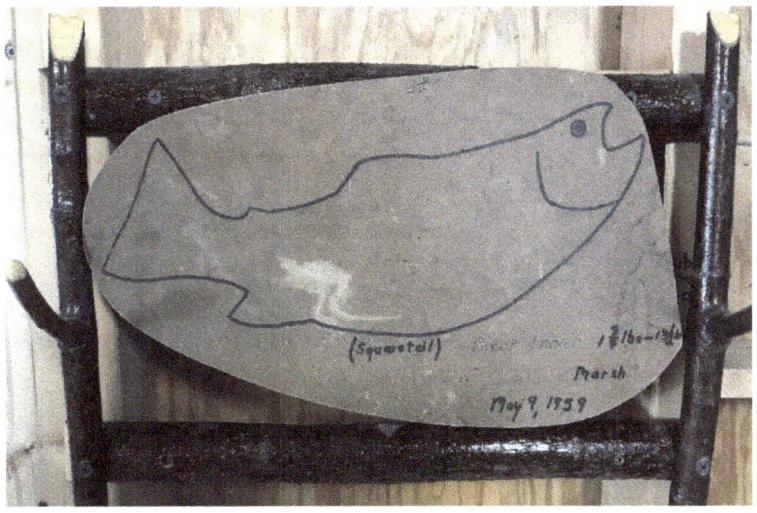

In 1959, when this sea-run trout was caught, the author was a junior in high school. The trout came from a local "trout epicenter" on Mount Desert Island known as The Marsh. It was only 13 ½ inches long but weighed a plump 1 ¾ pounds. The fish was snookered on a nightcrawler picked from his parents' lawn.

In the Grand Lake Region, we are talking *way* Downeast, home to blueberry barrens, Acadia National Park, the Narraguagus River, sardine factories (long gone), rocky shorelines with

16. Pine Tree State Has It All

seaweed, "lobstahs", Downeast accents, and wicked good sayings. Having been born and raised there, you would think I should know all of the Hex ponds and lakes in this region as well as I know the back of my grizzled hand. Wrong. I had never heard the terms *Hexagenia* or Green Drake until the 1980s, 20 plus years after I had moved permanently to Vermont. So, once again, I was reliant upon Maine's capable regional fishery biologists for valuable information, and in this case, it was Greg Burr of the Grand Lake Region.

After posing a multitude of questions to Burr (turns out we had a connection through basketball on Mount Desert Island), he reported that there are limited hatches of *Hexagenia* in the Downeast Region, but most notably in 389-acre **Schoodic Lake** in Cherryfield. He said that anglers anxiously await the Hex Hatch on Schoodic in late June and early July so they can cast dry flies to cruising salmon and brook trout. As an aside, Schoodic lies right in the heart of blueberry barrens and therefore is also quite popular with blueberry rakers during the so-called dog days of August, not because of a lingering Hex Hatch, but instead for a cooling off swim after raking tasty Downeast blueberries in the hot sun. There is a large population of smelt in Schoodic (maximum depth only 37 feet) and the last time biologists surveyed the salmon population, the fish were found to be in excellent physical condition. All the salmon had at least several smelt in their stomachs. That is a good thing since landlocked salmon are extremely dependent on rainbow smelt as a forage fish to become hale and hearty. As a bonus for Hex-Hatch anglers, Schoodic is also stocked with brook trout, including some hefty "brood fish" that are a strapping 18 inches long when stocked.

Burr also singles out **Beech Hill Pond** in Otis as producing some Hex mayflies although it apparently "does not produce

16. Pine Tree State Has It All

What a dandy Beech Hill Pond salmon (22 inches and just shy of 4 lbs.) landed by this youngster. It was caught trolling a streamer during the Hex Hatch and then released. The guide was Matthew Whitegiver of Eagle Mountain Guide Service. MATTHEW WHITEGIVER PHOTO

hatches of note", as he says. Beech Hill is a fairly large lake at 1,351 acres and most notably known for its lake trout (togue) fishery, and the mammoth state record of 31 ½ pounds caught there in 1958. That record held up for 62 years until a larger togue (39.2 pounds) was landed at Lower Richardson Lake in 2020. The emphasis on fishery management for this high-quality, coldwater sportfish lake is the wild lake trout population as well as landlocked salmon that are now stocked each spring to augment the fishery. As is true in all salmon waters, rainbow smelt are a key forage fish in Beech Hill, so smelt eggs have been stocked in recent years which has helped increase that population. In 2016, a survey of salmon was taken by fishery biologists and they were delighted to find that 22% of the salmon trapped were wild fish, a result of natural reproduction in one of the pond's tributaries. I wondered how often natural reproduction of landlocked salmon occurs overall in the state, and after reading a recent article in *The Maine Sportsman*, written by Christi Holmes, I had that question answered. Holmes stated that there are at least 57 Maine lakes in which natural reproduction of landlocked salmon occurs.

Sadly, Beech Hill Pond is another case of an illegal stocking with non-native fish, in this case, smallmouth bass sometime during the 1980s. That illicit stocking was at least partly responsible for a decline in the size of both salmon and lake trout. However, recent actions by biologists have begun to turn that decline around.

I also asked Burr about **West Grand Lake**, a large, well-known landlocked salmon destination, but he said that he has never observed or heard of a Hex Hatch on that lake. Burr added that there may be other deep, cold lakes and ponds in the Hancock County area that have limited Hex hatches such as **Branch Lake** (self-sustaining trophy brown trout and stocked salmon), **Green Lake** (salmon), and **Craig Pond** (salmon and brook trout).

Where-To Summary, The Pine Tree State

I warned you that Maine was going to be one "Hex-uva" trip. I did my best to cover the whole state from head to toe rather than listing just a few run-of-the-mill Hex ponds that most anglers have heard about. If it weren't for Maine's fishery biologists, though, being so open to answering my many questions there's no way I could have accomplished this "where-to" section for Maine. With their assistance, a little help from some outdoor writers and anglers, some serious digging, and my own experiences, I was able to chronicle a large, varied inventory of potential Hex fishing destinations, which by my count is over 160. I'd say there's a little bit for everyone. I'm hopeful that by mentioning a lot of Hex waters,

16. Pine Tree State Has It All

Baxter State Park is only one of many regions in Maine that produce Hexagenia mayfly hatches. DELORA REARDON PHOTO

the fishing pressure will be diluted, and therefore minimal, on individual ponds and lakes.

To illustrate the striking diversity of Maine's *Hexagenia limbata* waters cited in this book, take a gander at the following comparisons. (These water bodies are chosen randomly for each category and do not represent any special designation as "the best place" to go, except where noted.)

Stan Wass and son Eric are headed for a camping spot on Sugar Island in Moosehead Lake.

Lake/Pond Size... If you enjoy the challenges of big waters, there are jumbo lakes to fish such as Moosehead and Mooselookmeguntic Lakes. On the other hand, if you are partial to pint-sized waters you might find a liking to little dimples such as 7-acre Pickerel and 8-acre Celia Ponds.

Fish Size... Maybe you relish the opportunity to nail a blue-ribbon fish. If that is the case, you may like to visit trophy trout waters such as Pierce or Big Black Ponds. Or, maybe just catching trout is more important to you, and any fish is a "trophy in your book", so a trip to Little Lyford Pond or Sourdnahunk Lake will fulfill that need.

Location... Some Hex waters sit at the very top of Maine, in The County, such as Denny Pond and Square Lake. Yet a few are within a "stone's throw" of the Atlantic Ocean like Schoodic Lake and Little Pond.

Some Hex ponds require a little bit of elbow grease to access.

Ease of Getting There... A slew of these Hex waters like Russell and Sixth Debsconeag Ponds are perfect for the young-at-heart since they are isolated, in the backwoods, and require a hike to fish. Yet there are many roadside waters to entice those who prefer to follow an easier route, or those with less available time to fish, such as Thompson Lake and Daicey Pond.

Familiarity... No doubt, more than a few places I have targeted are well-known to anglers including Slaughter Pond and Parmachenee Lake, but a handful are so secretive that most fly

Some Hex Ponds are so secret that only the moose know. DELORA REARDON PHOTO

fishers probably have never heard of them, like…Secret and Bowler Ponds.

Depths… A few of these Hex waters are seemingly bottomless at over 100 feet deep like Beech Hill Pond (104 feet) and Clearwater Lake (129 feet), yet others approach frying pan depth as you will find at Brown (6 feet) and Second Currier Pond (9 feet).

Accommodations… If you want to enjoy the comforts of home at one of Maine's fine sporting camps, places like Maynard's in Rockwood of the Moosehead Region or Red River Camps on Island Pond will certainly pander to your wishes. But if instead you prefer roughing it with primitive camping, the Deboullie Region and Baxter State Park will accommodate you just fine.

Roughing it to fish Hexagenia mayfly ponds always requires a good campfire. DELORA REARDON PHOTO

Stocked or Not… Maybe you prefer to fish waters that have never seen a stocked fish, or at least not in the last 25 years. Heritage waters such as Kelly Pond or Dixon Pond are two you can select from a rather long list in that case. On the other hand, stocked fish may suit you just fine, so Hex waters like Alford Lake or Lower South Branch Pond certainly will do the trick.

16. Pine Tree State Has It All

Brook Trout… You may be a crazed brook trout nut and want to see squaretails sipping your dry flies. You could look to Island Pond or Kilgore Pond to satisfy that impulse.

Salmon… It could be you have a hankering for feisty landlocked salmon during a Hex Hatch. If so, Sebago or East Grand Lake may bring about that special choice.

Brown Trout… Maybe it's brown trout that get you lathered up. If indeed that is the case, you should put Hancock Pond at the very top of your list.

Anything as pretty as a brook trout??

Rainbow Trout… Any rainbow trout fans out there? Thought so. You need to get your *Maine Delorme Atlas & Gazetteer* out and find the way to Long Pond.

Blueback Trout… I know a lot of fly fishers would love to add a blueback trout to their "been-there-caught-this" list, and as difficult as it might be, there is a smidgeon of a chance at Deboullie or Gardner Lake to accomplish that feat.

Mixed Bag… And for you "conglomerate anglers", there are plenty of waters where you never really know for sure what species of fish might take your optimally presented dry fly, such as Branch and Rangeley Lakes.

Monikers… And finally, on a whimsical note, there are Hex-water names I have listed that probably

Spawning color of a Maine blueback trout (char). DMIFW

16. Pine Tree State Has It All

won't fire up your internal fishing engine at all, like Mud (meh) and Grass Ponds (vanilla). But looking at the bright side of things, I have listed a few waters with beguiling names like Nesourdnahunk, Little Enchanted, Wassataquoik, Lone Jack, and Rum Ponds that are total winners with just their expressive names.

Despite all the "Hexible" waters that I have mentioned for anglers to choose from, you may wonder how many other ponds and lakes with Hex hatches can there *possibly* be in Maine. Scores! So many that it would be hard to fish them all in a lifetime. Who knows? Maybe you will locate your own Maine Hex fishing spot. Maine has it all…and then some.

17. A Triple Play, A Dunk and Strawberry Shortcake

It's time to go fish a Hex Hatch! Here are some points to ponder: Is it strawberry season? Will the weather do a number on your fishing? Do you want a companion? Have you heard from a reliable source that mayflies are hatching, or, is the water's surface temperature 65-70 degrees? Can the lawn wait until tomorrow?

It's time to choose a Hex-fishing destination based on how much time you have available, what you plan to use for watercraft, and what species of fish you want to target.

Let me expound on some of these questions just a bit. As soon as I see the first newspaper ad that says, "Pick Your Own Strawberries", I *know* it's time. Strawberries usually ripen by the end of June to early July, and that my friends *is* Hex time. I even carry this whole strawberry season thing a bit further (as you are well-aware by now) by making homemade strawberry shortcakes and taking some with me fishing (real whipped cream of course).

Got a spoon?

17. A Triple Play, A Dunk and Strawberry Shortcake

I've plowed this ground earlier in chapter 12, but some information is worth repeating. Don't rely on what you see at the water's edge for upcoming weather, but instead get a good hour-by-hour prediction for the afternoon and evening *ahead of time*. A "light and variable winds" report is what you hope for. This kind of weather invariably produces zephyr winds and calm water, and that corresponds to perfect fly-casting conditions as well as the ultimate safety. With strong or even moderate winds predicted (depending on the lake/pond), my advice is to stay home and tie a few more flies for the next day. (And get the blasted grass cut too.)

This is what we called "flat-ass carm" when I grew up in Maine, and you can bet your LL Bean boots that trout will be up as soon as the Hex Hatch is on.

Will mayflies be popping is the critical question. Building a network of folks whom you can rely upon for accurate information is a big plus. Organize some connections with friends who troll and can spot empty Hex cases on the water while they fish. I have used "spotters" like this a number of times. You can also get to know the people at local fly shops. Then, close to the beginning of Hex season, call or drop by the fly shops and ask if anyone has reported seeing Hex mayflies yet. But no matter how much you

17. A Triple Play, A Dunk and Strawberry Shortcake

buy at the store, don't expect them to spill ALL the beans since many of these fly shop owners/employees are guides, too.

Your choice of Hex turf can sometimes be difficult. Should you rely on last year's fishing success? Not always, but it can help. How far can you drive and still have time to fish *at least* from 8 PM to dark? That depends on the time needed to pick up a companion, how busy the access area might be, the time it takes to get from the boat access to the fishing location, and any stops along the way. I *try* to plan so everything is taken care of ahead of time. And what about that lawn that needs cutting? You know, I've never yet seen a dyed-in-the-wool fly fisher get upset about a day's delay (or two) in mowing grass ... unless they happen to be a golf course superintendent.

By what means do you plan to fish the hatch? In most cases, it comes down to the mode of water transportation, but there is one other method – wading. In Northern New England, very few

A chunky rainbow came to Terry Van Veghten's Hex fly as he waded Caspian Lake. MARY VAN VEGHTEN PHOTO

anglers fish the Hex Hatch by wading from shore, primarily because of inaccessibility and shorelines that inhibit casting or are too far from the Hex fishing area. In fact, I can count on one hand

17. A Triple Play, A Dunk and Strawberry Shortcake

the number of fly fishers I know who have fished a Hex Hatch this way. Husband and wife team Terry and Mary VanVeghten fish by wading, but it's limited to only two Hex waters, **Caspian Lake** in Vermont and **Profile Lake** in New Hampshire. One other angler, Peter Shea of Essex, VT, loves to fish hike-in ponds and he shared one pond with me (see chapter 14) that he has been able to wade while fishing the Hex Hatch.

Caspian Lake is wall-to-wall camps, summer homes, and all-season homes. So, unless you are casting from your private dock, there's not much opportunity for the public to use its shoreline. Enter the Van Veghtens. Knocking on doors to ask permission for access to private land for deer hunting, turkey hunting, moose shed hunting, and mushroom foraging has been a regular part of their outdoor experiences for years. (Social-distancing is *not* their thing.) So, knocking on the door of a seasonal summer camp to garner permission to park, and fish the shoreline at Caspian, was as natural as tracking deer for this duo.

Pure VT, NH or ME maple syrup is a great gift for a private landowner who allows access to their land.

Their very first try at Caspian was a success. The kindly camp owners and Van Veghtens hit it off, and the "go-ahead" was issued. The first time wading this spot, Terry and Mary discovered a huge bonus. It just so happened that a sandbar extended from shore allowing them to wade further than expected, giving them an even better opportunity to cast directly into (Leighton's) prime Hex-water. I might add that they have caught more than their fair share of feisty rainbows (and a few perch, brook trout, and bats) from that sandbar. A token of appreciation never hurts when private landowners give permission to use their land. In this case, it was Vermont maple syrup.

17. A Triple Play, A Dunk and Strawberry Shortcake

How about using a floating "U Tube" like this during a Hex Hatch? Jeff Reardon says for those remote places with no canoes available, they are indeed a viable option. DELORA REARDON PHOTO

Canoes are considered by most to be THE vehicle to use when fishing the Hex Hatch, and I believe it's primarily due to an inherent feeling of nostalgia, sentimentality, and a little romanticism. Canoes are to Hex fishing as plaid green and black wool is to Maine deer hunting. I would be willing to wager a grilled 'lobstah' roll that more canoes are used when fishing the Hex Hatch in Maine than any other watercraft. They are whisper quiet as long as you stay away from aluminum, and they can be reasonably comfortable for short periods. On the other hand, canoes are more prone to capsizing than boats (a dunk story coming up) and aren't as fast if your fishing spot is at the opposite end of a big lake. Canoes don't carry as much equipment without cramping your quarters, are more likely to get gear wet lying on the canoe floor, and generally are considered to be unsafe when standing and casting. Yet, I absolutely do love their charming rusticness. In recent years, other modes of water transportation have become increasingly common, including kayaks, float tubes, pontoon boats, and various types of inflatables.

17. A Triple Play, A Dunk and Strawberry Shortcake

Over my thirty-plus years of fishing the Hex Hatch, I have fished more often from a canoe than a boat, but in recent years I have decided that I much prefer using a boat when possible. My reasons no doubt correlate with age more than anything else, but I favor a boat mainly for the extra room. I want spaciousness. I want lots of casting clearance. I want to feel okay taking three fly rods and a lot of gear. (I won't take more than two fly rods in a canoe.) A newbie to Hex fishing might be asking, "Really, two

Take extra rods (three if possible) when fishing the Hex Hatch, so when this happens, you can lay that rod down and pick up another ready-rigged rod! The author calls it the "triple play". Then unravel your tangle the next day!

rods? Do you fish two fly rods at once?" An explanation is in order.

Let's take a moment aside to chat about this so-called "triple play" of taking three fly rods to an evening's fishing venture. Face it, because of the brevity and oftentimes frenzied action of the Hex Hatch, it's a time we need to fish or cut bait. And as all experienced Hex anglers know, it doesn't take much to foul up a fly rod in the heat of battle. A litany of causes ranges from a hurried cast to a rise (will getcha every time), an inadvertent gust of wind,

17. A Triple Play, A Dunk and Strawberry Shortcake

bad timing with a fishing partner, or a plain-as-day horrible cast. And sometimes we even manage to snap a fly off or leader-wrap a fly during a terrible cast, or…break a fly off on a lost fish. With trout making wash tub-sized rings around you while slurping mayflies and with a limited amount of time for fishing, this is not the moment to be rectifying such problems. Instead, just lay down the inoperative rod and pick up another that is all rigged and ready to wrangle.

In my early days of fishing the Hex Hatch, I naively spent critical time untangling a mess or tying on a new fly. And under low light conditions, it is at best an absolute misery. A headlamp helps (if you remember to bring it) but what a waste of time. Then one fishing trip it dawned on me. Why not just switch with another fly rod that's all set to go? Untangle the knots tomorrow, for crying out loud. Once I established a habit of bringing an extra ready-rigged rod to the Hex battle, it saved me considerable fishing time. But then I tangled *both* fly rods one evening with fishing time still left. Enter the "triple play"! Maybe I should take *three* rods all rigged and ready to brawl? This enlightened angler has brought three rods to battle ever since. Have I had an occasion to use all three rods from that eye-opening moment? Oh, yeah.

The author follows his own suggestion for saving crucial time during the Hex Hatch by taking three fly rods, ready-to-fish.

Has it helped me to continue fishing with an ear-to-ear grin? A double, oh, yeah. Has it helped me to catch more fish? Absolutely.

Another plus factor for using a boat is its comfort. I often get wretched muscle cramps after plying Hex waters in a canoe. Not

17. A Triple Play, A Dunk and Strawberry Shortcake

so much from a boat. I also like to stand when I'm casting. (Did I mention stability yet?) When fishing with a partner, I have also found that fly lines are less likely to tangle when casting from a boat. An electric motor also works well on most boats, and their stealth when moving your boat's position during a hatch is not only less likely to put fish down but is appreciated by other nearby anglers, as well. In some fishing locations, a boat will get me home a tad earlier, too, allowing for more sleep-in preparation for the next evening fishing. But I *still* love the dreamy wistfulness and grace of a canoe.

I bought a 14-foot Mirrocraft boat in 1973 and spent more than a ton of hours in it over the years. I added some modifications to make the boat easier to fish from, and the first was getting rid of that damned middle seat. I put in a ¾-inch plywood floor with indoor-outdoor carpeting and what a difference it made, especially when fly fishing. I also added a bow deck with a cubby hole, several shelves in the rear, and a boat box on one side to store rods and other paraphernalia.

The boat box was an original idea of another fishing friend, Angelo Ambrosini of Barre, VT, Mary Van Veghten's dad. Angelo is a big-time putterer. He was always doing something to his boats to make them more enjoyable and easier to fish from. My fish measuring board is a gift from him and I have made others for friends and relatives that are replicas of his version. In recent years, Angelo has even been making homemade lures. He gave me several, and I took a liking to one he made from a piece of copper pipe. It had a nice wobble, was heavy enough to use for jigging, and was also a color I favor for togue. All of my recently jigged lake trout

Angelo Ambrosini can hold his own when it comes to fishing. He landed this 17.6-pound Caspian togue while jigging with a lure he had made the night before...on his very first cast of the day. MARY VAN VEGHTEN PHOTO

17. A Triple Play, A Dunk and Strawberry Shortcake

have been taken on that lure. Btw, Angelo was still fishing with Mary in the summer of 2019 at age 94 and is a robust 95 as I write this.

My boat eventually developed cracks in the stern that proved too costly to repair, so in the fall of 2018, I replaced it with a 14'-9" Discovery Crestliner. Wow. How boats have changed over the years. No need to lay down a plywood floor in this boat. Done. No need to build cubbies for gear. Done. No need to take any seats out for more room. Done. No need to build a fly-casting platform. Done. I'm sure all this is old hat to new boat owners, but also, the vinyl inside surface covering can be washed down with a hose, there's a bilge pump, a live well, cell phone charger and the seats are very comfortable and movable. I now also have electric start and trim with a tiller model that I think affords even more space for fly casting. My biggest question? *Why did I wait so long?*

Being a bit of a tinkerer myself, I had to add *something* to this new Hex machine, so I put in a prow anchor system that allows me anchor-rope control from the stern of the boat. I also added several sliding cover boxes for small odds and ends, a cell phone mount, and bumpers to use when docking. On the downside,

*A nicely colored togue from **Willoughby Lake** was deceived by jigging with one of Angelo Ambrosini's homemade lures. (MIKE SCOTT PHOTO)*

there aren't any waterproof storage areas, so I use dry bags. One item I am presently lacking is an electric trolling motor, but it's

17. A Triple Play, A Dunk and Strawberry Shortcake

just a matter of time before that becomes an accessory as well. The bow platform area in my new boat allows an angler to cast like a pro and if a second angler is present they have the whole aft area to use. What about three fly fishers in the boat? I never do it. In a canoe, it's way too dangerous, and even though it's doable in

A new boat, motor, and trailer in 2018 enabled the author to fish more handily overall, and especially during a Hex Hatch. A few things were added like the prow anchor system which allows anchor control from the stern when fishing alone.

a boat you are just asking for trouble. Even with two active casters, things can go awry. A few anglers suggest cueing your partner when about to cast, and I actually think that's a good idea. A caster can say "Up" or "Casting". Or upon completing the cast can say "Done" or "Go". But, one cause of fly rod entanglement is someone who false casts way too many times. You are waiting to time your cast once your sidekick has laid his line on the water, only to find as you start your cast, he adds another false cast or two. Maybe something said when starting to cast *and* after completion

17. A Triple Play, A Dunk and Strawberry Shortcake

would help in this case? After an evening of fishing, I feel pretty darned good if I haven't snagged another person's fly line. Does it happen? Hell, yes. And NO ONE is happy about it. If it happens in the "heat of action", and to untangle the two lines is a real problem, just drop the rods and pick up spares that are all ready to fish. Time is of the essence here.

I have learned from experience that there is one thing you can do to boats (or canoes) to make them the perfect Hex machine and that's to get rid of what I call fly-line-snaggers. Fly fishing lines seem to have a magnetic attraction to *anything* that protrudes, and it is a cussing experience. So, extra rods, gear bags with nasty little buckles, tackle boxes, boat cushions, and just about anything else needs to be stored out of the way. The boat must be "snaggle-proof". I've even found that some types of footwear can be prob-

What's the chance that the next cast will go smoothly?

lematic, especially if you tie double knots on them like sneakers or boat shoes. Wearing knotless footwear such as mid-calf boots helps, and they also keep the ankle-biting no-see-ums and mosquitoes at bay.

The extra fly line around your feet is always a potential pitfall and it is more so in a canoe. Does anyone know why a stripping

17. A Triple Play, A Dunk and Strawberry Shortcake

basket won't solve this problem? I've never seen one in use during a Hex Hatch but, geez, I'm wondering why not? Maybe it's just too cumbersome in a canoe?

You have to remember, the actual prime Hex fishing time is minuscule, maybe just 10-20 minutes in many cases. You want *nothing* to interfere with that golden time… including wardens! You must be doing the FOFS (Focus On Fish Search) relentlessly and *not* be constantly unsnagging your line.

Oh, yes, earlier I suggested a story. One evening on Caspian Lake, while fishing from my boat, I hit the Hex Hatch perfectly. Two canoes were fishing in the same area. Mayflies were coming off and rainbows (BIG rainbows) were into the duns like kids into s'mores. The hatch had been late that evening but at 9:10 I had a beaut, in the 20-

Wonder what's in the cooler?

inch range, engulf my home-tied Caspian Wulff. The fish took off like Vermont's Governor Scott laying rubber at Barre's Thunder Road racetrack. Zinnnnnnng went my reel. The rainbow then thrashed on the surface…and came off. Damn! About two seconds afterward I heard a gigantic splash. Turning to look in that direction I could see one of the canoes had capsized…a dunk smack dab at peak fishing time. Double damn. He seemed to be okay, but I pulled my anchor and headed his way. He was holding onto the canoe and his fly rod, so I towed him the short distance to shore, picking up most of his flotsam along the way. When he was safe and sound, he couldn't thank me enough but I noticed while talking that something was a tad amiss. Yup. His alcohol

17. A Triple Play, A Dunk and Strawberry Shortcake

breath pointed to a "Do NOT go canoeing with this BAC reading." He explained that the dunking occurred when he turned quickly to watch my fish that was screaming out line and splashing on the surface. Might have worked if he had been pie-eyed on lemonade instead of ethanol.

18. Getting There Early and Puttin' on the Ritz

If you are invariably late for most any event, you can skip this chapter and not miss a thing about how to fish the Hex Hatch. On the other hand, maybe, just maybe by reading about all the excitement that can happen *prior* to a hatch I can affect a change in your frequent unpunctuality...at least for fishing a *Hexagenia* mayfly hatch. Let's find out.

Why arrive early? Sometimes it's just unadulterated excitement. It's thrilling for me to see the very first *Hexagenia* mayfly of the year. At other times I may be expecting a banner evening for some reason or other and just can't hold back on the reins.

Seeing the first Hexagenia mayfly of the year lights this author's fire.

Sometimes I may want to get to *"my"* fishing spot before someone else does. Also, on a few ponds, you can "pound-up" fish (get rises with no fish showing) for as much as an hour before the real hatch begins. And for some, it's, well, just the relaxation of sitting...and waiting...and waiting. This latter reason doesn't fit my persona, so I usually opt for some kind of activity that has me fishing.

18. Getting There Early and Puttin' on the Ritz

What else besides casting to non-rising trout is there to do for early birds? Certainly, a big option is to fly fish with sinking lines, or as Ken Allen called it, Hi-D fishing while dredging the bottom. (Hi-D for high-density fly lines.) It is a fact; I have landed way more squaretails using Hi-D fly lines during the "Hex seasons" than I have on surface flies. The reason? It's all about fishing time. When visiting Maine's sporting camps for brookies, we spend way more time fishing with sinking lines than we do with floating lines. For the most part during *Hexagenia* time, fish won't be on the surface except (sometimes) for a brief period early in the morning and of course during the abbreviated evening hatch. As we all know, trout spend a very small amount of time inhaling food from

Using sinking lines prior to a hatch is a very effective method to land brook trout.

the surface. But they are likely still hungry and feeding. The DNA of a trout, through its eyes, sees a Hex mayfly on the surface and sends a message to muscles…MOVE, FOOD. That same DNA sees a "nymph wannabe" (your fly) near the bottom and sends the same message. You just need to go down and get them. Whatcha gonna do the rest of the day anyway? Play cribbage? Not me. I'd rather go deep with sinking lines and catch fish.

18. Getting There Early and Puttin' on the Ritz

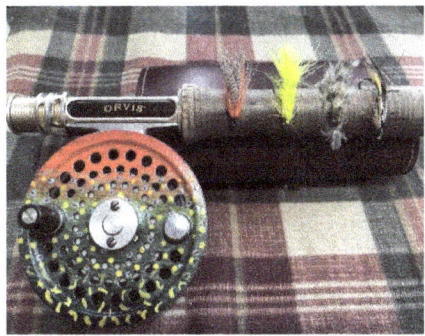

The Golden Demon, Wooly Bugger, Hex Nymph, and Campbell Fancy all work well for squaretails when using sinking lines.

When fishing this way, I anchor in depths between 10-30 feet outside the Hex area, or sometimes in another part of the pond. If there is no action after 20 minutes or so, I will move to a new spot and re-anchor. Casting methodically by "fishing the clock", I cover all likely spots within my range. If the water is fairly deep, I'll time the descent of the fly line based on the line's sink rate. *I want my fly right next to bottom.* Stripping speed is based on the type of fly used, fast strips for streamers, and slower strips when using nymphs. Some anglers, like my brother, will crawl a nymph in a teasing manner by slowly wrapping the fly line around their hands instead of stripping.

I like to use short leaders of 7 ½ foot length and tie on streamers or nymphs such as a Wooly Bugger (I prefer chartreuse or olive), Golden Demon, Campbell Fancy, Maple Syrup, or a Hex Nymph. When fishing this way it sometimes pays to vary your retrieval speed, set the hook with the line (not easy), keep the rod tip in the water during the retrieve, and move often.

I'll never forget the look on a guide's face at a sporting camp many years ago when he learned that my brother and I fished during the day (almost all day) with sinking fly lines – and caught trout, a lot of trout with a few lunkers thrown in. The guide told us that he didn't even *carry* a spool of sinking line when he guided during the Hex season. The sports would go out with him before breakfast and fish dry flies for an hour or two, and then he'd guide them for a couple more hours after the supper meal for dry fly fishing amidst the Hex mayflies. During the day? Everybody napped, played cards, imbibed, and socialized.

18. Getting There Early and Puttin' on the Ritz

Some anglers just don't enjoy Hi-D fishing, and that's understandable. Maybe that was the case with the sports this guide handled. It is true, casting a sinking line is not the hot knife through butter as is the casting of a floating line. It does take more effort and different timing, and I believe those are several of the reasons that sinking lines are not as popular when fishing still waters.

I do admit that a lot of my fishing done in this manner is when staying at sporting camps. Hell, I go there to fish, not play cards. And, it's worth noting that my largest

Fishing with sinking lines before the Hex Hatch can produce some very nice trout. This 18 1/4-inch wild trout was caught on a Hex nymph with sinking line...and released. (STAN WASS PHOTO)

squaretail (to date) resulted from this technique, a 20 ¼ inch fish at Red River Camps. Shucks. It doesn't bother me one bit to net a 20-inch trout when casting Hi-D lines near the bottom. Would I rather it had been on a surface fly? Is there jelly in a peanut butter-jelly sandwich?

Any jelly in there?

18. Getting There Early and Puttin' on the Ritz

The author's largest squaretail came to a fly fished deep on a sinking line prior to the Hex Hatch.

There is a very small contingent of fly fishers who snub their noses at using sinking lines… because it "isn't really fly fishing." To me, that's a fairly narrow scope of view, but whatever cues your cumber, I guess.

The opportunity to land the most fish usually favors the longer part of a day while casting weighted fly lines. Below is a chart depicting data from my fishing journals for the Deboullie Region over a few years. (The years aren't included because I didn't feel they were relevant.) I have compared the approximate time spent fishing with Hi-D (sinking) lines versus floating lines, to the number of trout caught, by two fly fishermen, over seven different days.

Red River Camps in the Deboullie Region is "headquarters" for wild brook trout fishing in Northern Maine.

18. Getting There Early and Puttin' on the Ritz

Date	Hours Hi-D	Trout Hi-D	Hours Floating	Trout Floating
June 29	7	15 (including one 17 inches)	1.5	3
July 7	6.5	35 (including an 18 ¼ incher)	1	3
July 8	8.5	19	1	1
July 2	6	2	1	3
July 11	6.5	7	1.5	6
July 10	6	27	2	1
July 7	6	10	2.5	4
Totals	**46.5**	**115**	**10.5**	**21**

As you can well see, more time was spent fishing down deep during the day, and more fish were caught on average that way, a 5:1 ratio compared to fishing the surface. On the other hand, an interesting comparison is the average amount of trout caught per hour using both techniques. It's very close to the same at two trout per hour of fishing. (Divide the number of fish by the number of hours.) And yet another observation is that the largest trout were indeed caught with sinking lines.

18. Getting There Early and Puttin' on the Ritz

Another variation of fishing with sinking lines before a hatch I discovered at Vermont's **Willoughby Lake** in 2004. This gorgeous lake boasts the opportunity for either salmon or rainbows during the Hex Hatch. (Yes, I know – suckers, too.) I tend to be early for a hatch so I can either jig for togue or cast sinking fly

A streamer the author ties to mimic smelts he calls a Flashabou Smelt, and it is a killer fly for enticing lakers with a fly rod.

lines. During one trip, I noticed that schools of small smelt were jumping out of the water as if they were being chased. Something with fins was scaring the bejeebers out of those smelt, and I wagered it was one of my preferred target species, a salmon or rainbow. I knew exactly what to do with no Hex showing yet. I carried a few single-hooked, smelt-like streamers that I tie and use for fly casting in deep water for lake trout. I call them Flashabou Smelts. They are my go-to fly for lakers, so why wouldn't they also work for other fish that are smelt-chasers? I tied one on my sinking line and started casting.

Shortly afterward, a fishing friend, Ron Frascoia, paddled his kayak up next to me wondering how I was doing. He was there

18. Getting There Early and Puttin' on the Ritz

waiting for the hatch too. I kept casting while we chatted until my stripping came to an abrupt halt as if I had hooked a submarine. It took off like a torpedo and went on a reel-screaming run taking out half of my backing. Wow! After several more zings and some surface splashing, I was able to net the Willoughby beauty, a handsome rainbow trout. Frascoia seemed to be more than impressed and he should have been. He had a front-row seat.

My measuring board certified that this wild rainbow was 21 ¾

One evening while waiting for the Hex Hatch, the author saw smelt on the surface acting like they were being chased by something with a much larger mouth. Casting a Flashabou Smelt on a sinking fly line, this handsome rainbow was tricked into becoming a meal for the author. RON FRASCOIA PHOTO

inches long and my scales dropped to an even four pounds. The Flashabou-fooled fish was a hen with an empty stomach… and tasted superb. The water temperature that evening was 64 degrees even though it was July 16, and the hatch was right on the verge of getting underway, as I noticed a few old shucks and saw one adult mayfly. I was able to hook one smaller rainbow that evening using the same setup but lost that fish.

For umpteen reasons, I have fished that way but only a few times since. When I did, there were no smelt being chased to the surface, and I was not successful. I guess the answer is to always

18. Getting There Early and Puttin' on the Ritz

be prepared for such an event (sinking lines, smelt-like streamers) even though you are really headed for a Hex showdown. So, where the heck is all this going? Simply this. Don't pass up fishing sinking lines before a Hex Hatch.

Casting to lakers can be a fun way to bide one's time while waiting for a Hex Hatch.

My next suggestion for whiling away the time on the front end of a hatch won't suit all fly anglers, nor will it work on all Hex waters. Are you ready for this? *Go catch a lake trout (togue).* You read it correctly, go catch a laker. Extend the day's fishing time and have some fun.

I have often fished for lakers in the time leading up to a Hex Hatch. Several lakes in Vermont fit the bill perfectly, including **Caspian** and **Willoughby Lakes.** For some reason, on these lakes where I target rainbow trout instead of brook trout during the Hex Hatch, I am not as successful with sinking lines and nymphs before the hatch and therefore I try something else. Since most of these rainbow waters also have lake trout, it is the species I fish for ahead of the hatch.

Tom McGreevy of Waterbury, Vermont jigged up this nice lake trout at Caspian Lake. What's with the white pants, Tom?

18. Getting There Early and Puttin' on the Ritz

Okay, so how do you land a togue before the Hex Hatch? Many guess by trolling. You could, but I don't. Instead, I catch them by jigging with a spinning rod, or…hold onto your Boonie hats…by fly casting with streamer flies. Here's my jigging technique without too much fanfare and detail. Using a fish-finder, locate a group of lakers in anywhere from 25-50 feet of water. It's not unusual for lake trout to be just on the outside edge of a Hex area, where they await the evening hours to swim on in and get their fair share of Hex nymphs.

It didn't take long for Ron DeVincenzi of North Hero, Vermont to catch on to the jigging technique.

After I've located a group of lake trout, I'll mark the spot nearby with a small buoy, then motor upwind 30-40 yards or so and drift over the marked fish. Any spinning rod will work and it's a real hoot on ultralight gear. Even though braided line is better because of little stretching, there's no need to go crazy and buy a whole new rod, reel, and line just for this purpose. I don't know too many fly anglers who don't have a spinning rod or two hidden somewhere at home.

18. Getting There Early and Puttin' on the Ritz

Locate a heavy lure that wobbles and gets to the bottom quickly. I favor Sidewinders, Goldfish, jigs (yellow and pearl), and homemade lures such as those made by Ambrosini. (See chapter 17) Various types of tube jigs also work. Once the lure reaches the bottom, I use a rhythmic rising and dropping of the spinning rod to give the lure some action. The fish will almost always grab it on the downfall. You can choose to just vertical-jig over the side of the boat or you can cast. When casting let the lure sink to bottom, jig a few times while reeling in, open the bail, let it fall to bottom again, and keep repeating until the lure is on the bottom below the boat, then vertical jig for a few minutes before reeling in and re-casting. When fish are showing over a fairly large area, instead of using a buoy just drift through that fishy stretch.

*Jigging (spin-casting) for lake trout can sometimes result in fish with gigantic proportions. This 17-pound laker lowered the water level in **Echo Lake** and was duped on a Sidewinder by Ron Frascoia of Barre, Vermont. DOLORES FRASCOIA PHOTO*

To be enjoyable, fishing for lake trout in this manner doesn't have to produce a state record or even a fish measured in pounds,

18. Getting There Early and Puttin' on the Ritz

although as you can see by the accompanying photograph, trophy fish are indeed possible. If you have never tried jigging my advice is to give it a whirl. It works, it's easy and more than entertaining.

A few lakes that I have already listed with *Hexagenia* hatches, and also have lake trout populations are:

Vermont...Caspian, Willoughby, Echo, Long Pond, Crystal

New Hampshire...Big Diamond, Big Greenough, Big Squam, Sunapee, Winnipesauke

Maine...Allagash, Richardson, Square, Thompson, Sheepscot

So, what's the deal with *fly casting* for lake trout during the summer? Doesn't sound quite right, does it? And for good reason.

Spud Man says, you can pass the time before a Hex Hatch by fly casting for lake trout. Use a fast-sinking fly line, a smelt-like streamer, and a very short leader. It works like beer and skittles.

Togue are deep in the summer months, and that means it isn't easy to get to them with a fly rod. In all my times fishing lakes that have a population of lake trout, I have never seen anyone else fish this way. Never. And I can't even come up with someone I know

18. Getting There Early and Puttin' on the Ritz

who casts for lakers in this manner, except maybe Drew Price of Master Angler fame. So how did I happen upon this apparent fishing anomaly? On a hunch. Really, that was it. And it helped to extend my fly fishing after the Hex season ended. I reasoned, if it works for brook trout why won't it work for lake trout? Just fish in deeper water. Use a fast-sink fly line. Tie on a smelt imitation streamer. Go *really* short on the leader—makes for easier casting. And find some fish. Seemed entirely plausible. If it worked, I figured it would be hellish fun and might even replace my jigging technique with the spinning rod.

Plausible, yes. Immediate success, no. My first attempts were in the years 1994-1995. I half-heartedly tried it a few times during that stretch and received no reward for my efforts. But I had this fisherman's gut feeling that it *should* work. My breakthrough year was 1996 when I boated seven lake trout between 17- 21-inches casting with a fly rod. Since then, I have landed as many as five lakers in one trip using this method and have caught several four-

Many times, it is best to use a buoy when marking fish like lake trout. Timing the fly as it sinks towards bottom helps to put your fly right in the laker's den, since you may be casting in as much as 40 feet of water. (Note: The measuring box was a gift from Angelo Ambrosini.)

18. Getting There Early and Puttin' on the Ritz

pounders. Not heavyweights for sure, but it is a blast to play these twisting chars of the deep on a fly rod.

This technique obviously will not work if the lake trout are too deep, so if you mark fish 50 feet or deeper, leave them for the trollers. Continue your search until you find fish at 25-50 feet. Those are the lakers you can reach with a fly rod.

The buoy marker is more important when using a fly rod. I typically anchor within a long casting distance (sometimes I can see the backing showing through on my reel, with a little help from the wind) of the buoy. If the sink rate of your fly line is known, as well as the water depth, you can determine the time for the fly to reach bottom, then use a watch or iPhone for counting. I tie my own single-hook flies to use when fishing like this and all of them have varying amounts of Flashabou. You need some highly reflective smelt-like material in the fly to attract these denizens of the deep. Sometimes I also use pearl Flashabou tubing, although the bulkiness makes it more difficult to cast. In lakes with a perch population (lake trout are big feeders on perch) a Barnes Special with some strands of Flashabou is a good choice.

You want to place that streamer right in Mr. Togue's den, where he's relaxing and watching the food channel on his DNA TV, then retrieve the line using nice long strips. Often a fish will strike right after the first strip, and other times they will follow the fly and grab it later. Whenever it is, be prepared for a rod-breaking jolt. (Yup, done that.)

After jigging for lakers and before the Hex Hatch, Steve Foster of Barre, VT prepares to barbecue some venison steaks.

Just remember if you do try this, don't get *so* caught up that you are late for the Hex Hatch! It's that much fun. And don't forget

18. Getting There Early and Puttin' on the Ritz

to pick up the buoy – which I have neglected to do more times than I care to admit. If the fly rod you use for laker-casting is a planned fly rod for the evening hatch, leave some time to change spools, flies, etc.

My last suggestion for whittling away time when early for a hatch is to…feast. Several times, in my boat, I have had venison steaks charred over a portable grill, followed by strawberry shortcake while awaiting the hatch. To me, that is **really** "puttin' on the ritz". (Btw, try THAT in a canoe…)

19. It's All About Timing & Temperature

I am willing to bet a Roman candle that *Hexagenia limbata* mayflies will be hatching somewhere in Maine, New Hampshire, and Vermont on the Fourth of July. Actually, one of my best ever evenings of Hex fly fishing occurred during a floating-fireworks display, and it was damned hard to keep my eyes on the fly.

Even though I have already addressed the topic of when a Hex Hatch occurs (see chapters 7 & 8), I feel the need to elaborate further before we start casting flies. Some of this may be a tad repetitive, but I'm hoping that the additional information will help you understand the fluctuations and timing of this "Hex-riffic" hatch even more.

Fireworks and Hex Hatches often coincide.

19. It's All About Timing & Temperature

It's fairly safe to say that a majority of ponds and lakes experience the onset of a hatch during the week on either side of July 1st. That said, I will add that I have recorded a hatch starting as early as June 22nd and as late as July 18-19. Why the differences in starting times? The answer is such variables as elevation, water depth, lake size, latitude, weather, and probably some other natural vagaries that we don't yet understand. This yearly difference of onset time can be as few as several days or as many as several

No matter the conditions, always be prepared for the Hex Hatch. (You should add a headlamp to the items seen here.) The black and yellow piece of equipment isn't necessary unless you want to be sure the surface temperature is optimum...or want to check your companion for COVID-19.

weeks. That's why you can't always depend on the hatch occurring at the same date from year to year.

The total length of the hatching period (from onset to hatch completion) varies as well, from a few days shy of a week to almost three weeks. This disparity is almost entirely due to the weather during the hatch. A few days in the 80s and 90s will bring a hatch to a swifter end (more mayflies hatching per day), whereas abnormally cold weather and/or heavy rainfalls will extend it. Without these extremes, the hatching period averages closer to a week to 10 days. On occasions, I have spotted a few Hex mayflies in late August and September. This isn't because of a 'hatch", but

19. It's All About Timing & Temperature

instead, these stragglers metamorphose late for some reason. I have even seen a Hex mayfly as late as Oct 8th.

The hourly timing of a hatch is more definitive, kind of a set-your-watch by event. You may see a couple of mayflies hatch as early as 4:00 in the afternoon, but that generally means little or nothing for an angler. The prime hatch time is usually somewhere from 8:45 to 9:15 PM. Some evenings it will just be a 10-15-minute blitz within that time frame.

I am a firm believer that the peculiarity of hatches from pond to pond is directly related to water temperature. Simply said, small, shallow, low elevation ponds warm up faster and get the Hex ball rolling first. Deep, large lakes take longer to warm up and the hatches start later. Sometimes as one water body is coming to the end of a hatch another may be just starting, or be in full swing.

In Vermont, some of the first water bodies to produce *Hexa-*

Small, shallow, low elevation ponds are usually the first to produce a Hex Hatch.

genia are **Eligo Lake, Nelson Pond, and Miller Pond.** Count on a hatch commencing in those waters around the fourth week in June. Next in this pond-to-lake "rolling opening" are typically

19. It's All About Timing & Temperature

Caspian and **Echo Lakes** and they occur closer to July 1st. My records show an average of a week's difference between Eligo and Caspian's onset hatches. The last hurrah goes to frigid, deep **Willoughby Lake**, with the hatch beginning around the second week in July. This so-called "rolling opening" fits perfectly with a dedicated Hex-angler's schedule.

Some ponds and lakes in Northern Maine start late but for different reasons. Elevation and latitude play a bigger part in that region of the Pine Tree State. But my guess is that the really late onsets, in all three states, are governed more by spring and early summer weather that I label in my journals as "cold, wet springs/summers".

All these dates and times I have indicated are my gold standards, based on fastidious record keeping over the years, but it's worth noting that my journals show a trend towards earlier mayfly hatches in recent years. I do believe that *climate change* could be the culprit for this earlier trend, but keep in mind that my data is anecdotal, not scientific, so you can take it for what it seems to be...or not.

Wild brook trout like this are caught on top during a Hex Hatch as long as the surface temperature is suitable for brook trout. Sean Fowler nailed this chunky trout on a home-tied dry fly.

19. It's All About Timing & Temperature

There are times during a hatch when the surface temperature (ST) is just too warm – not good for the fly fisher nor the fish. 2020 was one of those years. My initial fishing trip was on June 22nd to a small, shallow Vermont brook trout pond. In the past, a fishing partner, Sean Fowler, and I could expect to see mayflies there by July 4th, but each year since then, the hatch has started a little earlier. So, even though we adjusted and started to show up with fly rod in hand a few days prior to the preceding year, we still found the hatch to be already ongoing. In 2020, we bumped our first day up to June 22nd, partly because of a hot spell that occurred May 26-27 and another longer one that was going on at the time. The words we shared went something like, "We had better get our asses over there pronto or miss the hatch again!" Keep in mind that it was early for a Hex Hatch; it was only June 22nd. For crying out loud, we hadn't even celebrated National Catfish Day yet, which was on the 25th. We just HAD to beat the hatch THIS year.

Now that I may have you on the edge of your seats, here are the results for this *very first* Hex-fishing trip of 2020: conditions were awesome with a cloud cover and no wind, mayflies started hatching around 8:15, and scads of mayflies were hatching at the key time, 8:45-9:00 PM. **BUT** the ST was a whopping **79 degrees**. Egad. (Keep in mind that brookies love water temperatures in the 55-60-degree range, and can maybe tolerate very brief periods up to 72 degrees.) No squaretail in their right mind would come to the surface with the temperature at *79 degrees*. And they didn't. Not one definite trout rise did we see, and that was with hundreds of mayflies dotting the surface. I never cast a dry fly at all. My partner made six or seven fruitless casts. I did briefly try a sinking line…halfheartedly. "Very disappointing," were the words said all the way home. Actually, the *real* words were something more like, "I can't effin believe it!"

As it turned out, that was the trend for 2020. Earlier than normal *Hexagenia* hatches also occurred on Lake Erie, starting on average a week to 10 days prematurely, with much warmer STs than

19. It's All About Timing & Temperature

normal. The day after we Hex-fished (June 22nd), **Lake Champlain** was a very swimmable 77 degrees, and a small local bass pond reached a record 85 degrees.

My first fishing trip was followed by a second to **Jabe Pond** in New York state on June 27th. Even though this was a new pond for me, Terry Van Veghten had fished it many years ago during a

Guru Terry Van Veghten eyes the biggest sundae east of the Mississippi. The promise of such mountainous ice cream treats encouraged the author to try the Hex Hatch at Jabe Pond in New York State.

Hex Hatch. "Wanna go?", he asked. At this time, it was five days past the last temperature-foiled Hex trip, so I was mighty anxious to try another spot. "Sure. Let's do it," I replied.

He spiced up the trip as much as possible by telling me about a fantastic creemee place along the way located in Addison, VT. He failed to say it was right next door to a huge dairy farm, and I'm talking a *few feet next door*. The prevailing wind that warm day was, yup you guessed it, due (north), towards the creemee stand. It was indeed very difficult to discern the true flavor of the hot

19. It's All About Timing & Temperature

Two great Green Mountain "flavors" - maple creamees and barnyard manure.

fudge brownie sundaes, yet after only several heaping mouthfuls, this clumsy oaf spilled his entire sundae on the ground, anyway. But heck, it was free-fishing day in NY that weekend and at least I could celebrate that money-saving aspect of the trip.

It's worth mentioning that New York State has abundant Hex Hatches in hundreds of ponds and lakes, especially in the Adirondacks, but covering three states (VT, NH, ME) was all I wanted to tackle for my first book venture, so I left the Empire State out of the mix.

After paddling the Winonah canoe across Jabe to the further shore, we immediately saw cedar waxwings grab several Hex duns as they flew off from the pond's surface. That certainly was encouraging. But I still had suspicions that this trip was going to mimic my last one, although Jabe does have rainbows and browns which can handle warm water temperatures a bit better than brookies. But, with a measurement of the ST at 75 degrees, I

19. It's All About Timing & Temperature

wasn't that optimistic. Van Veghten brought a device that measures the thermocline (the depth at which temperatures abruptly change), and after several repeat measurements, the thermocline appeared to be at around 9-10 feet deep. Not good. That meant from the surface down to 9-10 feet, the water was bathtub warm, not exactly trout habitat.

Jabe Pond in New York State has a Hex Hatch but be wise and don't go if you are on the heels of a wicked hot spell...unless you plan to camp out and swim instead.

Eventually, what few trout rises we did see were at dark, but they were not taking the Hex duns. Instead, the rises were just swirls, with no splashy dun-taking rises, and no trout cruising the surface. At first, we couldn't understand why these fish weren't taking our flies. But after several more swirls, we noticed adult duns sitting on the surface briefly before flying off. Apparently, trout saw the nymphs swimming towards the surface from their cool hideaway in the thermocline, gave chase as their DNA kicked in, and maybe successfully nabbed the nymph. But once they got close to the surface, the trout abruptly turned around, creating swirls as they returned to their comfort zone. They did not linger,

19. It's All About Timing & Temperature

as many fruitless casts to the swirls proved. We never did see a fish take an adult mayfly.

I must add that these two experienced fly fishermen did miss the boat on their chance to pick up some fish, albeit not on the surface. We were expecting tough conditions from previous hot daytime temperatures, so we brought fly rods rigged with sinking

COVID-19 put the brakes on three Maine fishing trips for the author in 2020, one to Bradford Camps where he hoped to hoodwink squaretails like this pretty fish during the Hex Hatch. COURTESY BRADFORD CAMPS

19. It's All About Timing & Temperature

lines in the truck as a backup to dry fly fishing. While loading the canoe, Terry, my "Guru Guide" misunderstood and thought I *wasn't* bringing a sinking line out onto the pond, so he didn't put his in the canoe. Oops. It just doesn't work well if one guy is fishing deep (requiring deeper water) and the other guy can't because he's only casting dry flies. He might as well be tossing peanuts to a statue of an elephant. I did fish my Hi-D line for a while and picked up two small rainbows on a Hex nymph…while my partner was still tossing goobers.

And so that is how the Hex "season" went for me, one "woe is me" after another. Another kick to the seat of my pants came earlier this spring and started the year off on the wrong foot. I had reserved three different fly-fishing trips to Maine last winter before COVID-19 mounted its pandemic front. All three trips had to be canceled. I like Maine fishery biologist Tim Obrey's summation of 2020, "I feel 2020 has been cross-threaded from the start and now [Sept] we can [even] add drought to our list of grievances."

Another downfall to very warm STs is that trout will not be cruising for mayflies on the surface. That is a huge disadvantage to a Hex angler. (More on cruising trout in chapter 20.)

Just for the fun of it, I checked my fishing journals to see how successful I have been during a Hex Hatch when the ST was 74 degrees or higher, and fishing surface flies. These accounts ranged from 1991 thru 2019 and represented just the author's success…or more likely lack of success. Here's the chart; you add the numbers.

19. It's All About Timing & Temperature

Date	Location	Surface Temperature	Hex Hatching	Trout Rising	Trout Caught
July 13	Caspian Lake	74	A few	A few	0
July 21	Willoughby Lake	74	Very few	Less than 5	0
July 9	Caspian Lake	74	Yes	Few	0
July 5	Eligo Lake	75	Couple	A few	0
July 7	Caspian Lake	75	Yes	Yes	0
June 29	Caspian Lake	75	Yes	Very few	1 RBT
July 25	Caspian Lake	75	Some	A few	0
June 26	Caspian Lake	76	Yes	Yes	1 RBT
July 18	East Long Pond	76	A few	Scattered	0
June 30	Caspian Lake	76	Yes	Yes	0
July 2	Big Greenough Pond	76	A couple	None	0
July 10	Caspian Lake	76	Yes	Could count on one hand	0
July 20	Crystal Lake	78	A few	none	0

19. It's All About Timing & Temperature

Looks crystal clear to me. STs which are too warm can severely affect fishing success during a Hex Hatch, let alone also affect any fish that may be caught and released. At a microscopic 0.15 trout landed per trip (2 fish for 13 trips) with STs 74 degrees and above, we all might want to be a little more in control of the reins when Hexitis strikes us next time under these abysmal ST conditions.

Most of the trout and salmon caught during a Hex Hatch by the author have come when the surface temperature was less than 73 degrees. (The buttoned shirt was to keep pesky no-see-ums at bay.)

For a fair comparison, and to show that I actually do catch fish during a Hex Hatch (never large numbers), I scoured my journals from 1991 through 2019 looking for all Hex fishing trips in Vermont and New Hampshire in which the STs were no higher than 73 degrees. (I didn't include Maine since all the additional data would have tripped this codger's circuit breaker.)

With a varying amount of mayflies present, there were 58 of those days. Many times, I didn't measure/record ST for some reason or other, so those days were discounted. During those 58 days with STs 73 degrees or below, I landed 103 fish, including one brown trout, one white sucker (I just had to throw that in because it was a whopping 21 in.), 18 brook trout, and 83 rainbow trout (including a 19 ½ and a 22-inch fish). I also caught some yellow perch, smallmouth bass, rock bass, chub, and one smelt. The average number of trout I caught on those 58 occasions was a little less than two per trip, which was about 12 times my catch rate for when STs were 74 and above. Mission accomplished?

Btw, don't expect to land a lot of fish during a Hex Hatch. The involved time is just too short. In those 58 journaled trips,

19. It's All About Timing & Temperature

the most I landed in one evening was six rainbow trout. Checking my Maine trips when fishing for squaretails and salmon, the most I eked out in one evening was five. Terry Van Veghten once netted an astounding 12 rainbows one evening at Caspian and he reports that the largest number of squaretails he has landed from a hatch in Maine was around ten. Fish numbers just are not typically high during Hex hatches. Instead, it's the anticipation, excitement of fishing the surface, and the hope of landing a trophy fish that makes it special.

Generally speaking, a Hex angler doesn't land more than a few fish during a Hex Hatch because of the limited time available. Van Veghten claims that wearing your hat backwards helps. MARY VAN VEGHTEN

20. Rising Like Bread Dough

You have now learned how to engage the "triple play" as well as "puttin' on the ritz" before fishing a *Hexagenia* mayfly hatch. You are now ready for the real fireworks to begin. Let's go find some rising fish.

I like to be at my Hex fishing site by 7:30 PM. Sometimes I'll look for a shaded shoreline since fish seem to start rising there first. My initial decision is whether to anchor or to drift. If there's little to no wind, I'm likely to drift at the start. After "reading the

A single rise from a trout or salmon...what to do? With two anglers, one should cast left of the ring and the other to the right.

water" for a short time, I'll then decide where to anchor. If there are other anglers already there, drifting may not be a viable option, as it could nose you right into someone's "front yard", introducing the possibility of a little "Hex rage". Typically, I anchor, but the

20. Rising Like Bread Dough

decision of where to anchor should be considered carefully since picking up the anchor and moving late in the game is not always a wise decision. Anchoring depth is usually between 10-20 feet, although that can vary depending on many factors.

So, the first fish of the evening makes beautiful concentric rings. What to do? If it's just one rise and within casting distance, most of us would cast to it. The problem is if you are not quite ready and a tad slow on the uptake, it's advantage trout. In all probability, the fish is no longer there and you won't be sure what direction it went. With two anglers, the best choice is for one to cast left of the swirl and one to cast right, and hope for the best. If the fish swam left or right after coming to the surface, you may then have a 50-50 chance of enticing it. If the fish moved away from you or even came towards you, it's probably no dice. Be sure to lead the fish in the direction you think it swam, and *not* cast to the ripples, as fish are almost always moving during a hatch.

Another option when spotting a single rise is to have your arm and fly rod cocked, but hold off for the fish to come up a second time. This takes a little backbone but it will help you determine the direction of travel, allowing for an ambush. Advantage angler. Bob Mallard says that he can often detect a "pillow" of water on one side of a rise to determine the fish's

If a fish is cruising it's best to determine which way the fish is moving before casting. Lefty Lawrence Pyne has his eye on a cruising fish and plans to drop his fly about ten feet in front of it.

20. Rising Like Bread Dough

direction of travel, but I'm guessing that's more likely in moving water. I'm not sure that my eyes are that sharp anyway, so I look for fins instead.

You are in luck. Fish are rising like bread dough and are within casting distance.

Once the evening moves along, and if all the Hex stars are lined up, there will be some fish cruising the surface. They will take a mayfly, then instead of dropping down in the water column, will continue to swim just under the surface until they find the next mayfly, and so on. When fish are cruising the surface like this, it is the essence of what anglers will refer to later in life as the "salad days" (good ole days) of Hex fishing. Cruising fish are much easier to catch because you can determine their direction of travel more accurately, and that makes it easier to plop your fly in front of them, not behind. How far you should cast in front of a cruising fish, depends on how quickly you can cast to the fish and how fast the fish is cruising from rise to rise. When there are few mayflies on the water, fish swim faster looking for the next one, and vice versa when there are many mayflies. And even though you may think that you have accurately doped out the direction a fish is moving, the little devils may still give you the fin and make a right-angle turn *just* as you cast.

20. Rising Like Bread Dough

Let's say the fish are rising like bread dough and a few fish are within casting distance. Learn to pick out the larger fish and cast to them instead of any rise. That's not always possible, but when you see a dorsal fin followed by the tail after a second or two, that Mr. Man, is a fish you want to snooker.

During most mayfly hatches on still water bodies (lakes/ponds), trout and salmon will be cruising the top if there are enough insects. Generally, this is not true in moving waters like streams, where the fish station themselves at an ambush site, and wait for the mayfly morsels to come to them.

Steve Long nets a nice brook trout that came up for his dry fly during a "Recurve Hatch" on Seyon Pond.

I have observed this stationing by trout in only one pond, **Seyon Pond** in Vermont. There is an annual *Litobrancha recurvata* mayfly hatch that occurs during the afternoon at Seyon. This mayfly, you may recall, is super large like *Hexagenia* and is often referred to as a Dark Green Drake. To help avoid the confusion surrounding the oft used term "green drake", on a fisherman's whim I decided to call it the "Recurve Hatch", after its scientific species name, *recurvata*. At Seyon, this mayfly starts to hatch when surface temperatures reach about 60-62 degrees, around the last week of May and the first of June. An appealing characteristic of this mayfly at Seyon is the time of day that it hatches, usually commencing around 2:30-3:00 P.M., and shutting down between 5:00-5:30 PM. This is not a crepuscular hatching time like *Hexagenia* at all. And do I love it, for there are NO late-night trips home after fishing this hatch.

The other fascinating element about this Recurve Hatch is that these wild brookies at Seyon do not cruise the surface. Instead, they **station** themselves in about 4-6 feet of water, or wherever the mayfly larvae swim up from the bottom muck. That could be due to Seyon's shallowness coupled with its tannin-stained, low transparency water. I'm really not sure. But the trout rarely cruise the surface to pick up adult mayflies as happens with the later occurring Hex Hatch.

When fishing Seyon's Recurve Hatch, if I miss a better-than-average trout, I line the missed strike up with a rock or tree along the far shoreline and rest the fish for 5-10 minutes. Then I'll repeat a cast to the marked site, and four times out of five, that trout will come to my fly again. The fish stays right at that site as if it were anchored. A few times when I have had a trout miss the fly a sec-

Because trout station themselves in one spot during Seyon's "Recurve Hatch", you usually will have a second, and maybe even a third, chance at a nice trout that misses your fly on its first attempt.

ond time, I have again rested the fish and also had it come back for the third time. If during one of these fish-angler skirmishes, I

20. Rising Like Bread Dough

happen to nick a fish with the hook, that 5-10-minute rest is not likely to work.

There are several other strategies to try during a *Hexagenia* hatch that can also help you go home pleased as punch. Sometimes it seems like all the fish rises are 3-4 casts away. Once in a while maybe one of those fish will work its way towards you if you lead a charmed life. But too often those fish will just teasingly mill around making rings out in left-field. This poses a *difficult* decision...to chase rises or not. Have I done it? Oh, yeah. Many times. Does it work? Sometimes.

If chasing rises becomes a part of your agenda, it works best while paddling a canoe, or if you are fishing from a boat, an electric motor is best. One important item for you to consider, though, is encroaching upon someone else's turf. If so, an "iceberg" may be dead ahead. (Unfortunately, "Hex rage" does happen, although rarely.)

The game plan when chasing rises is to quietly get close enough so you can cast to a cruising fish without putting it down. Easier said than done sometimes. But, when fishing is otherwise slow, I don't think twice about resorting to this somewhat controversial tactic.

If you have ice running through your veins, you might want to try the stoic, cast-and-wait approach...even with fish rising in the distance. The eternal hope here is that a fish will eventually find your fly and inhale it. (Remember the elderly couple at **Sourdnahunk**?) You do, however, have to keep a constant eye on the fly, because these fish *know* when you are looking elsewhere. I have fished with several anglers who are very successful

Nah.

20. Rising Like Bread Dough

at this cast-and-wait tactic, but for me, not to cast to a rising trout is akin to taking a kid's Halloween candy. I just can't do it.

You may recall earlier in this book my plaudits given to fellow angler, Ken Grimes, as a master fly tier and Hex angler. In Grimes' "heydays" he landed a lot of large rainbows during the Hex Hatch, and with Metamucil regularity. So, I asked this former teacher, "What the heck are your secrets?" He admitted there would have been a day that loosening his tongue about fishing secrets wouldn't have been quite as easy, but as most of us do later in life, he has become more willing to share.

One of his tactics revolves around *patience*, specifically, not casting to every rise but instead being *selective*. Grimes waits until he sees a large fish flaunt its dorsal fin when gulping a mayfly, and then gamely waits until the big riser comes close enough for a cast. Placing his fly about 10-12 feet in front of the fish, he then seduces the overgrown trout by giving the fly a little jiggle. Slurp.

Another stratagem by Grimes involves setting the hook on a

A 14 ½ inch trout is nothing to sneeze at on Seyon Pond, especially when caught during the "Recurve Hatch". Carl Decoster pictured here is another fishing friend who is not with us anymore.

rise…or I should say NOT setting the hook, but letting the *fish* do it instead. That takes some practice. Our DNA wants our muscles

20. Rising Like Bread Dough

to react immediately. I *hate* to admit how many large fish I have issued a free pass to by setting the hook so hard that I broke the leader.

The third reason he gave for his success at catching the larger trout is the way he constructs his leaders. For that explanation and to learn what flies Grimes prefers during a Hex Hatch, see Chapter 21.

Just before dark, blanket hatches from a blizzard of mayflies may occur and present a problem. By this time the fish have been gorging themselves on nymphs and adults and actually may be starting to let up a bit, becoming a bit pickier. I do one of three

Blanket hatches can prove to be a problem. How in hell will a fish distinguish your single fly from 100s of the real thing?

things during a blanket hatch. 1) I try to cast to open spots where there are no shucks or mayflies. This might be just outside the main hatch area. 2) I might switch fly rods and start using one that is spooled with a floating fly line but has an unweighted Hex nymph on it. 3) I may just go home.

What about fishing *after* dark? Personally, I don't enjoy it. Why? Tangles increase exponentially, it's more dangerous to each other flinging flies around, you miss out on so much daylight fun of catching fish, and I just prefer to see what the heck I am doing. Can trout still be caught after dark? For sure, but not usually with the same regularity. There is one exception, and that would be nights with a full moon, or nearly so. I recall once fishing with a fellow teacher, Pat McCormack, on a clear, full moon night. He kept his large, dry fly right in the moonshine so he could watch it carefully. He was rewarded with a feisty, 2-pound rainbow... at 10:00 PM.

Clear, full moon nights during a Hex Hatch can extend an angler's fishing time...if you enjoy fishing after dark.

Many salmonids don't see as well in the obscurity of low light. That, and complete satiation, are the primary reasons for fish activity to dwindle after full darkness during a hatch. Brown trout are considered to be able to see the best, rainbow trout and brookies the least.

Below are some tips that I have learned from fishing *The Hatch* over the last 32 years. Maybe they will help give you an edge next time you choose to do battle.

20. Rising Like Bread Dough

1) Check your fly often. I once unknowingly fished a fly backward because of a leader tangle and missed several nice trout because of it.

2) Use the "triple play". Do **not** try to change a fly during a *Hexagenia* Hatch, or risk the chance of losing much of the valuable fishing time.

3) While waiting for a rise, lay out about 10 feet of line on the water instead of having the line way out and fishing blind. When a fish does come to the top, it's just a matter of lifting the fly and casting, all in *one* motion. No false casts needed at all.

4) Be prepared for biting insects, usually mosquitoes and/or no-see-ums. (Most blackflies are gone by Hex time.) Lather up with your choice of repellant *before* the hatch begins and wear long pants.

5) Carry a camera but realize that good photography during the frenetic time of a Hex Hatch is difficult at best. Fishing duos

Strike up conversations with geezers, codgers, and old-timers. There is a lot to learn from their past experiences.

can offer to photograph each other's good fortune, but that means putting fly rods down. Or, you can go fancy with today's myriad

20. Rising Like Bread Dough

of hands-off cameras. You could also bring along a non-fishing friend.

6) As the hatch moves along from the middle days towards the end of the hatch, fish tend to get more selective, so don't be afraid to think outside the box and try a new fly.

21. What to Take to the Mayfly Dance

I may surprise or even disappoint some of you with my opening sentence to this chapter, but one thing I am not going to do is name a single, blockbuster fly that works all the time during every

Many flies work during a Hex Hatch.

Hex Hatch. There isn't just one. Ask around and you'll see what I mean. Instead, I'm going to tell you about a number of flies that will do the job more than adequately.

And, I'm not writing this book to promote any particular makes, models, or designs of fly-fishing paraphernalia. There are as many good fly rods (and reels) out there as feathers on a duck's back. What it all comes down to is personal choice.

21. What to Take to the Mayfly Dance

Casting from a canoe works best with fly rods that are 8 ½ to 9 ½ feet long. Shorter rods are certainly fine, but they aren't as easy to cast to distant rises (which always seems to be the larger fish) while sitting in a canoe, low to the water. I prefer to use a 9 ½-foot rod with a large arbor reel that will hold plenty of backing and will cast large dry flies tied on size 6-8 hooks with relative ease.

A dry fly is the classic "roadster" of our fly boxes. It is the fly that most of us started using as a beginner. It is the fly everyone wants to use successfully. It is a fly that casts easily with a floating line. It is the fly that allows us to see the fish take our "bait". It is the fly that elicits the angina-producing excitement from a surprise splash on the surface. *It is **the** fly for Hex fishing.*

Dry flies are the classic roadsters of your fly box. HYMANLTD

For a dry fly to work its best for you, it needs to mimic the general size and shape of the *Hexagenia* adult dun. The overall color can vary from white to tan, yellowish to light or dark brown, and yes, even pink. I'm often torn in the waning minutes of daylight as to what color to use for my dry fly. I can see light-colored flies better on the water, but I think that it's easier for fish to see dark-colored flies. It's often a toss-up with little time to decide.

As far as dry fly desgn goes, Wulffs are one of the most popular styles of dry fly for fishing the Hex Hatch. They all have great floatability coupled with high visibility and they damn sure catch fish. My brother has a love affair with the Wulffs, especially a Royal Wulff, and swears by it during a hatch. In the Greenville

21. What to Take to the Mayfly Dance

and Sourdnahunk areas of Maine, the Grizzly Wulff is popular, and I saw an angler land seven rainbows one evening using a pure White Wulff. I met a guide in Northern Maine who used only a Pink Wulff, and he caught squaretails up to five pounds on that fly. I tie a ginger-hackled version with light tan deer hair for wings that I call a Caspian Wulff, named after the Vermont lake where I first used it, and quite successfully I

Fluffy and winged, Wulff dry flies are an extremely popular fly for Hex fly fishers.

Stan Wass swears by a Royal Wulff on the end of his leader during a Hex Hatch.

21. What to Take to the Mayfly Dance

might add. You can't go wrong with a Wulff, and it is one of my top five go-to flies.

Another fly style that rocks during a Hex Hatch is the Comparadun. This fly exhibits a well-defined profile to fish because it has no hackle and thus is low-riding on the water surface, like a mayfly. I tie a version that I have named the Hex Hybrid Comparadun. The largest fish I have ever caught on a dry fly was a 22-inch wild rainbow out of **Lake Willoughby**, and this Comparadun style fly was the trout's downfall. It features moose hair for the tail, yellow floating yarn for the body, and medium brown deer hair for wings. It has no hackle. After tying in the deer hair for wings, I lay the butt ends across the top of the fly to about the bend in the hook, tie them down, and then trim. This gives the fly more floatability. The hook is a size 8, fine wire with a 3X

Comparadun flies are known for their high catchability-rate when fishing for trout during a Hexagenia Hatch.

21. What to Take to the Mayfly Dance

A comparadun-style Hex dry fly tied by commercial tyer, Ken Grimes, is a total winner for enticing salmonids to the surface when a Hex Hatch is on.

(sometimes 4X) long shank. I've even been known to trim all the bottom hackle from some Hex flies to achieve this Comparadun look.

Ken Grimes also ties a great Comparadun-style Hex dry fly. He varies the colors a bit, but essentially, they have a yellow body, are striped on top and underneath with a magic marker, sport a tail of yellow or brown calf tail, and have thick undivided wings made from tan bucktail with a little yellow dubbing mixed in. The hook is a size 8 long shank. As much as I want to shy away from naming so-called dynamite flies, this dry fly is at the apex of my top five go-to Hex flies.

Author Peter Shea coughed up his favorite Hex fly named a Mansfield Hex. PETER SHEA PHOTO

21. What to Take to the Mayfly Dance

Author/Hex angler Peter Shea has a favorite dry fly that he ties called The Mansfield Hex. On a Size 8 hook, he ties in a light cream-colored hackle for the tail that is split and then uses the same hackle as a parachute around an exaggerated, tall wing of white calf tail. The body is made from a poly dubbing mix (chartreuse, yellow, and white). Shea says he ties it for as much his benefit as the trout's, and that he has "astounding luck" pounding up trout with this fly even without an ongoing hatch.

Fishing friend Sean Fowler and author/activist Bob Mallard tie foam-bodied Hex dry flies. Fowler's version, named Martin's EBH, uses an extended foam body, some dubbed rabbit fur, tan-colored deer body hair for wings, on a size 10 short shank hook. He believes the smaller hook, being less weighty, allows the fly to float better. Fowler ties it both as a dun and spinner. Mallard's fly, dubbed Hexagenious, has a foam body sectioned into segments by thread, long elk hair for wings, two folded rubber legs to make four total legs, tied on either size six or eight light wire hooks. Mallard believes the rubber legs help keep it upright and adds great twitching action to the fly.

Vermont Fish & Game Warden, Lt. Sean Fowler, ties a very successful foam-bodied Hex fly, called Martin's EBH.

Bob Mallard also ties a sharp-looking, foam-bodied Hex fly that he designed and calls Hexagenious. BOB MALLARD PHOTO

Two other groups of dry flies that get a lot of attention during a Hex Hatch are Parachutes and Haystacks. Like Comparaduns with no hackle, they sit tight

21. What to Take to the Mayfly Dance

to the water's surface giving a better outline image to hungry fish. I first learned about Haystacks on a visit to **Pierce Pond** in Maine where a guide told me that he considered it as one of the top flies for trout and salmon on that pond during a hatch.

Often you will see Hex dry flies in stores with exaggerated tails that curl upwards by several inches. To be honest, I think they are more for catching the angler instead of fish, but I saw one tied by Brett Damm of Rangeley River Sports Shop this summer called a Two-Feather Mayfly, and I have to admit it looks like a winner. Online I could find statements describing this fly as "a model of efficiency", "floats like a cork", and "easy to tie". It was also suggested that if trout are into a refusal mode, you can just trim the bottom hackles and magically start catching trout again. Since I haven't actually fished with this fly yet, I'm not sure how much of this is just blather, but there's one sure way to find out. I now have several in my dry fly box ready to assess during the next Hex season.

Here are four excellent flies to tie on your leader for a Hex Hatch. They are (from the top and clockwise) the Grasshopper, Emerger, Two-feather Mayfly, and a Stimulator.

Stimulators and Grasshoppers have taken their fair share of Hex-gulping fish too. I have on occasion used large Stimulator flies at dark since I think trout can see them better than a less "hairy" fly. Grasshoppers have put a lot of brookies in my net when fishing the Recurve Hatch at Vermont's **Seyon Pond**, so it seems to me that if they fool trout during that mayfly hatch, they should also work during a Hex Hatch.

21. What to Take to the Mayfly Dance

Another category of flies that is popular during a Hex hatch is the emergers. One that is in my top five go-to list is Ken Grimes' design of a Hex Emerger. It's not an insult to say this fly is quite ugly, but like a rabbit's foot, it works like a charm. I don't think Grimes uses this fly anymore and the reason is rather telling. He was extremely successful with it but noticed many of the fish he caught swallowed the fly too deeply, and it was, therefore, difficult to revive those fish. So, he stopped using it and went to his dry fly version instead. I haven't had the same problem, maybe because I tend to set the hook instead of letting a fish do it.

Ken Grimes' Emerger is as ugly as sin, but fishes the pants off many other flies during a Hex Hatch.

As my mother was fond of saying, "The proof is in the pudding." This brookie still has Ken's Emerger pattern hooked in its jaw.

21. What to Take to the Mayfly Dance

The logic behind Ken's Hex Emerger is to mimic the emerging dun as it first comes to the surface. At that time the mayfly's head and thorax break the surface tension first while the abdomen and tail are still below the surface. So, the fly is tied such that the body and tail feathers are made from materials that don't float well, allowing those parts to sink easily just below the surface, while the deer hair in front keeps that portion of the fly on the surface. I like to accentuate that logic by greasing (adding floatant to) the deer hair at the front end of the fly.

Grizzly hackle and deer hair on a size 8 hook that is 2X long are all that's needed to tie this fly. Grimes uses some hackle as the tail then wraps some of the marabou portions of the feather around the body. The final touch is adding deer hair to the front. The deer hair doesn't stick up straight in a wing-like fashion as it would in a dry fly. Instead, he ties it so the deer hair lies forward, ahead of the hook's eye. I have used Ken Grimes' emergers in all three northern New England states and it has proven to be very successful.

As mentioned earlier, rubber legs are used on some Hex flies, like Mallard's Hexagenious. Terry Van Veghten clued me into a

Flies with rubber legs attached are very popular with some Hex anglers. They tend to be a little harder to cast (use a heavier leader) but do as advertised...deceive fish during a Hex Hatch.

Hex rubber leg fly tied by a western company a few years back, and it really did the job on rainbow trout. It seemed that I caught larger fish with this fly, too. I foolishly bought just one. So, after the rubber legs started to break off from rainbow abuse, I tried to order some more, but the company wasn't selling them anymore. And do you think I could find a facsimile on the internet? I could have tried tying one, but as of yet, have not. I do now have some different rubber-leg Hex flies, although I haven't tested them yet. These flies don't cast as easily as flies without rubber legs but I'll give that up for their catchability. Due to the huge success that I had with my original fly, Hex flies with rubber legs have earned a spot in this author's top five go-to list.

Fishery biologist Tim Obrey of Maine ties a Hex emerger that he learned about from a Pierce Pond guide. The name of the fly is a taunting Sexy Hexy. I had to do a little wheedling to get Obrey to give up this fly

Tim Obrey is one of the many fishery biologists who has helped the author in identifying waters that have known Hex Hatches. He ties this fly, called a Sexy Hexy, and says it's a corker. (TIM OBREY PHOTO)

as it's on his "bees-knees" list. And even though he was kind enough to send me one, I haven't had the chance to do a test run with it yet. But I am expecting good things.

Obrey ties the fly on a size 10 streamer hook with red feathers for a tail and yellow floating yarn for the body. He uses an underwing of yellow calf tail which is topped by natural wood duck flanks (mallard flanks in a pinch). He ties one wood duck feather on each side and two over the top and shapes them to a point at

21. What to Take to the Mayfly Dance

the tips so they are tent-shaped. Then he adds Dave's Flexament to make them stiff. A large brown hackle is tied in front, along with a head made from yellow/green deer hair that is shaped like a bullet and cut flat on the bottom. As most fly tiers are prone to do, he has modified the original creation to some degree.

One other emerger I have used successfully was designed more to imitate large caddisflies than Hex duns, but it has worked extremely well for me at times during a Hex Hatch. I call it a Hud-

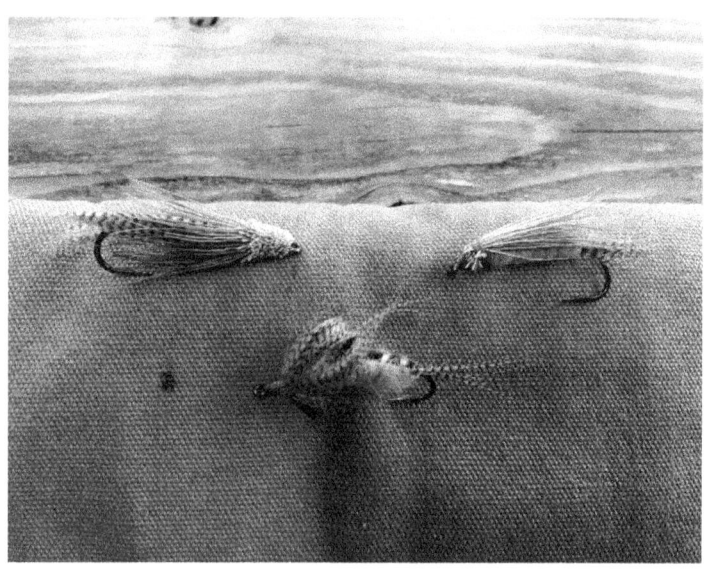

Simply put, these three different emergers catch fish. From the upper left going clockwise, they are a Kennebago Muddler, Huddler, and Selene's Hexamongus.

dler. It has features of both a Muddler and a Hornberg. There are no upright wings; instead, the wing feathers lie along the dorsal side of the fly, similar to Obrey's Sexy Hexy and the Kennebago Muddler. A little yellow or tan floating yarn is tied in before adding the wood duck feathers or mallard breast feathers that are tied flat across the top. I then place the deer hair on top of the feathers and tie it such that it becomes both the head and tail. After trimming the deer hair head, a Huddler is born. Though this is my basic pattern for the Huddler, I must admit that I have varied this fly's recipe many times to suit my mood at the time of tying. It floats really well because of the deer hair but I still grease the deer hair before using. Yup, it's another of my top five go-to flies.

While in Rangeley, Maine this past summer, I met fishing and hunting guide Bob Duport. When he found out that I was writing this book, he said, "Wait just a minute." He left the shop, walked to his truck, and came back with a fly box. He picked out a fly and kindly offered it to me, saying something like, "You need to try this emerger and look out, it's a killer." Now, when a guide makes a statement like that, *everyone* listens! The fly, named Hexamongus, was designed and tied by "Selene of Maine" out of Readfield, Maine. (What fun we have with that scientific name *Hexagenia*...) It's a great-looking fly and it, too, has been added to my "Be Sure To Try It Next" list.

While visiting with Bob Duport at Brett Damm's fly shop in Rangeley, I asked about the Kennebago Muddler since I had recently read excellent reports about this fly during Maine's Hex Hatches. Brett produced one from a fly case and I immediately liked it. It is an emerger-type fly and quite similar to my Huddler. I helped the economy and bought several to add to my fly book. Popular colors are olive and tan, and I will definitely be tossing one to trout during the next Hex Hatch.

These nymphs all work with sinking fly lines, and there are times when they also do the trick on a floating line, as well. On the left is a Fox Buff. On the far right is a Hex Nymph, and top to bottom are a Wiggle Nymph, two versions of the author's Modified Maple Syrup, and a Maple Syrup.

So, what about nymphs? They work, both before (with a sinking line) and

21. What to Take to the Mayfly Dance

during (with a floating or sink-tip line) a hatch. My favorites are the Maple Syrup (I usually modify it with a grizzly hackle tail and a palmered body), Wiggle Nymph, and Fox Buff. You may recall the Wiggle Nymph consists of two short shank hooks (size 8 or 10) joined by a piece of monofilament that gives the fly some tantalizing action when retrieved. (Be sure to clip off the front hook's bend before using it to avoid hook tangles.) The Fox Buff was introduced to me by Don Hibbs of Nahmakanta Lake Wilderness Camps in Maine. He said the fly came from Alvin Theriault's Fly Shop in Stacyville, Maine, and Hibbs praised the fly to no end. After using it on several ponds in the Nahmakanta region, I clearly understood his enthusiasm. This nymph is what Theriault advertises as a "Fancy Maple Syrup" and sports "legs" (feathers not rubber) as well as a wing case. When I got back to Vermont, I immediately went to my fly-tying table and whipped up a few based on the remnants of two flies that Hibbs had given me. I now always carry a few in my nymph wallet. Add it along with my Modified Maple Syrup as a runner-up to my top five go-to list.

You may have noticed that I haven't mentioned the ubiquitous Hornberg. This fly should be on every top ten list for trout flies. But strangely, I have never tried one during a Hex Hatch, and not sure why. There is absolutely no reason in the world that it wouldn't work, especially if it stays upright on the surface.

As mentioned earlier, I prefer a size 8 hook for the majority of my Hex flies, but I own a few tied on a size 6 long shank hook as well. When I tie Hex flies, I purposely tie a few with more deer

Pinching down barbs on flies that are used during a Hex Hatch will result in fewer fatalities when fish are released.

hair/calf tail than others. When there's a lot of wave action on the surface from wind, I go to my larger, fluffier flies, sometimes in a size six. But with calm water, I tend to stick to my smaller, less bushy flies.

I always pinch down the barb when I tie any kind of Hex fly. Oh boy. There's an odorous can of worms I just opened. One reason for barb-pinching is that it is required by law on a few waters, and if I don't pinch the barbs when tying I'm apt to forget when fishing. Also, I am a *firm* believer that any fish has a better chance of survival when released if they are landed with barbless hooks. There is just too much scientific evidence out there not to believe otherwise. That smell from the open can of worms is all about losing fish. Some fly fishers believe that more fish are lost when using barbless hooks, and as a result, prefer not to use them. My journals provide no data

The author has learned through painful experience that when tying on a leader to fish the Hexagenia Hatch, it's best to opt for heavy leaders instead of skinny ones.

21. What to Take to the Mayfly Dance

or anecdotal evidence that would suggest one way or the other, but I am not an adherent of the "lose more fish" belief.

Take me to your leader, but which one? I mentioned earlier that Ken Grimes thought he was more successful than other anglers, especially when landing large fish, for three reasons. He waits with the patience of Job for larger fish to work within casting distance. (I call that *selective casting*.) He also lets the fish hook themselves instead of yanking the rod like a beginner. The third reason is the way he constructs his leaders. He uses what he calls a "60-20-20 formula", the numbers referring to the ratio of three lengths of leader sections. The longest component, tied to his fly line, consists of 20-lb test monofilament, followed by the middle but shorter segment of 10-12-lb test, and finally the 15-18-inch tippet of 3-lb test. (And to think that some Pierce Pond regulars use nothing less than 8-lb tippets.) So, the total length of his leader is about 12 feet (15-18-inch tippet, 15-18-inch midsection, and a 9-foot butt section). Grimes says he has lost very few fish with this set-up and he even dropped down a notch to 2-lb tippets for a while to see if he could improve on his system. But he said he lost too many fish (rainbows measured in pounds) when they went skyward, so returned to using 3-lb tippets. Grimes' approach is certainly one very effective way of utilizing a leader.

Another faction of Hex anglers pooh-poohs the need for a light tippet, and because Hex flies tend to be large and bushy, suggest going to heavy tippets to minimize flies from spinning when casting. They prefer to use 5X-4lb leaders for smaller flies but suggest 3X-10 lb. leaders for large flies, claiming that a fly will not only spin less but is much easier to cast and lands more naturally. And for sure, with heavier tippets, hard setters are less likely to break fish off. I tend to go heavy on my leaders since I have a history of an uncontrollable urge to yank a fish inside out when setting the hook. My guess is that, once again, it comes down to personal preference as the deciding factor.

21. What to Take to the Mayfly Dance

No need for saddle shoes when planning for the Hexagenia mayfly dance.

So, what do you take to the mayfly "dance"? Recalling my "triple play", I bring three 9-9 1/2-foot rods, when possible. In most cases, one of the rods is rigged with one of my "go-to dry flies" that is "greased" for long-lasting action. Another rod has one of my "go-to emergers" and a third rod is armed with a nymph, or the "special of the evening", a new fly that I may want to test. No need for saddle shoes, bobby socks, or leather jackets at this dance.

22. Trophy Trout and the Four Qs

What exactly does the word trophy mean? One of Webster's Dictionary definitions is, "A reward for a specific achievement, and serves as recognition or evidence of merit." The word in itself connotes different imageries under different settings and can be admired by just one, a few, or many. For example, a trophy could

The author's daughter, Kara, was a blue-ribbon jumper as a teenager. Here she is jumping with Flip Side as she looks ahead for the next jump.

be a wide-racked whitetail deer for hunters or even a young hunter's very first buck. A trophy could easily be a blue ribbon in jumping for horse riding competitors. It might be a setter puppy's first point or a Labrador's first duck retrieve. You get the point. So, how about using the word "trophy" as an adjective for fish? Generally, we use trophy to refer to larger fish than usual for a particular species, such as the record togue caught out of Lower Richardson Lake in Maine this past summer. The enormous squaretail trout that have been coming out of **Moosehead Lake** over the past few years are magnificent trophies, as are super large landlocked salmon caught in the Fish River Lakes.

So, in general, when we think of a trophy brook trout it is beyond the scope of average-sized fish, but *how* large to be labeled a "trophy" fish? That whittles down to some considerations such as where it was caught, possibly how it was caught, when it was caught, and a matter of opinion. I have what I consider a trophy squaretail trout adorning my wall (three pounds) that was caught in northern Maine quite a few years back. (I would never keep a wild trophy trout such as this unless it was sure to die. They are *way* too valuable a resource to keep for eating and/or mounting.) But this trout, although a trophy to me at three pounds, would not come close to being called a trophy fish on the Nipigon River or in parts of Labrador.

I have a wooden cut-out of an 11-inch brook trout that I caught when I was about 10 years old. My father outlined the fish then cut it out on a piece of wood. It was probably my first trout over nine inches and I'm sure I was as proud as a peacock over it, as was my father. Is that 11-inch trout a trophy? You bet it is.

This cut-out of an 11-inch brook trout caught by the author when he was 10 years old is still a trophy in his mind.

22. Trophy Trout and the Four Qs

As mentioned, the really large trout are much too precious to keep, but you can still "preserve" the essence of trophy trout (actually, any fish) for a wall and memories, by taking quality photos of the trout. These photos, coupled with a quick measurement, are enough for many of today's taxidermists to make excellent replicas for you if so desired.

Maybe this is a good place to bring up an interesting topic regarding Maine's Moosehead Lake brook trout. Photos in recent years showcasing wild brook trout taken from that lake are mind-boggling and have graced the covers of a number of outdoor magazines such as *Northwoods Journal*. The majority of these trophy trout have been caught during the ice fishing season, although some have also been landed during the open water fishing season. (I'm still trying.)

These huge, wild brook trout in Moosehead Lake are on shoreline spawning grounds in November. Look closely and you can see several more in the background. MDIFW

22. Trophy Trout and the Four Qs

Tim Obrey, a fishery biologist for that region, estimates that more than 500 brook trout between 20-25 inches were caught and *kept* during the winters of 2019 and 2020. Zounds. That is one pile of trophy squaretails eliminated from that body of water. The majority of these fish were caught in January and therein lies a HUGE problem because of where most were caught – over spawning grounds. What? Don't trout usually spawn in October or early November? They do in most places, but recently biologists have determined that these particular Moosehead trout are spawning in the lake as late as January, even up to the last week in January. As Obrey says, "Spawning in January is unheard of, but here it is, right in front of us!"

It doesn't take too much deciphering to see that many, if not most of these trophy squaretails, are caught and killed while they are spawning, or even before the spawn since reproductive milt and eggs were seen running out of freshly caught January trout from this area. That is obviously not a good thing and if continued would severely impact this very unique wild trout population.

Three dips of the net to Obrey, as he has pounced on the problem like a lynx on a hare.

Fisheries Assistant, Maddie Killian, displays a 5-pound, wild Moosehead squaretail that was radio-tagged at a shore spawning site. MDIFW

22. Trophy Trout and the Four Qs

He met with a group of Moosehead Lake stakeholders called the Moosehead Lake Focus Group who are deeply associated with addressing the problem. The members include fisheries staff and primary representatives of the lake's user groups that comprise the fishing community of Moosehead Lake.

They hashed out several proposals for the protection of not only these magnificent wild spawning brook trout but for all the brook trout in Moosehead Lake year-round. As of Aug 12, 2020, the MDIFW was proposing an area closure to ice fishing, (similar to what already exists in Spencer Bay and Socatean Bay) for the Lily Bay narrows to protect these trophy, lake-spawning brook trout. The area affected would be marked with red posts. In addition, the MDIFW proposed a new regulation for the 2021 fishing season, that all brook trout between 18-22 inches be released immediately. Trout in excess of this slot limit (within the lawful limit) could still be kept by anglers if so desired, and trout between 14-18 inches could also be kept for a trout dinner if wanted. This slot limit of 18-22 inches would essentially protect 3 to 5-pound brook trout and could push even more trout into the 5+ pound range over the next few years. The proposals have been accepted and enacted for the 2021 fishing season. Kudos to the Moosehead Lake Focus Group.

There has been some discussion in the past few years regarding the "catch and release" slogan. The nucleus of the discussion that I have read centers around the dilemma of whether it is overdone, thus negatively affecting a fish population. A few believe that the popularity of "catch and release" may have a deleterious effect on a fish population for a specific body of water by inadvertently increasing their numbers, and thus causing a decline in food resources to the point that large fish become more uncommon.

22. Trophy Trout and the Four Qs

A well-known author and brook trout advocate once wrote, "You don't have to eat a golf ball to enjoy the sport." Of course, that's a very clever way of saying you don't need to eat the trout you catch to enjoy fishing for trout. Most of us certainly agree with that analogy, but what about keeping fish to eat that don't fit the definition of a trophy, or wild native trout? Both my wife and I enjoy a meal of brook trout on occasion, and I have some friends who are more than thankful when I drop off a few cleaned trout to tickle their palettes. I just don't feel guilty at all when killing a few, small trout for those purposes. With that said, there are many waters where keeping even small trout shouldn't be done, and I'm thinking especially of Heritage ponds and lakes.

The author believes that it's alright to take a few trout home to eat in some situations, although, as a rule, he is against keeping trophy trout for that purpose. It pays to be smart and know the history of places you fish, as well as its present situation...and the laws.

A favorite brook trout haunt of mine in Vermont, 37-acre **Seyon Pond**, also known as Noyes Pond, is a spot that you are

22. Trophy Trout and the Four Qs

Seyon Pond in Vermont's Groton State Forest is Vermont's "trout factory". Not only that, it also offers spectacular scenery, all year round. Its wild trout fishery is managed by the VTF&W department, while the use of boats and canoes is controlled by the state's parks system. There is a fee charged to fish there, the only public water in all three Northern New England states to do so.

becoming very familiar with while reading this book. According to Vermont fishery biologists, Seyon Pond, in Groton State Forest, has a higher population of wild trout than anything ever recorded in Vermont, or even Maine. This shallow but extremely productive pond is Vermont's own "trout factory". It was stocked regularly in the past (the last time was 2000) but biologists eventually determined that natural reproduction was more than adequate to maintain a healthy population of trout, so it hasn't been stocked since and were they ever right. But there is only so much food to go around, and because of that, the growth rate and maximum size of these trout have been determined to be depressed.

The "catch and release" mantra is in full swing at Seyon, despite a generous limit of six trout of any length. It's rare to see Seyon anglers take trout home to eat, and I'm convinced that guilt (not abiding by the catch and release catchphrase) is a big part of the reason.

22. Trophy Trout and the Four Qs

Jud Kratzer is one of Vermont's fishery biologists who was of help to the author. He enticed this fall brookie at one of the Northeast Kingdom's remote fishing spots, Notch Pond. COURTESY JUD KRATZER

I asked fishery biologist, Jud Kratzer if encouraging anglers to harvest more fish at Seyon would help increase the growth rate and result in larger fish. He said, "I think it is unlikely that fly fishers would be motivated, or able, to harvest enough trout to really make a difference." He then continued by saying, "But anglers should *not* feel bad about taking home fish from Seyon. If anything, there are too many trout in the pond." What I am trying to point out by using Seyon Pond as an example, is that killing and eating trout (salmon) is not *always* a bad thing.

What are the ways that we can minimize the injuring of fish before releasing them? We've all seen the suggestions put out by organizations such as Trout Unlimited and state fish and wildlife departments, so I'm going to try and condense them into what I think are the most important. As I see it, there are three critical factors: reducing fish exposure to air, eliminating (when possible) contact with a dry surface, and decreasing handling time.

22. Trophy Trout and the Four Qs

The year 2020 brought us many things to worry about, especially the Coronavirus. It also gave us record high temperatures coupled with drought conditions. The resulting very warm surface temperatures of small ponds, in particular, should remind us of one more important factor regarding the handling of fish – playing time. Playing fish for an excessively long time when water temperatures are (especially) 70 or above certainly can do them harm. There are some anglers (bless them) who won't even fish when water temperatures are so warm. I haven't quite reached that level yet because I like to fish with sinking lines down deep where the water is appropriately cold. But even so, I must remind myself that after I have hooked a fish, and when it is near the surface, I need to get it released as soon as possible.

And what about those times when fishing is so good that you wonder if it's only a dream? No matter what fly you throw at them, the fish take it like there's no tomorrow. Ah, if we could only be so lucky more often, but it does happen. Unfortunately, though, probably a fair amount of those fish will die from injuries sustained in the process of landing them. Studies I've seen indicate that upwards of 35% of hooked fish may die after being released. And that's not even counting fish swallowed by hungry loons lurking near your boat or canoe, who love to prey on just released fish that are still a little dazed. If fish are rising, try casting to the largest fish. Maybe just a few of the big fellas will sate your piscatorial desires enough so that you feel totally comfortable casing your fly rods early instead of continuing to catch as many as possible. You can also set a personal limit ahead of time. These are things we all need to do.

*One way **not** to hold a fish that you plan to release.* (STAN WASS PHOTO)

22. Trophy Trout and the Four Qs

Ironically, this fish is being handled safely for a fish to be offered clemency. Hey, Mary, were you targeting white suckers during the Hex Hatch? TERRY VAN VEGHTEN PHOTO

As we age, we go through rather distinct stages in our life as it is related to fishing. I am at what I will call the "Four-Q Stage". Let this duffer explain. The **quality of fish** is much more important to me now than quantity. I also prefer **quality time** on the water in a **quality environment** rather than just anywhere to wet a line. And lastly, **quality companionship** is more important to me than ever. I will point to a fishing experience I had in the spring of 2019 as an example of these "Four Qs".

Quality Environment

I was fishing my favorite Vermont trout pond, Seyon, which is a true gem in the mountains, surrounded by mixed hardwoods and softwoods that are punctuated with huge glacial erratics. I have been atop each of the surrounding mountains numerous times (Spruce, Signal, and Mt 2755) and that adds even more of a delight to the gorgeous views from the pond. On most days, there is nothing else to be heard on this fly-fishing-only pond than the

22. Trophy Trout and the Four Qs

Steve Foster reflects on the mountains surrounding Seyon Pond after a snowshoeing foray to look for moose sheds. Steve is another fishing/hunting partner of the author who is now looking for moose antlers in the heavens above.

swishing of fly lines, the calls of loons, the occasional creak of oarlocks, and the joyful sporadic "sploshes" of trout. It is heaven. There is no other place I would rather be fishing in the Green Mountain State. And that my friends, meets my definition of a quality environment.

Quality Time & Quality Companionship

To add more to this trip, I was fishing alone, something I seem to have enjoyed less and less as I have aged, but there are still those moments when fishing alone that I sense an unexplained companionship with the water, fish, and surrounding mountains. It is exhilarating. Any frets or worries that I may have been saddled with are now temporarily and magically pushed aside. This was one of those times, maybe partly because it was my first fishing venture that year. Quality time doesn't necessitate a breathtaking sunny day, although I must admit, those sunny days are a mite more enjoyable in my latter years. In the past I have fished all day long in the rain, bound and determined to extract every bit of fishing that I could from the day. No more. I rarely fish in the rain

22. Trophy Trout and the Four Qs

these days and I don't need to fish all day long anymore. This particular day on Seyon, in 2019, was actually a tad on the chilly side for May. The water was cold. The fish were cold. I was cold. But I was alone. Not another soul was fishing on the pond. I loved it. Of course, there are other times when my quality companionship is less spiritual and may include friends, relatives, beginning fly fishers, or pet canines.

Quality Fish

On this raw day in May, I anchored and used a Seyon-go-to fly on my sinking-tip line, and caught several 8-inchers in the first 20 minutes or so. Looking for virgin waters, I pulled anchor and

An Olive Muddler hoodwinked this nearly 16-inch, wild brook trout into thinking that it was something good to eat. It was too early for the Hex Hatch, so the author was using a sinking-tip fly line.

rowed to a new spot, smack dab in the middle of the pond where it might be all of eight feet deep. First cast, *wham*! The throb on the rod and hard-to-move fish told me that I had on a much larger trout. Fish were still a little sluggish because of the cold water, so I wasn't sure how large – until I saw it flash sideways at the side of the boat. "Mistah that is one nice brookie!", could have been another way of saying what I actually said out loud, **"Whoa!"** I eventually managed to net the feisty trout, taking several photos

22. Trophy Trout and the Four Qs

before releasing it. Nary a soul saw me catch this wild squaretail, but I didn't need or even want verification from an audience.

After releasing the trout, I just sat there for a few minutes relishing my companion forests, mountains, and pond. Then I calmly put my fly rods away and slowly rowed back to the dock. I

Sometimes just one fish in a quality environs is enough to fulfill the author's "Four Qs". SEYON LODGE STATE PARK

didn't need or even *want*, to do any more casting that day. That one quality wild trout satisfied my fishing soul for many days to come. It was also my largest ever from this delightful body of water.

Let's call this brookie 16 inches, even though it was a whisker under, and I estimated its weight close to 2 pounds. *From this pond, it was a true trophy trout.* Of course, that same trout taken from Moosehead Lake or Pierce Pond would certainly rate as a very nice brook trout, but would not be considered a "trophy" for those waters.

At Seyon it's rare to see or hear of trout caught over 15 inches. The few that I can verify in my 40 some years of fishing there include a 16 ½ inch trout netted by my son, Andy, back in 1990, a 15 ½ incher nailed by Sean Fowler during his very first fishing

22. Trophy Trout and the Four Qs

Andy Wass, the author's son, landed this 16 ½-inch Seyon trout as a young whippersnapper in 1990. This fish was fooled by a Hornberg during a Recurve Hatch.

trip there in 2011, and a beauty just under 16 inches landed by Mary Van Veghten in 2014. It's interesting to note that each of these trophy Seyon trout was caught on a different fly. I can't confirm any other large fish that may have lowered this pond's water level, but a fairly large number of rumors signify that there have been some.

As author Dee Dauphinee says in his book, *Stoneflies And Turtleheads*, "I don't know if fly fishing is really a sport unto itself…it's more like a life partner."

I believe as you live with this life partner, that you will eventually stumble upon the "Four Qs" and say, "Now I know what he was talking about."

23. The Value of a Chesster Ice Cream Sandwich

With thirty-plus years of fishing the Hex Hatch, you might assume that there were a couple of memorable moments, snags/hiccups, amusing times, maddening incidents, and even some appalling situations along the way. And of course, you are absolutely correct in that speculation. I have devoted some of those tales to this chapter and I hope you get as much enjoyment from reading them as I have had remembering them.

Angler's Best Friend

I am a lover of dogs. I have had as part of my household over the years an English Setter, four Brittany Spaniels, and four Labrador Retrievers. I often took them fishing with me, although that sometimes became an issue with fly fishing because of loose fly lines, three fly rods, and darkness when fishing the Hex Hatch.

One evening, I was fishing out of the wind in a cove where I usually didn't go but knew that *Hexagenia* mayflies hatched there. It was a "one-dog night", with Toller, our male yellow lab accompanying me. He was on full alert the whole time, perking his ears, listening for the slurps and splashes of fish on the surface. The excitement of the hatch and rainbows chasing mayfly duns was later than usual that evening, starting around 9:00 PM, and was over in 20 minutes. I had on an extra-large Umpqua Emerger thinking that because the evening was darker than usual because of a cloud cover, the trout would be able to see that fly more easily.

My problem soon became obvious; I could *hear* fish on the surface but couldn't spot them in the near darkness. But I noticed that Toller seemed to be both hearing and seeing them. Hmmm.

23. The Value of a Chesster Ice Cream Sandwich

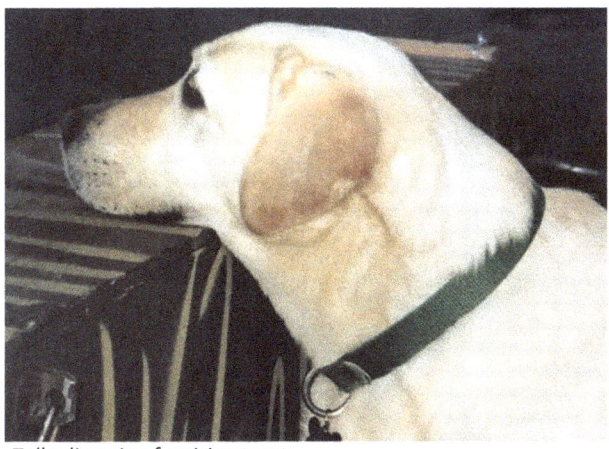

Toller listening for rising trout.

Soon I heard a walloping splash, close by, but I couldn't tell exactly where. So, checking Toller, I could see that he was looking intently in one direction, with ears cocked. I quickly cast in that direction and, slurp, I had the fish on. After a heckuva battle and several jumps, I eased the rainbow into my net. After a quick measurement and a sniff from Toller, I slipped the fish back into the water. I was tickled pink. Toller could determine where that fish was much better than I, and for sure, *he was the reason* I caught that 18 ½ -inch rainbow, which was just ¼ inch shy of my largest to that date.

Zebra Fish & Ice Cream Sandwiches

Frozen custard, sandwiched between two chocolate chip cookies called Chessters, were a great treat after fishing trips.

23. The Value of a Chesster Ice Cream Sandwich

The Chesster Ice Cream Sandwich (yup, it's spelled that way) was a very popular Vermont treat for around twenty years before going off the market. I have read that it may be resurrected in the near future, and that bodes well for my sweet tooth. I was introduced to this specialty of frozen custard, sandwiched between two chocolate chip cookies, by a former student of mine, Chris Crumbley. Chris took a number of my biology classes and I will add that he enjoyed teasing the bow ties right off me. During his post-graduation years, I helped him get started fly fishing by practicing on my front lawn, and then eventually getting him out fishing a few times in my boat.

On one of our trips, we went to **Eligo Lake** here in Vermont to fish the Hex Hatch, one of the first water bodies to produce hatching Hex mayflies. I had decided this small lake was worth trying after hearing a report from guide, Bob Shannon, of The Fly Rod Shop in Stowe, Vermont. He told me that one of his fishing parties had landed a 26-inch rainbow trout during the hatch there in 1999, so I decided that lake needed a little attention. There is one snag when fishing Eligo and that is the ample yellow perch and smallmouth bass populations that also enjoy the protein-laden mayflies.

Chris and I often stopped for a Chesster after our fishing trips, but this time at Eligo we added a touch of fun; we decided that whoever caught the first fish would be treated to a Chesster by the other on the way home. The whole time I was thinking, this poor kid will rue the day. He better have enough money. After all, here was this grizzled fishing veteran and former teacher with thousands of fish notched in his belt versus a happy-go-lucky teeny bopper, former student, with girls galore nipping at his heels. This kid simply had *no chance.*

Even though Chris still doesn't believe it, when I said, "first fish" I was thinking "first rainbow trout". Unknown to me, Chris was thinking all along that the "first **any** fish" would win.

23. The Value of a Chesster Ice Cream Sandwich

It wasn't long before Chris had a fish on and did he ever let me know about it. Damn, I was thinking, this cocky upstart is going to win the bet unless he somehow loses that fish. Of course, he played the fish very carefully, crowing about winning the bet the whole time. When the fish got close to the boat, we could see it was a yellow perch. Joyfully and quite loudly, I said, "Sorry Chris, **zebra fish** don't count." Well, you would have thought I had just accused him of cheating on a test! "You said **first fish** and that **is** a fish!", he retorted, as I took it on the chin. But just as he was getting ready to net it, the strangest thing happened. A strong gust of wind blew my fly rod tip right into his zebra fish and be darned if he didn't lose it. "*Saved by the bell,*" I chortled. His next two words have haunted me ever since that trip, "**You cheated**!!" Ouch.

Yellow perch ("zebra fish") can really muff up a bet.

Chris Crumbley learned the knack of fishing a Hex Hatch as seen here with this really nice rainbow trout.

This discussion still continues today as 42-year-old Chris, who still politely calls me Mr. Wass, pursues an advanced master's degree in cellular molecular nutrition. He hopes to teach at the college level, or possibly work with a medical professional who helps heal people nutritionally. Geez, maybe something I said in high

23. The Value of a Chesster Ice Cream Sandwich

school *did* rub off on him? By the way, I ended up paying for his Chesster that day. Guilt is an excruciating feeling. And, oh, yes, Chris also landed a nice 2 ½ pound smallmouth bass that same evening on a Hex dry fly, showing up "the master" in a blue-chip way.

Sneaking A Peek

I have to admit unabashedly that I "stole" this heading from a great article written by editor V. Paul Reynolds in the October 2020 issue of the *Northwoods Sporting Journal*, but I don't think he's gonna mind one iota.

I've been fortunate enough to hoodwink fish a majority of the time that I go on fishing trips. I'm not sure why, either. Maybe it's because I think like a fish? (That's not very complimentary when you ponder it I suppose.) Maybe it's because of good "fishing genes" passed down from my ancestors. Or, maybe it's because I'm just plain lucky. I really don't know. But I **do** know that on those fairly rare occasions when other folks nearby are catching fish and I'm not, that I can get pretty edgy, and even downright dour. After all, there is a perception of the "old-timer who can catch fish in a bathtub" to uphold. (I guess that's also a definition for pride.) Do I want to know what the successful anglers are using? You bet your ass I do. From a distant examination, I can at least determine if they are casting floating lines or sinking lines. I also can get some sort of an idea of how they are working their flies, but that's about it. I'm pretty much left to groveling after that, asking the hated question, "What are you using?"

Thankfully, I don't have to resort to such abominable temptations very often. But several years ago, I was fishing with someone new to me, and while we talked to a very successful angler, I asked the dastardly question, "What did you catch them on?" Without a hitch, the old-timer gleefully told us. Later, when my fishing partner and I were alone, he admonished me *severely* for asking that question. "You NEVER ask that question", he sternly said to me. (Huh. I guess I was unaware of that particular fishing law.)

23. The Value of a Chesster Ice Cream Sandwich

While fishing, I have had a fair number of anglers ask me what I was using for flies, and without hesitation, I tell them right down to the hackle if they want to know. At other times, a fly fisher may be close by and keeping a close eye on me, but doesn't ask what I

What did you catch that nice trout on, Sean? SEAN FOWLER PHOTO

am up to...I suppose because of that "law", never to ask. If this angler is not doing well, I'll ask *them*, "What are you using?" They tell me, and then I will say, "Try a (whatever I am using)" and often will also add a comment on my stripping technique. Why not? I don't mind at all sharing my success. They always reply with notable appreciation.

On occasion, the unsuccessful parties may be too far away for me to vocalize the gold-standard fly that's working for me. And sometimes those same folks appear at the take-out launch the same time that I do. Hmmm. At that point, fishing success and non-success are discussed endlessly until we leave. I rarely case my fly rods until getting in the truck, so whatever flies I was using are still attached to my fly rods. I have seen more than one curious angler "sneak-a-peek" at my fly rods when my attention is diverted

23. The Value of a Chesster Ice Cream Sandwich

while chatting with other anglers, or as I put my gear away. That's okay. I would tell them anyway if they asked. It's all just a part of the great game we play called fly fishing.

Passion

Early in our marriage, my wife, Jane, decided that she wanted to go fishing with me one evening and see for herself why in the world I spoke so passionately about the Hex Hatch. We got there early so we could jig a bit for lakers before the evening hatch. Learning fast, she soon had a laker on but lost it and I, quite improbably, caught an 18-inch rainbow while jigging. Following that, we anchored the boat in a pleasant spot and ate our supper.

After eating, we cruised over to the Hex area. She tried a few casts and did quite well for her first time, but despite my patronization, decided to put the fly rod down and just watch me. It was approaching that time, shortly before 9:00 PM, when the adrenalin starts to flow a tad faster and the feverish search for fish on the surface reaches its peak.

When THE time arrives, and Hexagenia mayflies are about to hatch, scanning for rises becomes feverish.

I must have looked like a nervous turkey while scanning left, right, behind, and beyond for rainbow rises. It was her first time watching my antics during a hatch and it has indelibly left a mark on her memory, even though I didn't hook a single fish.

23. The Value of a Chesster Ice Cream Sandwich

On the way home, she said, "You know, if I had fallen overboard, I don't think you would have even noticed!" I chuckled and replied, "I do get a bit fixated, don't I?", to which she replied, "*Fixated?!* You were *riveted!!*" I believe she has told that story to others a few more times than a lot.

Hex Rage

The following quote is from editor V. Paul Reynolds' article in the 2020 October issue of the *Northwoods Sporting Journal*: "Although there are exceptions, most fly fishermen that I have encountered over the years tend to be friendly, polite, even to the point of being thoughtful." I certainly agree with that assessment. But, quite often there is a hitch to statements like that, and here is mine.

I have come across only one angler who doesn't fit V. Paul's description, and though I have debated with myself on end if I should write about him, I finally have decided that I can make it somewhat humorous, informative, appalling, and memorable, all at the same time. Even though I have had other more unattractive names in mind, I'll refer to this person from now on as "Iceberg". (I actually don't know his real name.) It all started back in July of 2002 as a "two-dog night", with my labs Toller and Widgeon accompanying me on a Hex excursion. Overall, the year had been memorable even before my adventures with Iceberg. Earlier in the season, I had landed a new personal best for rainbows on this lake at 19 ½ inches. And that fish supported one of my hunches about what fly to use when daylight is at a bare minimum—a dark-colored fly. That handsome wild fish fell for a dark brown, deer hair emerger that I tie. Dark is indeed good at dark.

It was also the year that my friend, Lawrence Pyne of Weybridge, VT, taped a Hex fishing session with me for his show on VPT, "Outdoor Journal". We landed rainbows that were 13, 13, and 17 ¾ inches for the show. Not only that, but we played up "strawberry season is Hex time" by devouring homemade strawberry shortcakes on the boat, with the camera running by producer, Neil Hilt.

23. The Value of a Chesster Ice Cream Sandwich

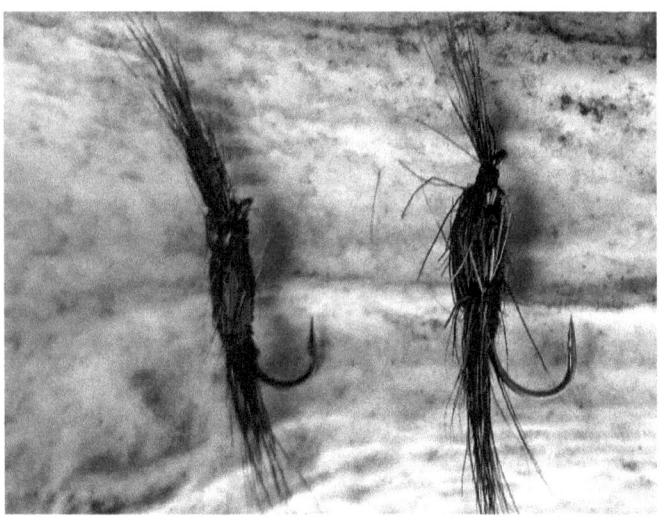

Deer hair emergers sometimes work well when the evening light has almost disappeared.

But I guess I have to break our bubble here. This *wasn't* the first time that we had tried filming! Nope. About two weeks before, Pyne had his filming and recording crew there on another boat, but try as we might, all that we could come up with was one perch and a bat. "UGH", I wrote in my journal. So, the truth is finally out there, Lawrence. Oh, yes, when we filmed the second and successful time, I met Pyne in the parking lot, and with a smug grin, he said, "Leighton, I have become even *more* of a fan of your "take 2 rods when fishing the Hex Hatch". He had forgotten to bring a fly rod to his own show production. Yup, back then my rod belief was a "double play". I graduated to the "triple play" several years later.

Returning to the latter memorable day with Iceberg, I was trying to edge my boat in close to where I had had success earlier in the week and noticed this single guy in an aluminum canoe, using a kayak paddle aiming for the same spot. Uh, oh. *Iceberg ahead.* Neither of us was willing to give much way. (I know. *Shame* on you, Wass.) Pretty soon I could hear him muttering something, but not having the best hearing, I had trouble making out *exactly* what he

23. The Value of a Chesster Ice Cream Sandwich

was saying. I just knew that it was said with some toxicity. I didn't say anything and just kept on casting. It wasn't long before he hollered out, *"Maybe I should come over and pound on your boat!"* Those were his exact words and I understood them quite clearly. I replied in a raised, but noble voice, "Go to Hell!" Now, this is NOT the Leighton Wass I knew. In 33 years of teaching high school teenagers, I had never raised my voice but once, and I have been forever penitent.

Iceberg never muttered another word that night, but in following years he continued to display his icy demeanor. Another time, I was fishing with Lawrence Pyne once more, and Iceberg came very close to creating another confrontation with a

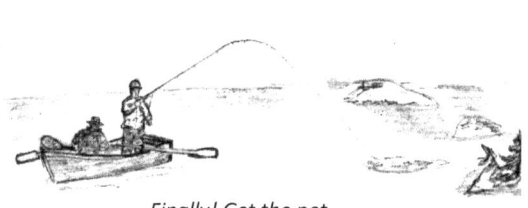

Finally! Get the net.

hissy fit. And yet in another later incident, I was fishing with Sean Fowler (a game warden), and once again, Iceberg was on the edge of trying to put down the Titanic. Now, these two fellers I was fishing with are not 96-pound weaklings. They are big Kahunas with big "guns" and if provoked too much, can turn quite nasty. (Should I also mention that Fowler was an Army Ranger? Okay. I won't.) For some reason, both of these times Iceberg just muttered unintelligible words when he thought we were too close to him. To be honest, I was hoping that Iceberg would vent like a volcano, and then I could hear a little indignation from my fishing friends. Not to be.

More recently, while launching my boat, a state warden on his off day, was also launching a boat. And guess what? To go Hex fishing! Aha. Warden Sean Fowler was fishing with me again that evening, so the two of them had much "business" to discuss. Eventually, our "friend" Iceberg came up in the discussion, and I learned that my boat wasn't the only one that he had run-ins with.

23. The Value of a Chesster Ice Cream Sandwich

This local warden, who covered the lake, reported that many anglers had complained about this angry, uncivilized fisherman.

Geez, maybe a class in anger management or some vitriol from a warden would straighten this guy out. I'm not sure. I do think the majority of us would agree, though, that the world would be a much better place if people would be a little more responsible and in control of themselves. Here's hoping.

Batman

Anyone who meets Terry Van Veghten for the first time learns right off that he loves to tell stories that get a good laugh, and often at others' expense, although he is humorously self-effacing, as well. So when someone can get the tables turned on him it's worth every single sniggle.

When he and his wife Mary fish **Caspian Lake** from shore, they wear waders and vests to get out "where the big ones are". Ten or so years ago when bat populations were at a much higher level than they are today, it wasn't unusual to have quite a few flying around at dusk picking up mayflies off the water or in midair. I have caught several on a fly and partly because of that, I typically quit fishing when the bats arrived en masse. One evening the Van Veghtens were still flinging flies as the bats arrived, and one of the bats managed to climb up Terry's back to his collar, then got down inside his vest. Being somewhat terror-stricken by this rabies carrier, he put on quite an amusing show trying to rid his clothing of the bat while

Is it much safer to fish a Hex Hatch with Batman at your side?

standing in thigh-deep water. So much so that anglers in nearby boats were laughing up a storm and the name "Batman" was wafting across the water. Even though I've heard people call him plenty of other names, the term Batman seems not to have stuck.

Milkshake Heaven

Another Van Veghten story materialized on their way back from a Hex fishing trip in Maine. They often stopped at McDonald's in Lancaster, NH to get some late-night fodder and drinks. As Van Veghten recalls, they ordered a couple of milkshakes from a most pleasant cashier, but as they and others were waiting, all hell broke loose. After the cashier started the machine, it wouldn't stop running and kept pouring milkshake contents down the side and all over the floor. She punched and pulled all the buttons and levers she could find but to no avail. At that time the cashier must have figured that there just wasn't much else she could do but holler, "Mayday! Mayday! Mayday!"

This gal obviously had a great sense of humor and knew exactly how to soften the situation with a good dose of laughter. The entire joint was chuckling as an astute worker finally reached behind the machine and pulled the plug. Only with Guru Van Veghten present would something like this happen. By the way, whatever happened to the *coffee milkshakes* at Mickey D's anyway?

An A For Effort

This anecdote doesn't really fall within my Hex fishing adventures, but I think it is amusing enough to earn a few lines here.

I started fly fishing when I was around 11-12 years old and carried it through into my college years. But for some reason that I don't recall, I left fly fishing for trolling during my first few years

23. The Value of a Chesster Ice Cream Sandwich

of teaching. I picked up a fly rod again in the 1980s and it has been part of my life ever since.

A Silver Doctor Bucktail is no flash in the pan; it is a great trout fly. They fish better for the author when tied with jungle cock eyes.

Going back to my college years at Norwich University, an interesting event relating to fly fishing happened my senior year. I was taking a physical education course with a well-liked professor, Major Wallace Baines, and each of his students (all males back then) was assigned a project that involved a paper and a demonstration of some physical activity. Most of the class members were players on Norwich's sports teams, and they naturally wanted to demonstrate an activity that they were familiar with, such as how to block in football, or, as my close friend Jim Call did, execute a basketball hook shot.

I did play basketball at Norwich as a freshman, but I didn't want to be like all the other "jocks" and show an aspect of a sport that almost everyone already knew. After pondering it a while, I wondered what about *fly fishing*? It's a physical activity and I could write a decent paper about it. The only question I had was where would I do my fly casting? It was mid-winter and the classroom certainly was not large enough. Why not the gymnasium which was in the same building? Other classmates were using it to show soccer kicks, jump shots, and wrestling moves. Why not me, showing the class how to cast a fly? So I brought it up to Professor Baines and he thought it was a great idea. (Just imagine how many basketball set shots, soccer headshots, football catches, and hockey slap shots he had seen over the years.) No wonder he had a bit of a gleam in his eye.

When my time came the class all moved to the gym and I had them sit along with Professor Baines, on the edge of the stage with

23. The Value of a Chesster Ice Cream Sandwich

their feet dangling down. I don't recall everything that I demonstrated that day but I do remember doing a roll cast for them coupled with an explanation of when it would be useful. But I saved my eye-opener for last. I moved way out on the gym floor and said, "Pretend there is a nice brown trout right under Professor Baines' feet. This is how I would get the fly there." (I didn't even know what a double-haul was back then.) Of course, I could have blown the whole enchilada by hooking the professor accidentally, or even casting forward too soon and wrapping the fly line around myself. But my timing was perfect. With only two false casts I laid that sucker right at his feet. The Silver Doctor Bucktail was so close to the professor, he had to bend over and look down. Yup, that somewhat ballsy Norwich cadet, from Downeast Maine, earned an A for his project…I guess for angling a professor.

Overboard

My brother Stan and I patronized Red River Camps north of Portage, Maine many times. It seems that every trip had its signature memory, including late one afternoon in 2013 when we anchored the canoe on **Island Pond** to try some casting with sinking fly lines before the Hex Hatch. When I dropped the anchor (a tethered rock), somehow one of my fly rods also went overboard without either of us realizing it. After I tied off the anchor rope, I noticed that the fly from my fly rod was hooked onto my pants leg. Of course, that's not an uncommon occurrence. I unhooked the fly and normally would have just tossed the fly and leader back in the water. But for some unfathomable reason, I held onto the fly, which was some kind of miracle since I soon realized that that fly was the *only* connection to my fly rod and reel …sitting on bottom in 25 feet of water!

I held onto the fly for dear life and explained to my brother what an improbable incident had just occurred. We pondered the

23. The Value of a Chesster Ice Cream Sandwich

Pulling his fly rod and reel from the bottom was a hair-raising experience for the lucky author. STAN WASS PHOTO

next step and decided there was only one reasonable way to address the situation – pull in the leader, then the fly line *very slowly*. Of course, as I started pulling, the rest of the line kept spooling off the reel on bottom, including the backing. When the backing finally snugged up, we had a bet as to whether I had tied a sturdy knot to the reel. I usually do, so I guessed a timid, yes. Just to be miserable, my brother said, "Maybe not *this* time!", with a Maine lobsterman's belly laugh.

As I pulled, and the line became taught, I was sweating bullets, but the rod slowly gave way and started coming to the surface. Thankfully the knot *had* been securely tied and finally, the rod tip broke the water's surface. (Can you believe we took time to take photos right then?) Quickly I grabbed the fly rod with a thankful sense of relief. If that fly hadn't hooked onto my pants as the rod went overboard …gulp. The Green Mountain codger lucked out on this one and in the process produced another fishing memory.

23. The Value of a Chesster Ice Cream Sandwich

Score: Fish One, Angler Minus One

Speaking of submarining fly rods, I just have to mention one other fly rod caper, but it is totally owned by author, Peter Shea of Vermont. (New book out in 2021, titled, *Vermont Trout Hikes: A Guide to Its Backwoods Ponds*) Seems Shea had finished fishing the Hex Hatch one night and was rowing back to the access area. Surely a dedicated angler wouldn't consider rowing all the way back to shore without trailing a fly behind the boat. And that he did. Partway across the lake, he had a tremendous strike from a fish, but before he could grab the fly rod, overboard it went. At about the same time a massive rainbow trout jumped behind the boat, I'm sure giving

Author and Hex angler Peter Shea gave up his fly rod and reel to the depths of Caspian Lake after a whopping rainbow decided he didn't need it. But this photo shows Shea can land stunning brook trout without giving up the ghost. CLEM NILAN PHOTO

Shea the fin. I have to believe that the words bellowed by Shea upon realizing his casualties that night are still echoing from the surrounding hillsides.

The Banana Boat

In 2017, fishing pal, Lawrence Pyne, and I decided that Maine's **Pierce Pond** should be fished once again. He picked me up, trailering his boat, on June 26. Due to inaccurate navigating and gas station mix-ups, we arrived late at Cobb's Camps and were darned lucky that we didn't miss out on a roast beef supper.

23. The Value of a Chesster Ice Cream Sandwich

We pulled out all the stops to fish the evening hatch, with, as usual, the elder of the two (me) slowing down the Pyne Parade. As in previous trips, boats and canoes were lined up along the "hot" shoreline – nine to be exact. We did quite well, landing three salmon between 18 ½ and 19 ¼ inches on dry flies, and losing two. The hatch was not from the Hex mayfly but turned out to be a hatch of the Dark Green Drake, (*Litobrancha recurvata* or Recurve Hatch). It lasted from about 9:00 PM to 9:20 PM. Not a bad start we surmised. (This was a totally different timing than when this hatch occurs at **Seyon Pond**.)

A Dark Green Drake Hatch provided the surface fishing at Pierce Pond on this trip. It typically hatches a little earlier than Hexagenia mayflies, although can be at the same time.

The following day we fished hard, casting to likely looking shorelines, reefs, and drop-offs, looking for one of Pierce Pond's blue-ribbon trout, but just a couple of small trout came to net. We were thunder-stormed out for the evening hatch which always hurts when your days are limited.

NEVER take a banana on a fishing trip. CLIPARTS.COM

The following day, we fished even harder, casting our flies to (it seemed) every square inch of shoreline. Nada. Zippo. Not a fish on at all. This was quite unsettling to two pretty damned good fly fishermen. But then it happened. Pyne discovered the cause for such a poor fishing day. A banana. I was eating my lunch which included a banana, and he yelled quite succinctly, "You NEVER take a banana on a fishing trip! It brings nuthin but effin bad

23. The Value of a Chesster Ice Cream Sandwich

luck!" "*What* in hell are you talking about Lawrence?", I laughed. "Don't you know that bananas are considered bad luck when fishing??" he barked. "Never heard of such a foolish thing," I retorted. We continued to banter about the veracity of bananas and fishing for some time and he reiterated several times how shocked he was that I had never heard of that bit of fishing lore. I was too.

He pulled his boat up to the dock at the launch area so he could retrieve some sunglasses from his truck, and that's when my mischievous mind started to click. While he was gone, I stuck the banana up straight in his coffee cup receptacle right by the steering wheel of his boat…and devilishly awaited his return. I *knew* this would get his goat because he thought I had gotten rid of it.

Watching him like a hawk for a reaction, he returned, cast off, and started the boat moving back out onto the lake and then suddenly saw that yellow monolith sticking out in front of him. As fast as a snake flicking its tongue, in one fell swoop, he grabbed that banana and hurled it a good fifty feet so it landed on the dock (he was always a good athlete but I never knew *how* good in the banana throw). Without saying a word, he wound that Merc up and sped out of there like A.J. Foyt out of a pit stop.

Ya ya nah ya ya. CLIPART

I guess you could say I went to school that day. After all, we didn't have even a strike all day long, and I also put my partner in a pretty foul mood. I was laughing; he was serious.

When I got home after the trip, I just *had* to look up bananas and fishing. Yup. It's out there. This weird bit of fishing lore was all over the internet, so just for my friend's sake, I copied a large photo of a "Don't Do This Sign", a red circle with a red slash and a banana pictured underneath, and posted it by my fishing bench. Oh, yes. The banana day that we did so poorly? After the supper meal, with not a banana peel in sight, we hooked six landlocked salmon during the evening hatch. Hmmm.

23. The Value of a Chesster Ice Cream Sandwich

Orchestral Hex Fishing

I grew up as a teenager in the 50s and I loved to listen to the likes of Fats Domino, The Coasters, The Everly Brothers, Johnny Horton, Perry Como, Elvis Presley, and a whole host of others. And yup, I even wore saddle shoes. Back then we all called classical music "longhair music" and the vast majority of teenagers didn't care for it one iota.

Years later, when I was teaching, the art teacher next door was always playing classical music on days that we had no classes but had to work in our classrooms. I kept thinking, how can anyone listen to music like that and enjoy it? (I was playing "oldies" in my science room.) But I have to admit, as I fumbled along in the aging process, I actually began to enjoy a little Mozart or Beethoven. Mind you just a little.

The next time I dealt with this so-called long-hair music style was while Hex fishing. Sounds nuts, doesn't it? As you know by now, one lake that I have fished the socks off in Vermont is Caspian Lake, and as I mentioned before, it has a jewel-studded shoreline with many, very expensive camps and homes.

One quiet evening, when sounds were carrying across the lake like a foghorn, I thought I could hear classical music at the far end of the lake. What? After I changed my fishing location, the music got louder and louder. I could see a collection of watercraft, mostly canoes, and kayaks, kind of milling around in the distance, maybe 100 yards offshore from a very nice camp. I kept fishing but also became more and more curious about what was going on. Could there be some kind of a concert event?

As I recall, at about 9:00 PM the music stopped and the gathered canoe/kayak flotilla dispersed, paddling off in different directions to their camps. I had landed two rainbows of unsubstantial size before leaving for home and on the way home marveled at what I had just witnessed that evening.

23. The Value of a Chesster Ice Cream Sandwich

As it turned out, some folks at one of the shoreline camps had decided to play classical music (I believe from the VT Philharmonic Orchestra) every Sunday night for about a month, to entertain anyone who was at the lake. They used tapes and amplifiers so the music could easily be heard a mile away at the other end of the lake. Lots of folks would paddle over to that area before the music started and listened from their watercraft while, I suppose, sipping some wine. This went on for several years and was thoroughly enjoyable. It got so I looked forward to those evenings and consumed that long-hair music like a connoisseur of gourmet food. Of course, I never stopped fishing to listen. I wouldn't want knowledge of something like that to get out and around.

As you may suspect, this photo is not one of Caspian Lake's "orchestral nights", but instead a Dinner Cruise on Adamant Pond in my Vermont hometown. Word is that there was a similarity though, such as wine being plied by a few participants. JANET MACLEOD PHOTO

Snags & Bob Newhart

A few years back, my brother Stan and I stayed at Nahmakanta Wilderness Camps, a few miles northeast of Kokadjo, Maine. Both of us were hurting from preexisting injuries, a bum leg for my brother, and a sore Achilles' tendon for me. To ease the pain, we began our fishing at nearby ponds that didn't take much hiking, but the lure of distant waters (of course with bigger fish) recommended by host Don Hibbs eventually won over the Wass

23. The Value of a Chesster Ice Cream Sandwich

mindset, and to far off ponds we slogged. We were there during the onset of the Hex Hatch so any place we fished "required" staying through the bewitching hour of 9:00 PM. Every trout pond that we fished called for a hike of varying lengths and difficulties, including one where a little hand/foot climbing was a bit challenging to geezers like us. But we did it – twice. Another great Hex water required a much longer walk on a trail that was peppered with rocks, boulders, and roots but, heads down, we tackled it like a couple of old goats. While trudging onward, neither of us saying a word, it reminded me of the old Bob Newhart Show that was based in Vermont. Do you remember Larry and his brothers Darryl and Darryl from that show, following along behind each other as they walked? I swear that we could have been good replacements for any of those brothers, Larry, Darryl, or his other brother Darryl. This style of plodding along, cost us dearly several times when we veered off the pond trail onto a moose trail for some distance before realizing our mistake.

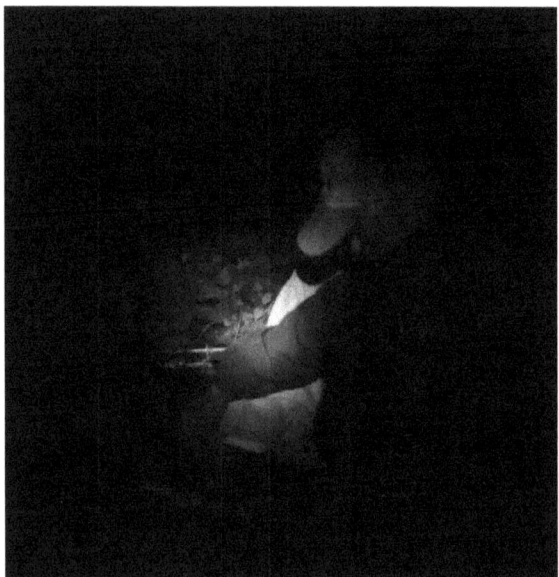

Trudging back in the dark after fishing a distant Hex Hatch became a tad more worrisome as the headlamp batteries faded. The Wass brothers were so late on the return to their cabin that owner Don Hibbs was about to launch a search party.

It took us one hour and 45 minutes to get to the shores of this particular, hallowed Hex pond where a rowboat awaited us. The fishing was excellent, and we stayed until 9:10 PM, realizing we had a brutal walk

23. The Value of a Chesster Ice Cream Sandwich

back in the dark, requiring headlamps to light the way. Part way back, our headlamp batteries began to die and the nanoscopic rays that they then emitted made the trip even more perilous and slow.

We ambled into Nahmakanta Camps at 11:15 and were greeted by Hibbs and his questions. "What happened to you guys?" "Are you alright?" "I was just about ready to come looking for you with my 4-wheeler!" We explained that being Wasses we *had* to stay for the full hatch and that we didn't always make sound decisions. We apologized for creating such a ruckus and again, with our heads down "Larry and Darryl style", limped back to our cabin.

Hex Hatch-caught brookies were a helluva hike from camp...but well worth it.

As I recall, Hibbs didn't smile too much during that brief conversation and probably had been in bed. Nope, that's *not* the way to impress a sporting camp owner. But, dammit all, we caught wild trout up to 15 1/2 inches, *and* – we even limped in there one more time before going home, but this time we gave Hibbs more than a fair warning. (We returned to camp that second time at a quarter to midnight.)

By the way, this was the same trip that I was involved in a much more upsetting snag. I broke two out of my three graphite fly rods.

Wardens and Fishing

I admire game wardens. They have a dangerous job, deal with some miserable people, and often work hours that would flatten the average person. When you stop to think about it, almost every

23. The Value of a Chesster Ice Cream Sandwich

person they deal with during hunting seasons is carrying a gun. It certainly is not an occupation for everyone.

As you know, when fishing the Hex Hatch there is a very short-lived time when the fishing is likely to be optimal, maybe 20 minutes if you are lucky. *This* is the time to score. It's do-or-die time. Knowing that, I was a tad annoyed one evening many years ago to see two wardens arriving on the Hex-fishing scene by boat. Quite a few boats were fishing that evening, so I could see that the wardens were going to consume most of the prime fishing time…and they did.

Heck, I know they have a job to do and I am one of their biggest supporters. One of my best friends is a Vermont Game Warden, and we have shared woods and waters recreationally many times. But really, right during the Hex Hatch? I fussed and fumed over that all the way home.

Then, a week or so later the same thing happened again. Okay, fellers, once is sort of okay, but twice is downright agonizing. I just have to vent. And I did so but pleasantly, as they checked my license. They explained that there were reports of Hex anglers keeping more than their limits of rainbows, thus the timing. Okay. But for some reason that didn't mitigate my feelings

Vt Game Wardens not only check anglers for violations, but they help anglers in many ways. Stocking trout, as Warden Chad Barrett is doing here, is one example. (VTF&W PHOTO)

23. The Value of a Chesster Ice Cream Sandwich

very much. At least maybe now, I thought, after listening to me, they could see that possibly it *wasn't* the best time to accomplish their goals and that checking anglers post-Hex time at the launch area would have been much less vexing.

Since then, I have become friendly with one of the wardens involved and be durned if he isn't a fly fisherman as well. In addition, he loves to fish the Hex Hatch. You don't suppose that there was more on these wardens' minds than just patrolling the waters for wayward anglers? Were they checking our flies? Nah.

The last time I was checked by a warden, several years later, I was fishing in a spot that is out of view of the cove where most anglers fish, including the Van Veghtens, and I knew that they were wading in that prized spot. This warden *may* have asked me if anyone else was fishing in the cove around the point, and I *may* have told him, yes, Mary and Terry were there. He knew who they were so the last thing I saw was the warden's boat speeding off into the sunset – exactly west, towards the Van Veghtens.

Terry and Mary Van Veghten getting ready to fish the Hex Hatch. Maybe you should attach licenses to your vests next time?

23. The Value of a Chesster Ice Cream Sandwich

The warden soon approached the wading couple and, yes, asked for their licenses. Their licenses were buried deep within the bowels of their waders and they had quite a struggle to display them to the warden. Oh, yes, it was the "heart of the hatch" time, too. After the warden left, Terry and Mary must have discussed the whole thing and concluded that I, the guy fishing out of sight, their friend, had purposely sicced the warden on them as a prank. Ouch.

Did I ever hear it from them the next day! *Why* did you tell that warden we were fishing? I bet you did it on purpose you scumbag! I denied everything, of course. How does it go? "Try to tell the truth but lie through your teeth?" I think I know several wardens who will get more than a chuckle out of these stories.

Success when jigging lake trout is bound to get the attention of roving wardens. But sometimes it can lead to a bonanza for the angler.

I'll end this warden section on a positive note since I must give credit to a warden for keying me into the Hex Hatch fishing on Caspian Lake. It was June 25, 1991, and I was fishing alone at Caspian trying to jig up some lakers. I did boat one decent fish at 22 inches and 3 ¾ pounds and lost four others, so I was having pretty good action. That may have attracted some attention because while I was drifting and casting for lakers, I was approached quickly by a warden on my blind side who wanted to check my license.

280

23. The Value of a Chesster Ice Cream Sandwich

Warden Chris Clark was very genial and offered information that he fishes the lake, too, but only during "the hatch". Not knowing about any hatches at Caspian at that time, I immediately grew elephant ears. I had been fishing the Hex Hatch in Maine for several years by that time and was quite familiar with its profound magnetism on fly anglers. So, the prospect of a hatch going on in my "backyard" was indeed exciting news.

I started peppering him with questions and determined that he was, indeed, talking about a full-blown Hex Hatch. He continued to offer valuable information, including where he fished the hatch, right in front of a brook in the western cove of the lake. He added that the day before he had seen several shucks on the water, indicating that the mayfly hatch was beginning. Oh, my stars and garters.

We shook hands and off he sped. Even though I hadn't planned on staying late, this news took on a whole new significance for fishing the lake that day. Believe it or not, I had even included a fly rod along with my other fishing gear before leaving home. So, I decided to bide my time (with more jigging) and then give the shoreline full scrutiny at dusk.

Even though Warden Clark said that the mayfly hatch occurs along most of Caspian's lakeside, I pointed the bow straight towards that western cove with the little brook. I got there late, and trout (to my jubilance) were already chasing *Hexagenia* mayflies. According to my fishing journal notes, I tied on a Gray Wulff (with shaking hands) and quickly started casting towards the rising rainbows. Before all the activity ended at 9:30 sharp, I had 3-4 rises and had hooked a corker of a fish, that broke off when it jumped. I found that moving the fly a dite helped to entice strikes and noticed that sometimes the rainbows would make really splashy rises while chasing an adult mayfly. But at other times the fish rises were slurps or even noiseless which I surmised was fish taking nymphs near the surface. Some of the fish were quite close to shore, maybe in only 3-5 feet of water, but the majority of the fish I saw rising were in water from 10-20 feet deep. I had it all to myself until 9:30 PM when all activity stopped as if a curtain had

23. The Value of a Chesster Ice Cream Sandwich

The author's first time ever fishing a Hex Hatch in Vermont occurred along this shoreline on Caspian Lake.

been dropped. As I slowly motored away towards the boat launch, I said to no one in particular, "I'll be back." That turned into a bit of an understatement. I have been back, and back, and back…120-plus times since that day to fish the Hex Hatch at Caspian. Thank you, Warden Chris Clark.

SOS

My last Hex anecdote isn't humorous in any way and can't be blamed on anyone. It was just one of those unexpected close calls that can happen to anyone who fishes from a boat. As mentioned earlier in the book, there is a "rolling opening" for lakes and ponds with a Hex hatch. Small, shallow ponds at low elevations tend to record the first hatches, whereas, large, deep lakes come later. In Vermont, Willoughby Lake is last during this rolling opening. It is a gorgeous lake at five miles long, covering 1690 acres, and is glacially-gouged to over 300 feet deep. By Vermont standards,

23. The Value of a Chesster Ice Cream Sandwich

Dogs are great companions when fishing alone, and they add to the scenery such as here on beautiful Willoughby Lake.

discounting Lake Champlain and Lake Memphremagog, which are only partially located within the state's boundaries, Willoughby is one of the largest lakes in the state, taking fourth place on the state's lake-acreage list. Willoughby is classified as oligotrophic (low nutrient level and high dissolved oxygen) and is exceptionally clear. Because of its huge mass of water content, it tends to warm up quite slowly.

Willoughby also harbors some strapping salmonids. The state record lake trout of 35 lbs-2oz, landed by Shawn Dutil of Plainfield, Vermont came from this lake. The leviathan togue was yanked from its depths in July of 2003, and I'm proud to say that Dutil was one of my former students. Hey, maybe he also learned

23. The Value of a Chesster Ice Cream Sandwich

something from me; I chatted up fishing quite often in class.

Willoughby's smelt population also grows robust rainbow trout and landlocked salmon. The rainbows are all native now as they haven't been stocked since 2011, although the salmon are still stocked annually.

Shawn Dutil of Plainfield, Vermont, holds the current state record for lake trout, of 35 lbs. 2 oz. It came from the depths of Willoughby Lake while he was yanking a "silvery spoon" (a Sutton, Shawn?) that fooled the goliath fish. Quite a few years before this extraordinary feat, Dutil sat in the author's high school classroom.

The year was 2008, and I had brought my two yellow labs, Toller and Widgie, along for companionship while fishing the hatch at Willoughby. As I launched my 14-footer, I noticed quite a bit of water in the boat that I thought was a result of recent heavy rains. Anxious to get fishing, I sped west to the Hex grounds and I opened the stern drain along the way.

I had modified my boat in previous years by taking out the middle seat to allow for more room, and in the process put a piece of plywood in the bottom of the boat. As a result, I couldn't see any water that was underneath the floorboard.

I know what you all are thinking. He didn't put the plug back in. But, surprisingly, I did. As I was speeding across the lake, I

23. The Value of a Chesster Ice Cream Sandwich

kept reminding myself *not to forget* to put the drain plug back in once I cut my speed, because when fishing, I am *so* focused that I fail to see or remember such things.

Landlocked salmon can be in the mix when fishing the Hex Hatch at Willoughby. PAINTING BY THE AUTHOR

I was pleased to see that I had the lake to myself and that rainbows and salmon were already surfacing for Hex mayflies. As usual, I was tense, excited, focused, and frantic all at once. After casting for maybe 20 minutes, I noticed that there were several inches of water *covering* the floorboard where I was standing and the boat was listing to that side! Bugger me dead, **what** is going on? I quickly checked the stern plug again, which was covered with water but it seemed fine. Damn, some quick thinking was now in order. I was about 75 yards from shore and was really more worried about my dogs than myself, even though they would have had no trouble swimming to shore.

I don't recall if I put on my life preserver or not, but if I didn't, I was an effing idiot. I threw my rod into the boat and decided to gun it back across the lake to the access, a distance of about ½ mile. I opened up my 15 HP Mercury as fast as the prop revolutions would turn, but there was one big problem. Water weighs about 62 pounds per cubic foot and a lot of water was already in the boat, with more coming in. The boat would only plow ahead at a few miles per hour. "Geezus, Wass. I don't like this situation *at all*," I muttered.

23. The Value of a Chesster Ice Cream Sandwich

I was a basket case while literally bulldozing across the lake in semi-darkness with my two companions. But you know, we made it safe and sound. You could almost hear my sigh of relief as I reached shore echoing from the two mountain sentinels that frame Willoughby, Mt. Pisgah, and Mt Hoar. Not a soul was there to greet us at the dock to ask, "What happened?" The story was only mine for the time being.

Hold on guys!

It still bugs the holy Swiss cheese out of me that I don't remember whether I wore my life jacket or not because I was just inches away from having one helluva long swim in the dark. I guess we all could learn a lesson from this very hairy, close encounter.

Oh, yes. You are wondering about the cause of the leak. The following day, I gave the boat a complete once over. The stern plug was solid. No problem there, but as I peered under the boat, I could see a crack in the hull's aluminum, right about where a trailer roller contacted the boat. That crack was the culprit.

A few years before, I had elected to buy a trailer with rollers instead of bunks, simply because it would be easier for me to crank the boat up on the trailer when alone. I also kept a full-sized, 12-volt battery for my trolling motor near the stern, inadvertently right over that same roller. I'm convinced that the extra weight of the battery (about 40 pounds) coupled with the pounding while driving on roads just put too much wear and stress on the aluminum, and finally produced that crack on that one-plus hour drive to Willoughby. Lesson learned. I was able to get a local machinist shop to weld it solidly and that crack never leaked again.

My new boat rests on bunks, and I will never use a roller-type trailer again. I now am always suspicious of excess water in my boat *before* motoring to a distant location, and I always try to remember to have my life jacket readily available for emergency use, *not stored away*.

I know, some of you are waiting for the fishing results for that evening. Okay. I'll cave into the unbridled pressure. I caught two fish before I realized what was going on. I'd like to report that the fish were 20-inch rainbow trout, but this time I can't tell the truth and lie through my teeth. I will say this much, though, that both fish were non-target species and leave it at that.

24. John-Boy's Journal

On some of our fishing trips to sporting camps in Northern Maine, my brother Stan and I brought food for housekeeping accommodations instead of eating at the lodges so that we would have a little more control over our fishing hours. My brother's wife, Noreen, always supplied us with many delectables including a lobster-scallop-shrimp stew, and for our sweet tooth scrumptious, chocolate-covered peanut butter bars. (Maybe *that's* why we chose the housekeeping option...) For one of our last trips, she handed me a cute gift, a ballpoint pen with the inscription "John-Boy Wass". She was well aware of my penchant for keeping journals on all these trips.

For younger readers, that inscription may not mean much unless you are a patron of watching old (very old) television shows. Back in the 1970s and early 1980s, an extremely popular television show called "The Waltons" aired on CBS. The hour-long drama was centered around a rural Virginia family during the Great Depression. The eldest son, named John-Boy, was an inveterate writer, and every night before

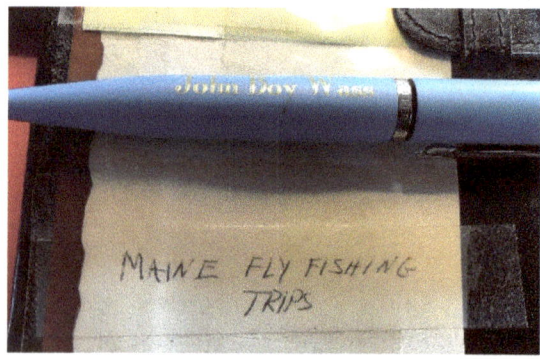

The author was gifted an inscripted pen to use for writing in his journals. It fondly says, "John Boy Wass".

24. John-Boy's Journal

going to bed he would write about his family and the day's experiences in a journal. Noreen obviously saw me as a modern-day John-Boy Walton, and she wasn't that far off. I have kept records in a variety of journals since I was 13 years old (still have them) and continue to do so today. In the earliest logs, I recorded all of my fishing trips, many of them salmon and togue fishing trips with my father at Tunk Lake in Downeast Maine. Also included were my traipses as a kid to local Mount Desert Island brooks where I caught wild brook trout (many were sea-run trout) mostly on worms. I also kept a log of duck hunting trips that my father and I had at a camp in Franklin, Maine, where we consistently were successful at bagging black ducks and whistlers over handmade decoys.

In each journal, I religiously recorded the following: date, where we hunted or fished, temperature, weather, accomplishments, and a written summary of the day. I can recall asking my father many times, as I was writing at the kitchen table of our Southwest Harbor home, "How fast would you say the wind was blowing today?", or, "How many strikes did you get on that Liggett Special streamer?" I'm sure my parents' affinity for keeping their own journals is what got me into also investing my time in such a labor of love. They kept diaries ranging from my father's fishing and hunting records (until I took over) to my mother's notes about family, bird watching, and the weather.

LEIGHTON Wass of Southwest Harbor displays a 12 pound lake trout taken from Tunk Lake. He was fishing with his father, Henry Wass

24. John-Boy's Journal

Today I still keep logs, although not quite as prolifically as in the past. I like to know the details of the past years' fishing trips or what success I may have had hunting, and why. I also keep tabs on what I make in my woodshop, including measurements, sketches, and any suggestions I may have learned from each project. And then there is firewood. I used to do all our firewood from start to finish, beginning with tree felling on our 40-acre property, blocking the logs, bringing the chunks down to the house in a trailer with my 1953 Ferguson tractor, splitting the firewood with a gas splitter, and finally stacking it. Because this process seriously ate into my fishing excursions and because my body protests fiercely when I attempt anything close to that today, I now limit it to a little blocking, splitting, and stacking.

At the end of a long day of fishing, it is sometimes a real chore to record the day's events in a journal. The cabin's bed can be a much more attractive choice. STAN WASS PHOTO

So, what in the heck is the value of all this journal-keeping? There's no question in my mind that one of the primary reasons I enjoy writing in journals is because it welcomes a chance to recall those events. Also, I am constantly checking my journals for a variety of reasons, such as to remind me of what I have learned in previous years because more than likely I would either forget most of it or possibly recall it incorrectly. The review might be for tidbits of data, such as what flies worked especially well on a given pond, or how long it took to drive to a particular location. Or it could be to see how much firewood I burned the previous year up to a specific date. I also sometimes read my journals just for the sheer enjoyment of reliving the experiences. It's somewhat similar to the additional knowledge you pick up after reading a book for the second time or re-watching a movie or television show.

One last reason for keeping records is its usefulness when writing an article or book. If you haven't already, you might want to add your name to the burgeoning list of writer-anglers and pen a magazine article or a book. Your journals will be indispensable. I can't begin to count the number of times that I have checked my journals for authenticity while writing this book.

Often it is difficult to find the time or energy to record a day's events, such as after a long, tiring day on the water, or when you

A game of cribbage sometimes fits into a fishing trip, especially on stormy days. This board was co-constructed by Warden Sean Fowler (the woodwork, made from teak) and the author (painting). That's a Warden's Worry fly the trout is chasing.

are ankle-deep in must-do projects. In cases like that, I am likely to wait until the next day, but if there is anything that I consider particularly salient, I will jot it down briefly on a piece of paper.

24. John-Boy's Journal

When I am on a multi-day fishing trip it can be very difficult to archive the stories of the day because of the many activities involved such as fishing, meals, chatting, napping, cribbage, more fishing, or just being dead tired. In those cases, I still try to squeeze in the important aspects but written in a shorthand format, instead of a full story of the day. Once I get home, I use those jottings to write a more complete record…sometimes.

Obviously, keeping a journal is not for everyone. But, if you are a "list person" at home or work, or if you often find yourself asking questions like, "I wonder what time that Hex Hatch occurred on Secret Pond last year?", you might want to give it a whirl. Nothing fancy is needed to log your daily records. Many of my journals are simply spiral-bound notebooks, although I do own a few others that are the real McCoy, leather-bound logs that are usually given to me as gifts from family members, such as my sister Janet, because of my known proclivity for being a John-Boy journalist.

If you are handy in a workshop, there are lots of "how to make a logbook" ideas on the internet that you can use to construct one of your own. I actually have had that on my "winter-to-do-list" for several years now. I am leaning towards making a logbook with covers of birch bark, or others that use various types of woods such as red cedar, walnut, and butternut. Once you have made a journal, it's no stretch of the

A homemade bookmark spices up a journal. This one has a favorite Maine brook trout fly painted on it, the Devil Bug.

24. John-Boy's Journal

imagination to make a wooden bookmark with something inscribed on it like, "Hex Stories" or "Five Steps to Heaven". Pinterest is a great place to look for ideas.

A consequence of keeping journals may be that you want to share those stories, either in writing or orally. In the majority of instances, that sharing is greeted with gratitude, appreciation, and as a great source for banter. On *rare* occasions, a negative aspect of this sharing can arise, that of attracting too many anglers to these spots like honeybees to basswood trees. Many years ago, I paid dearly for sharing some fishing information in an article about a prolific mayfly hatch that occurs on **Seyon Pond** in Groton, Vermont. Seyon Pond is unique in many ways, one being that fishing is limited to 10 boats/canoes, all of which are supplied by the state. Anglers are not allowed to fish from shore nor use their own watercraft, but you can reserve a boat as long as it's not too far in advance.

On this particular mortifying trip of mine, I did not bother to reserve a boat because I had always found one available in the past. I arrived fully charged because I knew the Recurve Hatch was still ongoing. What I hadn't considered was how efficient word-of-mouth can be after reading a fishing article. The Seyon

Seyon Pond has a maximum limit of 10 boats/canoes for fishing, and it's always best to reserve ahead of time.

24. John-Boy's Journal

Ranch attendant approached me as I started carrying my gear to the dock and said, "Sorry, but there are already 10 boats on the pond. You can wait until someone comes in if you wish." Of course, almost everyone was there to fish "the hatch" and therefore wouldn't be in until *after* it was over. Crikey.

I returned to the truck with all my gear, and on the hour's drive back home kept muttering something about, *"What is the matter with me?"*, and *"Why didn't I reserve a boat?"*, and *"Lesson learned."* I do like the 10-boat maximum regulation because Seyon is a very small, popular fishing pond, and the boat requirement helps keep the Seyon experience as it is intended. But never again did I gamble on getting a boat when a hatch is happening. And, ever since then I have been *much* more careful about what I have written and when it is published. Sometimes mum **is** the word in the world of fly fishing.

25. Endgame

As a teenager, I was fortunate to spend many hours in an outdoor sporting environment with my father. I loved it and those idyllic days paid huge dividends for years to come. I don't recall that our conversations covered much more ground than fishing and hunting, and that was fine with me. When we drove anywhere

Several trips to Old Stream in Downeast Maine with his father, helped to solidify the building blocks for the author's history of fishing. They stayed at Stanwood King's camp in Wesley.

25. Endgame

together, I pestered him with questions about every brook, stream, and pond that we went by. All of his stories were studded with tales about Maine characters he had met and I treasured those stories, especially when a tall tale came to an end and he laughed himself silly.

As an aside, for readers who are interested in a little bit of Maine sports history, my father was not only an achiever in the fishing arena but also in basketball. In short (sorry Dad), at 5'3" in height (for some reason that never seemed short to me), he played semi-pro basketball after graduating from Hebron Academy. He was a star on Maine teams such as the Bar Harbor Blackcats, the Bangor Five Aces, Bar Harbor Buicks, and the Augusta Five. My father was obviously best suited for a guard position, and old newspaper clippings reported that not only was he rabbit-fast and able to dribble through the legs of defenders, he could also drain a two-handed set shot as well as casting a fly rod.

Short in stature and tall in ability, Henry "Shorty" Wass was a stalwart guard on several Maine semi-pro basketball teams in the late 1920s and early 1930s.

I can recall those set shots from the 50s when he would ask for the ball on our backyard basketball court. As I recall, he usually would take one shot, drill it, and then return to the house.

25. Endgame

I honestly believe that my father's heartfelt interest in taking me afield so often as a youngster was at least partly driven by his desire to keep me busy. Idle time can be a Pandora's Box in many ways, and for a teenager, back in the 50s (as well as today), idle time could easily have been a precursor to delinquency. My father did his best to keep "social distancing" of a few country miles be-

The author spent many days of his teenage years at this duck hunting camp in Franklin, Maine, with his father.

tween me and inappropriate behavior, by whetting my interest in outdoor activities such as fishing and hunting.

So where is all this leading me? Back to fishing. Whenever my father went fishing in a boat, he performed a little ritual as we started out on a lake. He'd pick up our long-handled net and dip it three times in the water for good luck. But I like to think that this fun fishing rite was also a "good luck" gesture to his son for all the years ahead. And maybe, just maybe I recently received "three dips of the net" from somewhere up above for success while writing this book. Just maybe.

25. Endgame

In the early days of fishing the Hex Hatch, the author often found himself fishing alone. A fat chance of that nowadays! SEAN FOWLER PHOTO

When I started fishing the Hex Hatch in the late 1980s and early 1990s, I really had trouble understanding why there was such low participation by others fishing this hatch. Sometimes I would be the only one fishing a Hex Hatch which blew my mind. Let me quote a passage from Ken Allen in his 1984 *Maine Sportsman* article, 'Matching Maine's Great Mayfly', about Hex Hatches in Maine.

"In Maine, these hatches come and go, and few notice or even care. When people do notice, it is erroneously referred to as the Green Drake Hatch. It is odd and too bad, more anglers fail to take advantage of the wonderful fishing *Hexagenia* hatches offer."

It's a much different story today. I saved that yellowed article all these years, but primarily because Allen gave the recipe for tying a Hex dry fly, not realizing that his article might indeed make the pages of a book I would write someday.

25. Endgame

So, what *was* the issue back then? I'm guessing that the pull of moving waters was a more powerful magnet than that of still waters. Fly fishing streams was the dominant activity back then for the majority of fly anglers, especially since almost every article written in magazines focused on fly fishing streams and rivers instead of ponds. You can add the time of year to that magnetic pull

There is a magnetic pull from moving waters that may have kept fly anglers away from Hex Hatches 25-30 years ago.

since the end of June and the first of July were considered to be prime times to be fishing moving waters…*right* when the Hex Hatch occurred. I also believe that it was a matter of communication, as in very little hype and dissemination of knowledge regarding this hatch from participating fly anglers. The word of the Hex Hatch simply had not been shaken from the bushes at that time.

Today, of course, there's hardly a fly angler who hasn't at least heard of or fished the Hex Hatch. It's a term bandied about in fly shops all over New England and other parts of the United States, year-round. The popularity of this hatch has increased so much that it even becomes wise to carefully comb through Hex discussions to separate the true wheat from the chaff.

Recently as I reflected on all the work that I have put into this book, I wondered how I would answer someone's question as to

25. Endgame

what I had hoped to accomplish by writing this rather detailed book on just one aspect of fly fishing. After staring out my window at the leaf-less November landscape and watching chickadees contend for sunflower seeds, I found that the answers were as easy to come by as casting a fly to a trout rise. They materialized in the following order.

Entertaining

I enjoy reading non-fiction sporting books, especially those that are interspersed with humor and have abundant, captivating anecdotes. A lively read that is spirited and full of beans will get me every time. I'm hoping that the readers of this book will feel the same way.

Educational

As you may have gathered, I am proud of my career as a teacher and even though I am now retired, I just can't seem to quell the desire to educate. It's in my bones, or saying it a little differently, you can take the teacher out of the classroom, but you can't

Don't you just love it. A youngster, in this case, Kellon Mencucci, of Walden, Vermont, who is going to be one of our next Hex-fishing anglers. DANIEL MENCUCCI PHOTO

take the desire to educate out of the teacher. In this book, the chapters which detail the life cycle and biology of our celebrity, *Hexagenia limbata,* illustrate what I mean. I not only want anglers to know *how* to fish the Hex Hatch but also want them to know what makes this mayfly tick.

25. Endgame

Help For Beginners

We are in the middle of a new surge in fly fishing, past the "River Runs Through It" surge, and that means there are a large number of folks of all ages who have a desire to learn as many facets of fly fishing as they possibly can. Fishing the Hex Hatch is probably not at the top of most beginners' "to-learn-list", but I'm willing to bet a slice of chocolate cake that it won't be long before this remarkable fishing hatch bumps other fly-fishing elements aside and sits at the head of that list. As some might say, the cream always seems to rise to the top.

Tips For Experienced Anglers

I hope that my personal experiences of fishing the Hex Hatch have precipitated a few snippets of information that will enhance experienced anglers' capabilities on Hex waters.

If the author can bring the zeal and excitement of Hexgenia mayfly fishing to others as Neil Hilt demonstrates, he will consider his book an unqualified success. (Hilt was the producer of the award-winning VPT show, "Outdoor Journal".)

25. Endgame

Naming Hex Hatch Waters

This segment of the book was the most time-consuming and hardest to write. Giving up the names of special ponds and lakes takes a lot of soul searching, but I reasoned that if I am going to dwell on *how* to fish this hatch, I should certainly include a wide range of waters in this tri-state area that support *Hexagenia* mayflies. With that reasoning, I have cited 160 plus lakes, ponds, and rivers that are home to Hex mayflies in Maine, New Hampshire, and Vermont, and they span a distance of 300-400 miles. I believe that provides a bona fide opportunity for most New England fly fishers to find plenty of Hex waters within reasonable reach. Anglers from outside New England, with a tad more traveling to do, also have a similar prospect.

Since there are many methods today for directing anglers on how to get to fishing locations, I have left some of the research up to the reader. As much as possible, I wanted to avoid the likes of, "Go to Hannibal's Crossing, take a left, drive 10 miles …", or, "After driving on the logging road for 3 miles, turn right at the spruce blowdown, and go until you see a moose, then…" My preference was to cite an abundance of Hex locations in lieu of directional details and let you, the reader, figure out some of the specifics such as camping sites, sporting camps, and fishing laws. I didn't want to be a mother hen. In doing so, I'm proud to say that there is *no other source out there* even close to citing the number of Hex waters as are listed in this book. I hope it will become your go-to resource for the future. It's now in your hands as to whether I "pass the test" for accomplishing these five objectives while explaining the nuances of that seasonal disorder… known as Hexitis.

About The Author

Leighton Wass grew up in Southwest Harbor, Maine. He graduated from Pemetic High School in 1960. He attended Norwich University in Northfield, Vermont (1960-1964) and graduated with a BS in Science Education.

He taught high school biology for 33 years in Vermont. Since 1972 Leighton has written articles for magazines that include *The Vermont Sportsman*, *The Maine Sportsman*, *New England Game and Fish*, *Vermont Life*, and *Northern Woodlands*. He also writes outdoor articles for the *Bangor Daily News*.

Leighton has fished, including fly fishing, since he was a preteenager, and continues to do so today at age 80. He has used the outdoors as his playground for decades that has included hunting, foraging for mushrooms, searching for moose sheds, and, of course, fishing the Hex Hatch. He is also a fly tyer and woodworker.

Leighton lives in Adamant, Vermont, with his wife Jane and two Labradors.

He can be reached at walkingstickcrafts@gmail.com

Resources

Angers, Steve. *Fly Fishing New Hampshire's Secret Waters*. The History Press, 2020.
Animal Diversity Web. Museum of Zoology. University of Michigan.
Caucci, Al, Nastasi, Bob. *Hatches II*. Lyons & Burford, 1986.
DeLorme Atlas & Gazetteer. Maine, New Hampshire, Vermont.
Destination Northern Ontario.
Flyanglersonline.com
Google Earth.
Lake Stewards of Maine, "Brook Trout Heritage Lakes of Maine Map".
Mallard, Bob. "Maine: Cold Stream Forest". American Fly Fishing, Jul/Aug 2020.
Miner, A. "Hexagenia Limbata". Animal Diversity Web, 2014.
Native Fish Coalition.
Online Etymology Dictionary
Raychard, Al. *Remote Trout Ponds in Maine*. Thorndike Press, 1984.
State Fish and Game Agencies: Maine Department of Inland Fisheries & Wildlife, New Hampshire Fish & Game, Vermont Fish & Wildlife.
Van Wie, David. *Storied Waters*. Guilford, Conn: Stackpole Books, 2019.
Wikipedia

Index of Lakes, Ponds & Rivers

MAINE

1040 Pond..115, 119
Alford Lake..164, 171
Allagash Lake.......................................121, 122, 198
Aziscohos Lake................................79, 116, 137, 139
Beech Hill Pond..........................139, 166, 167, 168, 171
Big Berry Pond..108
Big Black Pond........................25, 42, 43, 132, 133, 170
Big Jim Pond..135, 143
Big Lyford Pond..113
Blood Pond..120
Bowler Pond...164, 171
Branch Lake...168
Brassua Dam...16
Brassua Lake..105
Brown Pond...105
Celia Pond..124, 170
Chase Stream Pond..109
Chesuncook Lake...115, 116
Churchill Lake...121
Clearwater Lake..145, 171
Cold Stream Pond...108
Craig Pond..168
Cross Lake..130
Currier Pond...133, 171
Daicey Pond..124, 125, 170
Deboullie Pond...132, 172
Denny's Pond..132

Dixon Pond..................150, 171
Durgin Pond..................108
Eagle Lake (Fish River)..................121, 129, 130
East Grand Lake..................7, 127, 128, 129, 172
Egypt Pond..................164
Ellis Pond..................109, 110
Fernald Pond..................108
Fish Pond..................150
Foss-Knowlton Pond..................124
Gardner Pond..................132, 172
Grace Pond..................110, 111
Grass Pond..................150, 173
Green Lake..................168
Hancock Pond..................155, 158, 172
Helen Pond..................150
High Pond..................150
Horseshoe Pond (BCGW TWP)..................113
Indian Pond (Greenville)..................105
Indian Pond (TC R12)..................121
Iron Pond..................110, 111
Island Pond (Deboullie)..................25, 132, 171, 172, 269
Jo-Mary Pond..................113, 114
Kelly Pond..................115, 119, 171
Kennebago Lake..................60, 135, 140, 141, 143
Kennebago River..................60
Kidney Pond..................124, 125
Kilgore Pond..................150, 152, 172
Lang Pond..................108
Little Berry Pond..................108
Little Enchanted Pond..................110, 111, 173
Little Jim Pond..................135, 143
Little Lang Pond..................108
Little Lyford Pond..................113, 170
Little Pillsbury Pond..................134
Little Pond..................161, 162, 170
Little Sourdnahunk Pond..................127

Lone Jack Pond..108, 173
Long Lake..130
Long Pond (Belgrade)........................159, 160, 161, 172
Lower Richardson......................135, 139, 144, 167, 243
Lower South Branch Pond....................................171
Magalloway River..60, 139
Moosehead Lake...23, 97, 103, 104, 105, 107, 113, 116, 117, 159, 169, 171, 243, 244, 245, 246, 254
Mooselookmeguntic Lake..........................135, 143, 169
Mud Pond (Fish River)....................................129, 130
Nahmakanta Lake................51, 52, 114, 115, 238, 275, 277
Nesowadnehunk Lake...........................3, 97, 98, 99, 101
Otter Pond (T3 R13)......................................115, 119
Parker Pond..164
Parmachenee Lake.........................135, 138, 143, 170
Peters Pond..164
Pickerel Pond..150
Pierce Pond 5, 145, 146, 147, 148, 149, 150, 151, 153, 154, 155, 170, 232, 235, 240, 254, 271, 272
Pushineer Pond...132
Quimby Pond................................135, 136, 143
Ragged Lake (T2 R13)..120
Rangeley Lake...............134, 135, 141, 142, 144, 145, 172
Ripogenus Lake..115, 117
Rock Pond..80
Rocky Pond..124
Round Pond (Chase Stream Township)................109, 110
Round Pond (BSP)..124
Rum Pond...................................105, 106, 173
Russell Pond...125, 170
Salmon Pond..106
Sanborn Pond...164
Schoodic Lake (Cherryfield)...........................166, 170
Sebago Lake...........................155, 156, 157, 158, 159
Secret Pond..67, 105
Sheepscot Pond..164, 165, 198

Sixth Debsconeag..170
Slaughter Pond..115, 170
Spectacle Pond..…164
Square Lake..129, 170
St. George Lake..…164
Thompson Lake.....................155, 158, 170, 198
Tim Pond..135, 144
Upper Pond..132, 152
Upper Richardson..........................135, 139, 141, 144, 198
Upper South Branch Pond.......................................124
Wassataquoik Lake 124, 173
West Branch Pond....................................113, 114
West Richardson Pond............................135, 144

NEW HAMPSHIRE

Back Lake..…91, 93
Big Diamond Pond....................................93, 139, 198
Big Greenough Pond..............84, 86, 87, 89, 90, 91, 198, 212
Butterfield Pond..93, 94
Chapin Pond..93, 94
Christine Lake..91, 93
Cole Pond...93, 94
Connecticut River...60
Echo Lake...91, 92
Lake Winnipesauke................................94, 95, 198
Lake Winona...95
Little Diamond Pond...92
Little Greenough Pond...................83, 85, 90, 91
Little Squam Lake..95
Lower Trio Pond..91, 92
Mirror Lake...91, 92, 93
Mountain Pond..91, 92
Munn Pond..91, 92
Nathan Pond..91, 92

Newfound Lake..94
Profile Pond...91, 92, 177
Simmons Pond...93, 94
Sky Pond..96
Solitude Lake..93
South Pond...91, 92
Spectacle Pond...95
Sunapee Lake...95, 96, 198
Upper Hall Pond...95, 96
Upper Trio Pond...91, 92
Waukewan Lake...94, 95
Wentworth Lake..94
White Pond..93

VERMONT

Big Averill Lake..72
Caspian Lake............22, 27, 41, 72, 77, 177, 185, 195, 198, 205, 212, 214, 266, 274, 280, 281, 282
Clyde River...81, 82
Connecticut River...60
Crystal Lake..72, 73, 198
Echo Lake (Charleston)....22, 48, 72, 73, 74, 75, 76, 77, 165,197, 198, 205
Eligo Lake..................................78, 204, 205, 212, 258
Holland Pond 72, 73
Island Pond..78
Jobs Pond..77
Lake Carmi..41
Lake Champlain....................................40, 42, 207, 283
Lake Groton...69
Lewis Pond...78
Little Averill Lake...22, 72
Little Rock Pond...80
Long Pond..78, 198

Maidstone Lake...72
Miller Pond..79, 204
Nelson Pond..78, 204
Peacham Pond..79
Seymour Lake... 22, 77, 78
Seyon Pond.........20, 126, 218, 219, 232, 247, 248, 249, 251, 253, 254, 255, 272, 293, 294
Shadow Lake..77
Willoughby Lake.........................36, 76, 193, 195, 205, 282

www.ingramcontent.com/pod-product-compliance
Lightning Source LLC
Chambersburg PA
CBHW042131160426
43199CB00021B/2874